RE-UNION

RE-UNION

How Bold Labor Reforms Can
Repair, Revitalize, and
Reunite the United States

David Madland

ILR PRESS

AN IMPRINT OF CORNELL UNIVERSITY PRESS ITHACA AND LONDON

First published 2021 by Cornell University Press
Printed in the United States of America

Library of Congress Cataloging-in-Publication Data

Names: Madland, David, author.
Title: Re-Union : how bold labor reforms can repair, revitalize, and reunite the United States / David Madland.
Description: Ithaca [New York] : ILR Press, an imprint of Cornell University Press, 2021. | Includes bibliographical references and index.
Identifiers: LCCN 2020034892 (print) | LCCN 2020034893 (ebook) | ISBN 9781501755378 (hardcover) | ISBN 9781501755385 (ebook) | ISBN 9781501755392 (pdf)
Subjects: LCSH: Labor unions—United States—21st century. | Industrial relations—United States. | Labor policy—United States.
Classification: LCC HD6508. M255 2021 (print) | LCC HD6508 (ebook) | DDC 331.880973—dc23
LC record available at https://lccn.loc.gov/2020034892
LC ebook record available at https://lccn.loc.gov/2020034893

To my family

Contents

Acknowledgments

I am thankful for the help and support of the many people who made this book possible.

I am particularly grateful to those who took to time to read chapters or drafts and provide valuable feedback, including Kate Andrias, Matt Dimick, Keith Ewing, Jim Stanford, Cathy Braker, Marc Jarsulic, Andy Green, Greg Kauffman, Alex Rowell, Danyelle Solomon, Sam Berger, Sara Slinn, Phillip James, Shae McCrystal, Karla Walter, Fred Wilson, Kevin Reilly, Becky Wasserman, Steve Kreisberg, and three anonymous reviewers.

I appreciate the assistance Malkie Wall provided on so many facets of the book. Adam Stromme, Divya Vijay, and Nathan Smith provided additional research help.

At Cornell University Press, I am grateful for the support that Fran Benson and many others demonstrated throughout this project.

Researching this book, I benefited from the ability to learn from and bounce ideas off numerous people, including Christy Hoffman, Kelly Ross, Damon Silvers, David Rolf, Ben Sachs, Sharon Block, Larry Cohen, Cam Dykstra, Brad James, Gavin McGarrigle, Angelo DiCaro, Tonia Novitz, Amanda Brown, Jennifer Abruzzo, Mia Dell, Arun Ivatury, Peter Colavito, Ian Campbell, Glenn Adler, Joe Isaac, Michelle Bissett, Iain Ross, Brian Lawrence, Matt Cowgill, Mark Bray, John Howe, Amanda Mansini, Tim Lyons, Tim Lee, Trevor Clarke, Margaret McKenzie, Scott Barklamb, Cath Bowtell, Andrew Stewart, Shae McCrystal, Rae Cooper, Tony Slevin, Ray Markey, Frances Flanagan, Damian Oliver, Kristina Keneally, Wayne Swan, Gerard Hayes, Tony Shelton, Michael Kaine, Adam Serle, Geoffrey Giudice, Elsa Underhill, Julius Rowe, Nick Wilson, Dario Mujkic, Imogen Beynon, Lowell Peterson, Judy Scott, Catherine Fisk, Paul Booth, Zack Fields, Joel Rogers, Richard Freeman, Amy Sugimori, Brishen Rogers, Carmen Rojas, David Socolow, Wilma Liebman, Nicole Berner, Cheryl Feldman, Julie Su, Geoff Betts, Ann Burdick, Jeffrey Bennett, Shelia Blackburn, Uta Dirksen, Earl Mathurin, Achim Wachendorfer, Tony Cheng, Roger Pollak, Lynn Rhinehart, Craig Becker, Bill Samuel, Carolin Vollmann, Matthew Finkin, Tom Kochan, Harold Meyerson, Andy Stern, Richard Heyman, Cynthia Estlund, Eileen Applebaum, Jennifer Gordon, Stephen Lerner, Jeffrey Vogt, Janice Fine, Ai-Jen Poo, Katherine Stone, Lyle Scruggs, Amy Rosenthal, Tim Lyons, David Socolow, and Kathleen Thelen.

Research for this book was also assisted by my receipt of an Australia Endeavour Executive Fellowship and a Friedrich-Ebert-Stiftung's EU Study Visit.

At the Center for American Progress, I have been fortunate to work in a stimulating environment conducive to exploring the future of the labor movement. I appreciate the support I received for this effort from Neera Tanden and numerous colleagues, including Ben Olinsky, Andres Vinelli, Olugbenga Ajilore, Christian Weller, Jacob Leibenluft, Marc Jarsulic, and Livia Lam as well as others who read drafts or helped in other ways, many of whom are named elsewhere.

I want to acknowledge the important role that Thomas Geoghegan's book *Only One Thing Can Save Us* had in sparking this book.

Finally, I am thankful for the support my friends and family provided while I researched and wrote this book.

RE-UNION

Introduction

The United States faces some of the most significant challenges in its history. For decades, the economy has failed to deliver for most people, the political system has been hijacked by corporations and the wealthy, political polarization has risen to extreme levels, trust between people fallen sharply, and racism and sexism have been stubbornly persistent. More recently, the COVID-19 pandemic hit the US so hard because too many leaders and citizens failed to take basic steps to protect the public health. Alarm bells are ringing, warning that things need to change or else the country's already grave problems will get much worse.

Many problems in the United States stem from the fact that working people have too little economic and political power. Most Americans have not been able to get a fair share of the gains they help create or been able to ensure that their elected representatives respond to their economic concerns. This powerlessness continues to compound as rapid technological change makes it easier for companies to contract out, control workers, and generally make work worse, and lobbyist-influenced legislation increasingly provides the wealthy with additional advantages.

The central argument of this book is that stronger unions operating under a new type of labor system could help address the country's underlying economic and political challenges. A new labor system would raise wages, reduce extreme economic inequality, strengthen the middle class, and increase the responsiveness of politicians to regular citizens. It would even help address the decline of trust and the huge racial and gender divides in society.

Unions bring together people who on their own have relatively little influence with employers or politicians. But when people join together in unions they have greater ability to negotiate for higher wages, better benefits, and improved working conditions and are significantly more likely to vote and participate in politics. Unions also give workers a voice in the behind-the-scenes battles where policy details are hashed out. In addition, unions bring together people across race, ethnicity, religion, gender, and even class, in ways that few other organizations do.

Yet simply trying to resurrect the labor system the United States had in the 1950s will not do. The world has changed since then, exposing the labor system's long-standing flaws.

In the first few decades after World War II, union membership was high—covering around one-third of the workforce—due to gains unions had made through the favorable policies of the National Labor Relations Act of 1935 and the pro-union policies enacted during World War II.[1] The United States was by far the strongest economy in the world, as war had decimated most competitors.[2] Social trust was strong, due to relative economic equality and the common bonds forged in the war effort, which helped people work well together.[3] The Cold War and communism in the Soviet Union put pressure on American businesses and politicians to treat workers better. Leading companies such as Ford and General Motors were large, capital-intensive manufacturing firms structured so that most of the work—from janitorial to engineering to parts to assembly—was done in-house and was hard to relocate.[4] A number of elected officials in both the Democratic and Republican parties supported, or at least accepted, unions as a part of the economy. These factors helped the US labor system deliver shared prosperity—though it left out too many workers, particularly women and African Americans.

But almost every factor that enabled the old system to work fairly well for the workers it chose to cover has changed. The law has become increasingly hostile to unions. It makes it very difficult for private-sector workers to unionize—just 6 percent of private-sector workers are union members today, virtually the smallest share of the private-sector workforce since the country industrialized in the 1800s—and public-sector unions have come under attack in recent years and are starting to lose density as well. Foreign competitors have chipped away at US economic dominance. Common bonds among all Americans have become harder to find, and social capital has withered away as economic inequality has increased. Cultural and economic norms have shifted to an especially cutthroat version of capitalism. Capital has become more mobile, enabling employers to more easily move jobs around the country and the world. The service sector increasingly dominates the economy as the more heavily unionized industrial sectors make up a smaller and smaller share of jobs. Modern firms are no longer vertically integrated: they now focus on their core competencies and contract out work as much work as possible. Even though large firms are structured differently, they have become more dominant in their fields and face less competition to increase wages. Leaders of the Republican Party have become more hostile to unions, while the Democratic Party has not always had labor's back.

US law does not provide enough support for unions to overcome the growing power employers have over their workers. It also fails to adequately address the basic collective action problem inherent in union membership. Unions provide a service that benefits society broadly—higher wages for most workers, including many nonunion workers, and political voice for the working class. Because people can benefit from these services even if they do not pay for it, society gets too little of public goods like unions. In the modern economy, public policy needs not only to provide workers with strong union rights, it also needs to actively encourage membership by providing unions with a platform to recruit members and incentives for workers to join unions. Just as the government supports small business with contracts, loans, and antitrust laws, it also needs to support labor unions with a range of policies.

The changing economy has also made it harder for workers to collectively bargain at their worksites—the place where US labor law encourages bargaining to occur—because worksites have become more mobile and companies can increasingly contract out work. Bargaining at a single worksite always left out too many workers compared to bargaining at a higher level, such as the sectoral level or regional level, but the problem has gotten much worse in the modern economy. Workplace-level bargaining also causes unionized employers to have higher labor costs than their competitors and thus increases employer resistance to unions. In the modern economy, unions need to be able to bargain for all workers across an entire industry no matter the type of workplace they have, no matter how their employment is structured. This is often called sectoral or broad-based bargaining.

The new labor system would provide strong incentives for membership and promote broad-based bargaining. In the modernized system, unions would deliver or help people access governmental benefits—including workforce training, retirement benefits, and enforcement of workplace laws—akin to how unions help make unemployment insurance work in countries like Sweden, Demark, and Belgium. This type of platform for recruitment and retention has proven effective at generating high and stable union membership in today's economy because it ensures visibility, provides access to workers, creates incentives for workers to join, and paves the way for greater recognition of the important work that unions do to support a fair economy. The new labor system would also foster broad-based bargaining to allow most workers to enjoy the benefits of collective bargaining whether they are union members or not, whether they are direct employees or independent contractors. This type of bargaining would also ensure similar pay for similar work, not only limiting opportunities for discrimination but also encouraging industries to more efficiently allocate economic resources and preventing good employers from being undercut by low-road competitors.

The new system would also include reforms necessary to provide real rights and protections for all workers—the kinds of changes that labor supporters have long advocated for. It would, for example, guarantee significant penalties for employers violating the law and ensure adequate strike protections for workers as well as their right to strike against firms that have power in their industry, not just their direct employer.

The new labor system would take the best of what works elsewhere in the world—such as the bargaining and incentive structures from places like Denmark and Belgium—and adapt them to the US context based on existing policies in US cities and states. The modernized system would build on broad-based bargaining models that exist in California and New York and in government contracts throughout the country, as well as incorporate incentives for union membership at use in the workforce training systems of states like Washington and Montana and the labor enforcement activities of a number of cities.

These reforms would raise wages for those who have a college degree and those who do not, for low- and middle-income earners, regardless of their race, gender, sexual orientation, or classification as independent contractors. They would help ensure that work has dignity, increase economic productivity, and help workers get a larger share of the gains they create. They would reduce inequality, shrink gender and racial pay gaps, and help average Americans have a stronger say in politics.

While a new labor system could help ordinary citizens gain economic and political power, unions are not perfect. Unions' flaws are often exaggerated by their opponents, but unions have weaknesses just as every organization does. Like corporations, their leaders can be shortsighted and sometimes corrupt. Like other advocacy organizations, unions can be captured by their leaders or swayed by the worst impulses of their members and even harbor racists and sexists.

But the harm caused by the near elimination of unions is far worse than that which stems from their flaws. Moreover, a new labor system would encourage more of what labor does that is helpful and irreplaceable and less that seems self-interested and shortsighted. Unions would have greater ability and incentives to help all workers and less of a need to focus on narrower issues. Unions would also be able to have an even more positive impact on the economy as a whole.

To some, the idea of a modernized labor system will challenge their notion of what a union is because it imagines a different role for unions than "pure-and-simple unionism," which focuses on servicing members through self-help and workplace bargaining and discounts broader political and social struggles. Pure-and-simple unionism is encouraged by US law, and some labor leaders have emphasized it, but unions are not and have never been just one thing. Rather, unions are multifaceted organizations that need to service members, build grassroots power, and gain greater influence in the larger economy and political systems.

While there are some inherent tensions between prioritizing the bottom-up power of pure-and-simple unionism and the top-down power of the new labor system, unions need to pursue both and have a long history of doing so. Unions are a way to aggregate the power of workers in the workplace, economy, and democracy, and they emphasize different roles to achieve their goals depending on circumstances. Further, US unions have a long history of doing all the tasks necessary in a new labor system—including bargaining at a higher level and providing multiple incentives for workers to join. In addition, these more expansive tasks would be layered on top of worksite-based roles, so unions would continue with many of their current functions even as they adopt additional roles.

Unions cannot fix America on their own. Other reforms are certainly necessary—such as those that increase investments in skills and education, raise taxes on the rich, strengthen government benefits, limit campaign contributions, ensure citizens can vote, and reduce gender and racial discrimination. But unions can help make these policies work better and compensate for their weaknesses.

Raising the minimum wage, strengthening public benefits, or even a job guarantee would help reduce poverty, but these policies are unlikely to do much for middle-class wages. More education is usually good, but it will not increase pay for people whose jobs do not require additional training or have the power to capture some of the economic benefits of their increased productivity. Campaign finance and voter reform policies would help address glaring problems in US election law but not build the organizations necessary to make the political system truly responsive to the people. A new labor system could raise wages for the poor and the middle class, no matter their education level, and have the scale and the mission to give regular citizens a political voice. Moreover, unions could help provide political muscle to pass other reforms and also help make these reforms more effective by ensuring they are properly implemented and enforced.

Because attempts at even modest labor law reforms have failed over recent decades, the politics of enacting a bold new labor system may seem daunting. Still, events are unfolding that make bold reforms more achievable in the relatively near future than they have been at any other time in recent history. Public opinion is moving decisively in favor of labor, with half of workers saying they would join a union, and public approval of unions higher than it has been in many decades.[5] Workers are increasingly taking direct action. More workers went on strike in 2018 than had struck in any year since the 1980s, and a similar number went on strike in 2019.[6] There has also been increasing activism among workers who do not have a clear path to traditional collective bargaining, such as teachers in states without collective bargaining laws, employees of fast food franchises, and domestic workers without traditional employers. A small but growing core of academics, union leaders, activists, and politicians are making the case for a new labor system. Elites seem to increasingly recognize the need to consider bold solutions and are more receptive to pro-labor policy than they have been in some time. A number of state and local governments have been experimenting with innovative models of collective bargaining and policies to support unions. Leading figures in the Democratic Party increasingly support bold labor reforms similar to those called for in this book.

While this book is focused on the United States, it is relevant to readers around the world. Its basic lessons about the need for labor reform and the types of reforms that work best apply broadly. Most advanced democracies face economic and political problems analogous to those of the United States, and most other countries need labor reforms to address these problems. The United States may be an outlier in its level of inequality and union weakness, but the downward trajectory in most countries is quite similar.

The twenty-first century version of extreme capitalism is exacerbating deep economic, social, and political problems, which even some of its cheerleaders are beginning to understand. As a result, people around the world have become increasingly interested in the long-standing debate about how to manage capitalism so that it delivers for most people and does not undermine democracy and societal values. Old worries like fascism and even communism no longer seem like historic relics. This book aims to be a guide for this debate by explaining why a new labor system is a necessary part of the path forward.

Chapter 1 explains in detail what the new system would look like. Its shows how public policy can actively support unions and encourage broad-based collective bargaining, and it explains how the newer elements of the modernized system would be layered on top of the existing system. The chapter discusses how the United States could adapt the "Ghent system" that several countries use to provide needed benefits to workers and a platform for unions to recruit members. It also describes how to move toward broad-based bargaining by promoting high union density as well as by creating supportive structures—including extending union contracts to similarly placed workers through more expansive use of prevailing wage laws and the creation of workers' boards in sectors with little or no union density. Examples from cities and states with these types of policies are highlighted. Finally, how unions would operate in the new system and build power in the workplace as well as in the larger economy is explored.

Chapter 2 steps back from policy reform to provide the building blocks to support the book's claim that unions can help address the economic and political challenges facing the United States. It highlights America's troubles—stagnant wages, extreme inequality, low trust, racism, and a weakened democracy—and the reasons why unions might be expected to help solve them. It then presents theory and evidence showing what unions do to raise wages, reduce economic inequality, increase political participation, and make politicians more responsive to ordinary citizens, as well as how they help reduce racial and gender discrimination and rebuild societal trust. Chapter 2 also discusses how unions achieve these goals with little to no harm to the overall economy.

The book then develops the argument for why a new type of labor policy is so vital. Based on economic and political science theory as well as empirical findings from the United States and countries around the world, chapter 3 explains why policies that encourage union membership and promote broad-based bargaining would enable labor to deliver much more for workers and the economy than they can under the current system. The chapter discusses why labor has been in decline in the United States and elsewhere but has been able to maintain strength in a few other countries with favorable policies. Policies that actively encourage union membership are needed to counteract the collective action problem unions present. The chapter also discusses why collective bargaining currently does not work very well in this country but could be much improved by shifting toward broader-based bargaining. Compared to worksite bargaining, broad-based bargaining raises wages for more workers, reduces economic inequality as well as gender and racial pay gaps to a greater degree, and is better suited to the way firms are structured in the modern economy.

Chapter 4 reinforces the lessons from the preceding chapter by presenting case studies from Canada, Britain, and Australia—the three countries most similar to the United States. The case studies highlight the importance of broad-based bargaining and strong incentives for union membership. Canada has the kinds of traditional labor policies that most union supporters wish for in the United States, including stronger strike rights and no "right-to-work" laws, but unions in Canada continue to lose density, and workplace-level bargaining is not working very well there either. Both Britain and Australia are suffering the consequences of moving toward US-style law and dismantling their systems that promoted higher-level bargaining and robust union membership. Importantly, major elements of the left in all three countries have begun working to promote the kinds of changes called for in this book. Comparisons with countries similar to the United States reinforces the need for a new US labor system.

The final two chapters discuss potential challenges that could prevent a new labor system from being enacted. Chapter 5 considers whether the new labor system could work as intended in the United States and whether alternative policies could better address the country's economic and political problems. It reviews some of the likely implementation challenges the new system would face, including determining the appropriate bargaining unit in a broad-based system and relationship friction between national and local unions, and finds, based on the US historical experience, that the challenges are likely manageable. It also reviews alternatives to the new labor system and argues that while most would be helpful, all have limitations. Other strategies to strengthen labor, such as increased organizing by unions and banning right-to-work laws, are necessary but on their own would not sufficiently increase union density or dramatically increase collective bargaining coverage. Nonunion policies—from increased training to a jobs guarantee to campaign finance reform—would do less to raise wages, reduce inequality, or increase political voice. These often rely on strong labor unions to work best. All told, the new labor system is practical and necessary.

Chapter 6 explores whether a new labor system could ever become law and overcome the massive political hurdles standing in the way. The path to victory is quite narrow. There needs to be sufficient grassroots activism to push labor issues to the top of the agenda, a strong majority of politicians willing to vote for pro-union policy, champions to drive the policy forward, and a favorable intellectual climate. As difficult as these are to achieve, they are possible if favorable trends continue and rise in intensity. The public must increasingly and more forcefully demand change, and the political and intellectual climate must continue shifting in favor of labor modernization. The chapter concludes by echoing the theme of the book—that a new labor system with broad-based bargaining and encouragement for union membership would help address the fundamental economic and political challenge that the United States faces. The more people recognize this, the better the chances for creating a new labor system.

1

THE PLAN

The proposed new American labor system would be built around two central ideas. First, public policy needs to actively support unions, not just be neutral about their existence. Active encouragement of union membership is critical because unions face structural disadvantages that limit their ability to recruit members—including the power employers inherently have over their employees and the basic collective action problem that encourages workers to take advantage of the efforts of others and free ride. Second, policy needs to encourage broad-based collective bargaining that seeks to cover all workers in a labor market, in addition to worksite-level bargaining. Broad-based bargaining is so important because it covers more workers and does more to raise wages, reduce economic inequality, and close gender and racial pay gaps. It is also well suited to the way modern firms are structured.

The proposed system would seek to push union density higher than it has been in US history and ensure that some form of collective agreement sets wages and benefits for the vast majority of workers. It would provide workers with strong rights as well as incentives to join unions so that unions would have more power to bring employers to the bargaining table, and it would structure collective bargaining to cover as many people as possible. While the new system would be a radical departure from the current American system that stifles union membership and severely constricts collective bargaining, it is based on elements that have proven to work in the United States as well as in countries around the world.

To actively support unions, a number of policy reforms are needed. Most obvious are the kinds of changes that would protect workers' basic rights. These types of changes have long been promoted by unions and would help reverse the obvious inequities in current law that advantage employers and disadvantage workers. All workers—including domestic, agricultural, and public-sector workers, as well as independent contractors—need union and collective bargaining rights. These rights also need to be sufficiently strong, and workers need a fair process for joining unions. Policies to achieve these goals include preventing employers from permanently replacing striking workers, allowing intermittent and sit-down strikes, permitting various types of picketing and protesting, increasing penalties on companies that violate labor law, ensuring that workers have a private right of action to access the courts for violations of their rights, and outlawing coercive tactics that allow employers to force workers into one-on-one discussions about the union with their supervisor. They also include banning so-called right-to-work laws that undermine union finances, requiring employers to recognize unions where a majority of workers have signed cards, and allowing first contract arbitration to prevent employer opposition from dragging on endlessly. Union-endorsed legislation such as the Protecting the Right to Organize Act and the Public Service Freedom to Negotiate Act include these types of provisions.[1]

As vital as these changes are, achieving truly strong unions will also take policies that provide unions with additional platforms for recruitment and workers with additional incentive to join. Union membership is notably high and stable primarily in countries that have the Ghent system, in which unions help deliver unemployment insurance.[2] Most countries, including the United States, have a system of unemployment insurance administered by government, but for a variety of historical reasons unions have been heavily involved in running the unemployment systems of several other countries, notably Denmark, Finland, Sweden, Iceland, and Belgium. The Ghent system gives unions greater access to workers, enables them to deliver important assistance, and provides a selective incentive for workers to join unions, which leads to higher membership levels. In the United States, Ghent-like incentives would be provided in a number of ways, including through reforms promoting labor-management workforce training partnerships, allowing unions to help workers navigate public benefits such as health care and retirement, and encouraging unions to help enforce workplace laws. Unions would be involved in the navigation and delivery of a range of governmental benefits that workers need throughout their lifetime. Additional platforms for recruitment, such as worksite access, are also helpful and can complement Ghent-like incentives.

Promoting broad-based bargaining will also take a big set of changes. In order for any type of collective bargaining to be successful, unions need enough strength to compel employers to bargain with them, which is why the reforms to ensure union rights and encourage union membership are so critical. But broad-based bargaining works best with additional tools because it seeks to cover all workers in a labor market and requires bringing multiple employers to the table, rather than just one.

The first step toward promoting higher-level bargaining is to undo the structural biases against it in current law. In the United States, the law is oriented toward a very narrow type of collective bargaining often known as enterprise bargaining—which means bargaining only for a particular group of workers at a particular worksite—for example, the butchers at one supermarket location. The law permits other arrangements on occasion, such as bargaining for all the butchers in a supermarket chain, all the workers at one supermarket, or even all the workers at all the supermarkets in a region. Generally, however, the system contains a number of features that lead toward collective bargaining based on small, fragmented units in particular firms or parts of a firm.[3] Current policy, for example, prevents workers from striking or picketing against "secondary" employers, which is an important way that unions can force multiple employers to bargain.[4] Current policy also unnecessarily gives employers a veto over whether unions can legally combine existing bargaining units or seek to bargain with multiple employers. These and other shackles that make it unnecessarily difficult for unions to achieve sectoral bargaining should be eliminated.

In some cases, getting rid of these restrictions on broad-based bargaining, combined with reforms that increase union membership, will help unions gain sufficient power to bring enough employers to the table to negotiate for an entire industry. This kind of bargaining is the ideal, but if reforms stopped here too few workers would benefit from collective bargaining agreements, given the current weakness of unions and the way many sectors of the economy are structured with multiple layers of contracted firms. Thus, the new system would also promote contract extension and workers' boards to ensure broad bargaining coverage.

Contract extension spreads the gains from union contracts to similarly placed workers—effectively extending the terms of collectively bargained agreements to workers in nonunion firms. Extension could be achieved through the expanded use of prevailing wage laws, such as Davis-Bacon, which requires that firms doing construction work for the government pay market rates, as well as through the creation of a new policy to promote master contracts. In areas where unions have been able to maintain, or could reasonably be expected to achieve, a decent level of bargaining coverage, extension laws help amplify union strength and ensure that all employers in a particular sector provide workers with similar wages and benefits. In regions or sectors where union density is too low and the sector too fragmented for independent collective bargaining to cover many workers, workers' boards—governmental bodies that bring together representatives of workers, employers, and the public and are sometimes called wage boards—would set minimum wage and benefit standards.

In order to imagine what this model of broader-based bargaining and incentives for membership would look like, it is helpful to consider a couple of real-life examples from the training for home care workers in Washington State and the bargaining by TV show writers. The analogies to other industries may not be perfect, especially because unique features enabled unions and employers to strike these deals, but the examples provide a good overview of what may seem like difficult concepts to see working in the United States.

Over recent decades, the State of Washington has worked to move Medicaid-financed long-term care from nursing homes to in-home and community-based care, allowing seniors and people with disabilities to continue to live in their homes. During this transition, the state worked to ensure that caregivers in the home had appropriate training.[5] Home care workers must now complete seventy-five hours of training to be certified as a home care aide, with ongoing continuing education requirements.[6] This training is provided by a joint labor-management partnership.

The home care labor-management partnership provides several kinds of support for union membership. The training is open to all, but the cost of training is covered by employer contributions for union members. This provides an incentive for union membership. The training also provides a platform for unions to recruit new members by increasing union access to workers and highlighting the role unions play in delivering important benefits. The home care partnership is now expanding beyond basic training to include apprenticeships for more advanced caregiving as well as building credentials to move to fields such as nursing, thereby providing additional help to workers and additional opportunities for unions to recruit members.[7] This system has delivered for unions (by helping support high density), for workers (by significantly increasing compensation), and for the public at large (by improving the quality of care). Indeed, Washington ranks among the top states for quality of long-term services and supports, likely in part because the training program has helped build a more professionalized workforce and a strong union that has been able to negotiate increased pay for workers.[8]

Under the new labor system, this type of union involvement in benefit delivery would not just be limited to training home care workers in Washington State. Rather, unions would be integrated into a wide range of federal, state, and local programs, including training but also such benefits as helping workers navigate health care and retirement programs and helping enforce workplace laws. Doing so would likely benefit not just workers and their unions but also the general public. Indeed, research on similar programs that involve unions in public programs suggest that this structure leads to improved outcomes for the public, such as higher take-up rates of benefits.[9]

Elements of the broad-based bargaining model can be seen in the contract television writers currently have. Two unions, the Writers Guild of America, East and West, negotiate a nationwide Minimum Basic Agreement with the Alliance of Motion Picture and Television Producers. The contract provides for minimum wages, portable pension and health benefits, a process to receive proper credit for one's work, and residual payments to writers when produced content is exhibited outside of its initial window. Writers can—and frequently do—negotiate for higher standards, but employers cannot pay less than the minimums agreed on. In 2017, for example, a writer of a story and teleplay for a thirty-minute prime-time network TV show received a minimum fee of $26,303, and roughly 40 to 50 percent of that amount for the first prime-time network rerun that aired, depending on the show's budget, followed by progressively smaller percentages for each subsequent rerun. Moreover, the production company is required to pay an additional 19 percent contribution on top of the writer's salary and TV residual payments to the Writers Guild of America's pension and health fund to cover the writer's benefits.[10] Minimum payments for non-network prime-time shows were smaller but followed a similar format. Even when a writer changed employers, their work was still covered by the minimum basic agreement, and they therefore continued to receive the minimum pay and benefits that the collective bargaining agreement guaranteed.

The writers' contract is negotiated between their union and an alliance representing hundreds of production companies and covers much of the writing work in the industry and thus approaches a sector-wide contract.[11] Still, it does not actually cover the entire sector of television writing, as it leaves out a number of reality television production companies and some production companies for streamed shows.[12] The union has been trying to organize much of this work and may succeed, even under current laws. But under the new system it would be more likely that writing for reality television would be covered—either because the union gained additional members and strength from the policy changes designed to promote union membership or because the terms of the contract were spread through prevailing wage-style extension.

To sum up, the new labor system would strengthen unions and workplace bargaining, create platforms and incentives to encourage union membership, and promote broad-based bargaining. The box below provides a high-level overview of the core elements of the new labor system.

Core Elements of the Proposed US Labor System

Robust union rights for all workers

- Fair process for joining unions
- Strong strike, picket, and protest rights
- Meaningful penalties and remedies for violations
- Arbitration to facilitate first contracts

Platforms and incentives to encourage union membership

- Union access to workers
- Union role in workforce training, enforcement of workplace laws, and public benefits navigation

Broad-based bargaining

- Elimination of current biases against broad-based bargaining
- Extension of collectively bargained standards to similarly placed workers
- Creation of workers' boards where bargaining hardly exists

In the new system, workers would have strong and effectively enforced basic rights—most importantly the right to strike and protest in a variety of ways, a fair process for joining unions that does not allow employers to override workers' desires, and meaningful remedies for violations of workers' rights. Rights would extend to virtually all workers—not just the select group of workers currently protected. In addition, workplace bargaining would continue and would receive additional aid, including arbitration to facilitate first contracts. These protections would provide a foundation for bottom-up worker power.

On top of these basic rights would come policies that would actively encourage union membership. Unions would play an important role in helping deliver workforce training, enforcement of workplace laws, and other public benefits such as unemployment and paid leave and would use this position to help recruit and retain members.

Broad-based collective bargaining would be supported by facilitating independent negotiations between unions and multiple employers as well as by creating structures that support higher-level bargaining. Legal barriers to broad-based bargaining, such as bans on worker activities that involve "secondary" employers, would be eliminated, as would restrictions on combining bargaining units. Contract extension to spread the gains of collective bargaining agreements would be promoted—for example, through widespread use of prevailing wage-style laws—and workers' boards would be created in places where collective bargaining is particularly difficult.

As subsequent chapters will highlight, especially chapter 4 with its discussion of Australia and Britain, there can be some degree of flexibility about the specific elements of the essential components. For example, an essential element of protecting workers' rights is the need to make the process for joining unions fairer. The process would be fairer if coercive one-on-one employer meetings were banned, though it is possible that a reasonably fair process could be achieved through other means, such as a union sign-up process, or through a combination of reforms. The key is the general direction of policy. It needs to actively support union membership with strong rights and incentives for joining as well as seek to cover most workers with collectively bargained agreements by encouraging broad-based and workplace-level bargaining. It is also important to note that these core elements are compatible with a number of additional labor reforms, as will be discussed in subsequent chapters, particularly chapter 5 with its review of alternative reforms.

The rest of chapter 1 will explain more about how the new system would work. It will discuss the role of unions in the new system and how the new system would fit with the current one. It will also provide additional details on the modernized system's newer elements, including contract extension, workers' boards, and the Ghent system. To help ground the discussion of these elements, the chapter will review how similar policies work in the United States today and touch on some history of broad-based bargaining in the United States. (Chapter 5 provides additional discussion of the history of higher-level bargaining in the United States). Finally, it will discuss the relationships between top-down policies to promote union power and grassroots organizing that develops bottom-up power.

First, a brief discussion of bargaining terminology is in order. This book uses the terms "broad-based bargaining" and "higher-level bargaining" as catchall terms for bargaining done above the level of the worksite or firm. Broader-based bargaining can be structured in different ways and called many different things, including "sectoral," "multi-employer," "industry-wide," "occupational," "national" "regional," or even "supply-chain" bargaining. There are important distinctions between each of these types of broader-based bargaining, but all are part of a similar family that is clearly distinct from worksite-level bargaining.

Various types of broad-based bargaining may operate slightly differently, but they seek to set a floor for the relevant labor market and ensure that employers provide similar pay to workers who do similar jobs in similar environments. Sometimes the relevant labor market necessary to set compensation standards among competitors is regional—such as for retail workers—but other times it is industry-wide, such as for auto workers. Often broad-based bargaining is a hybrid of types: the television writers' contract is a mix of industry-wide and occupational bargaining. More of these details will be covered in subsequent chapters, but the key point to understand now is that "broader-based bargaining" and "higher-level bargaining" are terms to represent a number of types of bargaining structures that seek to cover all workers in a labor market.

Workers' boards—governmental bodies that bring together representatives of workers, employers, and the public to set minimum standards for jobs in particular occupations and sectors—are also included under the terms "broader-based bargaining" and "higher-level bargaining" because they seek to set standards for whole sectors or occupations. However, it is important to note that they do not constitute truly independent collective bargaining because they give the government a seat at the table. The term "sectoral bargaining" is often used as a synonym for "broad-based bargaining" in the popular debate.

The Old and the New Systems

The new labor system would need to be layered on top of the current system. It is more feasible to build on an existing system than to create something from scratch. But layering is also an effective approach because no single method of bargaining works perfectly for all situations, and no single incentive structure is sufficient to recruit members. The ideal labor system is not one pure type but rather has a mixture of elements.

Higher-level bargaining is very good at setting broad floors that cover most workers, while enterprise bargaining has the benefit of providing greater flexibility to address workplace-specific issues. In even the most centralized bargaining systems in the world there is some room for workplace bargaining. Higher-level bargaining provides a framework and places some constraints on worksite-level bargaining, but worksite bargaining still plays an important role. The two types of bargaining can complement each other and maximize their individual strengths while minimizing their weaknesses.[13] Similarly, people join organizations for many reasons, and providing only one type of incentive would make unions too vulnerable to changes in that system. Even countries with a true Ghent system provide additional ways for unions to recruit members.

In the modernized US system, unions would continue to recruit members in some of the ways they currently do—from encouraging solidarity and workplace improvements to offering products to members—and charge agency fees to all workers covered by an enterprise-level collective bargaining agreement. But unions would also gain additional platforms to recruit members, such as through a much more prominent role in the workforce training system and deeper integration in enforcement of workplace laws and navigation of government programs. These Ghent-like policies would provide unions greater access to workers and provide workers with additional reasons to join.

In the new system, additional tools, opportunities, and incentives for membership would be critical because broad-based bargaining covers union as well as nonunion workers and thus creates additional opportunities for free riding. The opportunity for free riding often weakens unions, but these kinds of policies have proven powerful enough to maintain high and stable union density even in the face of the collective action problem. In the new system, unions would still have to work to organize and recruit dues-paying members but would have help in doing so. Requiring unions to continue to actively recruit members is important because it helps ensure unions maintain their independence and grassroots connections, which are essential to exercising power. All told, traditional methods of organizing workers and funding unions, combined with newer platforms for recruitment and greater ability to deliver for workers, will help significantly increase union membership.

Enterprise bargaining would also continue but as part of a bargaining system that would encourage broader-based bargaining. Unions would still be able to negotiate enterprise agreements (and charge workers at the firms for this service as they do now). But the new system would give unions additional tools to bring multiple employers to the bargaining table. In addition, if collective bargaining reached a certain threshold of coverage in a sector or region, the terms of the contract could be extended to similarly placed workers, a bit like how prevailing wage laws currently operate for government contracting. In sectors where there is minimal or no union density, bargaining would need to be bootstrapped through a workers' board, composed of representatives of workers, business, and the public.

The new system would require some significant changes for unions, and as a result not all unions will eagerly support or easily adapt to this new model. Some local and even national unions with significant influence with a particular employer could fear losing out as broader-based bargaining takes hold. And some unions will be challenged by a system that at times emphasizes working closely with government. But the union role in the modernized system would not be so different from what many unions have done in the past and some continue to do today.

In the new system, unions would play a more formalized role in providing public benefits—a role they have experience with. Since their inception, labor unions have been involved with workforce training, and today unions train thousands and thousands of workers every year through joint labor-management training funds and place them in good jobs. Unions help lead these training efforts in a variety of ways, from bringing groups of employers together to create an industry-wide training program, bargaining for employers to fund the program, seeking government grants, helping set training standards, and helping administer the public training system by serving on government workforce boards. Further, many labor-management training funds provide training to union and nonunion workers. In addition, unions help run funds that provide health care and retirement benefits to millions of workers. They help workers apply for and receive public benefits such as unemployment insurance and workers' compensation benefits.[14] Unions also enforce the contracts of their members as well help ensure that the legal standards in various workplace laws are adhered to.

Similarly, many unions have a history of bargaining above the enterprise level. Until the 1980s, higher-level bargaining was quite common in many industries, especially in industries like mining, trucking, steel, and telecommunications.[15] Estimates suggest that in 1980 roughly 10 percent of US workers were covered by multi-employer agreements.[16] This means that in 1980, approximately 40 percent of all workers covered by a collective bargaining agreement were covered by a multi-employer agreement.

Some of this broad-based bargaining occurred when a group of employers negotiated with a union or unions about the conditions in the industry, while in other cases it occurred through pattern bargaining, where a union would negotiate with a single firm and then uses its power in negotiating with other firms in the industry to ensure that they adopted the same contract, so ultimately many of the workers in the industry were covered by the same contract. Only in a few cases did this bargaining actually cover most of the workers in a relevant labor market and truly take wages out of competition, but in a number of cases it covered a significant percentage and approached this goal. This history will be explored more in subsequent chapters, as it shows how the current system makes broader-based bargaining difficult to achieve and maintain and also highlights why the new system would be much better. The point to recognize now is that many unions have experience with broader-based bargaining, so they would likely be able to perform bargaining roles encouraged by the new system. Indeed, higher-level bargaining exists in a number of sectors today, such as hotels in some cities and in sports and entertainment, to name a few examples—though it is nowhere near as common today as it once was.

With this baseline understanding of how the new labor system would operate, the details of its new facets can be explored. The new labor system's interlocking policies to strengthen unions and promote broader-based bargaining would not work well without all of these core elements. For example, workers cannot effectively bargain without enhanced strike rights and adequate penalties on employers that violate the law. But these and many other parts of the envisioned new labor system have long been on the labor reform agenda and are fairly well understood. In contrast, contract extension, workers' boards, and an American version of the Ghent system are less well known and deserve additional discussion.

Broad-Based Bargaining

Most countries in which sectoral bargaining covers a significant percentage of workers have what are known as extension laws, which spread the gains of union contracts to similarly placed workers.[17] Extension laws vary across countries, but the basic concept is that once a union contract is considered to represent a sufficient number of workers in an industry or region, its wage and benefit standards are extended though official action to cover all workers in that industry and region, regardless of whether or not the workers are part of the union. This helps to spread the gains of union contracts but also encourages employers to collectively bargain so that they can have input on these industry-wide or regional standards. In the United States, the most promising versions of this concept are based on prevailing wage laws that are already used for government contracts and the Baigent-Ready model being considered in Canada that seeks to extend master contracts.

In the United States, prevailing wage laws such as the Davis-Bacon Act of 1931 require companies working on government-funded projects to pay wages and benefits that, at minimum, match existing compensation levels in the industry and region. Prevailing wage laws are most commonly applied to government-funded construction projects, but they can also apply to service work and to grants, loans, and tax breaks, and they exist at the federal, state, and local levels. These laws ensure that government spending does not drive down market wages, and they lead to high-quality work and good value for taxpayers.[18]

Prevailing wage laws can also be seen as fostering broad-based collective bargaining and helping standardize wages across an industry—as the laws can, in areas where there is sufficient union density, effectively extend collectively bargained wages to other workplaces that contract with the government. Under these laws, governments must determine what wages prevail in the industry and occupation. This is often set at the rate that either 30 or 50 percent of workers are paid—a level that is possible for some unions in certain areas to achieve through workplace-level bargaining but still a relatively high threshold. But the way prevailing wages are calculated in some localities is particularly supportive of collectively bargained wages. Bergen County, New Jersey, uses collectively bargained wages from the union contract that covers the most workers in a given classification for prevailing wages for building service workers, provided that the contract covers at least two hundred workers.[19] Several states have explicitly use collectively bar-gained rates, without regard for a set coverage threshold, to determine prevailing wages for public works projects.[20] Still other states give significant consideration to collectively bargained wages.[21]

While prevailing wage laws already support collective bargaining and encour-age industry-wide coverage, the basic model could be applied more broadly.

A step toward promoting sectoral bargaining would be to ensure that all government spending—no matter how it is structured, whether it is a contract, grants, loans, or tax break—has prevailing wage standards attached to it. Cur-rently, prevailing wage laws tend to apply only to a fraction of overall government spending, so there is significant potential for expansion of this concept, at the federal level as well in state and local governments. As a second step, the prevail-ing wage should be calculated in a way that supports unions. One way to do this would be to set the percentage of workers covered by a contract necessary to be determined prevailing could also be set at more easily attainable levels, such as 20 or 30 percent. Alternatively, once a sufficient number of workers are covered by a collective bargaining agreement, for example 200 workers, the standards in those contracts become prevailing. A third and more dramatic step would be to use the prevailing wage model in the private sector outside of areas with significant government spending. Under this policy, once union contract coverage meets the representation threshold set by prevailing wage laws, employers in the same industry and region would have to meet the union standards.[22]

Prevailing wage-style extension would be particularly useful in industries and regions where unions already have relatively high levels of density. In those areas, the contracts that unions have negotiated would set the standards that other employers would need to follow. Unions would gain some stability knowing that their bargaining would not be constantly under threat from low-road employers. Unions that were close to the coverage threshold necessary to trigger the contract extension would have a strong incentive to organize additional workplaces. Fur-thermore, employers in these sectors would have an incentive to bargain, as they would want to have some input on the standards.

Still, many industries and regions are far from having the density levels nec-essary for prevailing wage extension to work and would need different types of extension tools. In lower-density sectors and regions, a kind of master-contract extension being considered in Canada would be necessary to promote broader-based bargaining.

Canadian unions and policy makers have increasingly recognized the impor-tance of promoting broad-based bargaining and have been considering a range of alternatives to achieve this goal. The Canadian labor system is quite similar to the US system, and one of its most notable sectoral bargaining proposals is the Baigent-Ready model, named after two commissioners on a labor reform panel.[23]

Under the Baigent-Ready model, once a union contract covers two different workplaces in a particular industry and region, each additional workplace that organizes would be automatically covered by the union contract. This means that if a union bargains a contract with company X at one worksite and bargains a similar contract with company Y at another worksite in the same industry and region, then each additional worksite where a majority of workers agree to join the union in that industry and region is covered by the same contract.

The policy works a bit like a master contract on steroids. American unions have a long history of creating master contracts, where they create a single contract that they negotiate with multiple employers to sign.[24] However, as unions have become weaker and the law increasingly hostile, they have had a harder time getting employers to agree to sign these agreements. Indeed, today only one-seventh of union organizing drives results in a union contract for workers.[25] Under a Baigent-Ready policy, unions would not have to compel each new employer to sign the master contract—they would only need to organize workers at the worksite to automatically achieve contract coverage, thus making master contracts much easier to extend to other worksites.

This master-contract extension can help get multi-employer bargaining started, particularly in industries with relatively low union density and a number of small employers or firms. In the early stages, when relatively few employers are covered by the master contract, this coverage would not constitute true sectoral bargaining. However, it would create an on-ramp to covering all workers in a sector in a manner that is quite compatible with the current process of worksite-level organizing. Unions would still need to organize worksite by worksite, but the process would be much easier. Workers would be more optimistic and less fearful because, once organized, they would immediately be covered by a union contract, and employers would not be able to deploy the common tactic of fighting to avoid signing.[26] Thus, the Baigent-Ready model would be a helpful tool to promote multi-employer bargaining in industries where a little push is necessary to get the process moving, as well as helping to strengthen unions.

There will still be regions and sectors in which traditional or even Baigent-Ready-style collective bargaining may not be able to gain a strong foothold. Examples include heavily fragmented industries with very low union density, such as domestic work, the gig economy, and fast food franchises. Policy makers also need to ensure that workers in these areas and other workers are not misclassified as independent contractors.[27]

Workers' boards—which bring together representatives of employers, workers, and the public to set minimum standards—are particularly helpful in these types of cases. In sectors where there is little or no traditional collective bargaining, these tripartite boards can significantly raise standards and help create the conditions that lead to more independent bargaining. Several states, including New York and California, have relatively limited versions of wage boards, but Seattle has a more robust version for domestic workers, and Washington State considered a particularly strong version for independent contractors.[28] The more robust versions of wage boards are often called workers' boards or worker standards boards.

In a new labor system, workers' boards would have the ability to set minimum wages and benefits, or floors, for jobs across an industry, as well as institute wage scales requiring higher pay for greater skills or experience. Individual workers and their unions could negotiate for improvements but could not go below set minimums. All workers in an industry would be covered, regardless of whether employees or independent contractors and whether or not unionized. The workers' board process would offer strong legal protections for participating workers, increase union access to workers, and provide incentives to encourage workers to join unions and other worker organizations that represent them on the boards.[29] These incentives would include involving unions in the enforcement of the wage board standards and enabling worker organizations to help deliver benefits or navigate workers through the process. These essential workers' board elements would help build union strength and potentially lead to more direct bargaining, especially because workers and employers would create a history of negotiating.[30]

There is a long history of wage boards in the United States—they were used to help set standards in dozens of states in the early 1900s as well as in the original federal minimum wage legislation, and they continue to be used in several states.[31] Even though the National Labor Relations Act preempts state and local governments from legislating around a number of bargaining issues for workers covered by the act, the model of setting minimum standards through a tripartite wage board is legally considered standard setting rather than bargaining, and thus state and local governments have some room for experimentation.[32]

Perhaps the most notable example in recent years of a wage board was for fast food workers in New York State. Fast food work in the United States is typically very low-paid, with extremely high turnover, and even though there are a few very large profitable firms, such as McDonald's, Burger King, and Taco Bell, most of the individual employers are relatively small franchises with low profit margins. If the majority of workers at a particular store location organized, they would be extremely unlikely to be able to negotiate for better working conditions—with the lead firm claiming no responsibility, the franchise claiming no ability, and the location possibly closing to prevent negotiations from occurring. Moreover, should the workers succeed in negotiating a contract—this one store would then have higher labor costs than its competitors, potentially creating a range of economic difficulties. In this context, broad-based bargaining would be particularly useful, but it could only be achieved with a wage board due to low union density in the industry.

In 2015 the governor of New York exercised his long-standing but infrequently used ability to empanel a tripartite wage board composed of a representative of workers, a representative of employers, and a representative of the public to investigate working conditions and make recommendations for the fast food industry.[33] The board conducted investigations into working conditions in the industry and heard testimony from workers, employers, and the public over a period of several months. The board recommended a $15 hourly minimum wage for the industry—which would be achieved more quickly in downstate New York than in the more rural upstate areas—raising wages for thousands of fast food workers and setting a precedent that would ultimately be adopted statewide.[34] The states of California and New Jersey also have similar wage board laws.

A related but more expansive version of a worker board comes from Seattle, which in 2018 passed a groundbreaking bill for domestic workers such as housecleaners, nannies, and home care providers.[35] This policy provides one of the most important and innovative models for the future of bargaining and worker organization. Domestic workers—as well as agricultural workers and independent contractors—are exempt from federal labor law, which provides state and local governments greater room for experimentation with forms of higher-level bargaining, as well as incentives for membership. The industry is characterized by low pay and poor working conditions, and it has long been fissured with many independent contractors and very small employers. Some consider domestic work to be the original "gig" work, as it can be quite difficult to get steady well-paying employment and workers often need to piece together multiple gigs.[36] These industry conditions occur in part because domestic workers have not been covered by federal bargaining law or minimum wage laws, because the workers often are immigrants with low levels of education, and because barriers to entry into the industry are low.

In this context, typical enterprise-based collective bargaining is very difficult. A lone house cleaner or nanny does not have much ability or structure to bargain collectively with the employing family. Nor does a group of "independent contractors" have much ability to negotiate with the agency that contracts them out, and, even if they somehow could, standards would be easily undercut as only a very small part of the industry would be organized.

The Seattle solution was to bring together representatives of employers, workers, and the government in a workers' board to negotiate minimum industry standards for domestic work. Because of the structure of the industry and the fact that most of the workers are unorganized and have little ability to compel employers to bargain, it was necessary for the government to create a bargaining table and force all the parties together. Over time, the board may evolve into a more direct kind of multi-employer bargaining, affirming, and helping spread the contracts agreed upon through collective bargaining.

The Seattle domestic worker law does far more than just create a structure for broader-based bargaining, because it also creates several incentives for membership. The law creates a process for selecting board members that provides an impetus for groups to organize workers and for workers to participate. More directly, the policy can create a fund to help provide the kinds of benefits other workers often receive but are virtually impossible for domestic workers to get, such as sick leave, training, and workers' compensation. Such a fund would be managed by worker organizations and help provide a key tool for recruitment because it would authorize worker organizations to help deliver public benefits and provide them with access to workers and an incentive for workers to join them.

Incentives for Membership

The portable benefits fund is an example of how a Ghent-like system could be created in the United States. The Ghent system—named for the city in Belgium where it originated—relies on labor unions to administer unemployment benefits. Today variations of the Ghent system exist in Denmark, Finland, Sweden, Iceland, and Belgium. While each country's system works slightly differently, the underlying logic is the same. The Ghent system provides worker organizations with a formalized role in delivering unemployment insurance that is subsidized by the government. In some versions of the Ghent system, workers are required to join the union to access the benefits, but in other versions unions use the insurance sign-up process and the relationships built through this process to recruit and retain members.

In Belgium, the government is responsible for funding the unemployment insurance system, and people can either choose to go through the government or a union to access the benefits. The union receives government funds to help administer the program; however, it has to keep that money separate from other union finances. Workers do not have to be union members in order to receive the benefits, but many still choose to go through the unions because they find it easier and the service better. Unions make it easier to navigate bureaucracy by providing help with paperwork and ensuring that workers receive their payments and enroll in training.[37] On top of supplying a needed public benefit, the system also gives unions a chance to interact with workers outside the workplace.[38]

In short, the Ghent system creates a framework that incentivizes and encourages union membership.

The benefits of the Ghent system can extend to the public as well. There is some research to suggest that, despite the voluntary nature of Ghent—as opposed to the "universal" nature of most countries' unemployment insurance systems—take-up rates in Ghent countries are actually higher than in other European countries or the United States. For instance, one study found that in both Denmark and Sweden, 85 percent of unemployed people received unemployment insurance in 2005, compared with only 47 percent and 20 percent of unemployed people in Germany and the UK, respectively.[39] What's more, studies find that the Ghent system can help achieve much higher coverage in an efficient and cost-effective manner.[40] Other research suggests that the key role unions play in the Ghent system helps make it work well.[41]

In the United States, there is clear evidence that public programs designed to help workers—such as unemployment, health care, and retirement benefits—can be difficult to navigate alone and that involving unions would likely improve outcomes. For example, only about 40 percent of unemployed workers apply for unemployment insurance and less than 30 percent receive it.[42] Studies suggest that union members are more likely to receive workers' compensation and unemployment insurance (UI) than nonunion members.[43] Indeed, blue-collar workers who were laid off from union jobs were about 23 percent more likely than comparable nonunion workers to receive UI benefits. Professors John W. Budd and Brian P. McCall speculate that unions drive higher take-up rates by acting as a "conduit of information." They argue that unions reduce the "costs" of applying for benefits by providing information about how and where to apply for benefits, helping collect evidence in case of disputed claims, and providing representation in hearings over disputes.[44]

The basic concept behind the Ghent system—unions delivering or helping people access governmental benefits—already exists in a number of forms in the United States. In the new system, these models would be expanded on so that unions would play a key role in helping provide a range of public services that workers need, including program navigation, workforce training, and enforcement of workplace laws.

This benefits navigation concept could be applied to a variety of government programs, from unemployment insurance to healthcare to retirement, and is currently being modeled in several areas. Somewhat mirroring Seattle, with its domestic worker benefits fund, New York has had a portable benefits fund for independent contractors who drive limos, known as the Black Car Fund, for two decades.[45] In recent years, the fund has also covered Uber and Lyft drivers. For drivers injured on the job, the fund provides workers' compensation insurance—something that most employees but very few independent contractors have. Benefits are funded by a legally required surcharge on each ride.[46] The International Association of Machinists and Aerospace Workers District 15 helped push for the creation of the fund, and its nonprofit affiliate, the Independent Drivers Guild, has been working to make the fund into even more of a recruitment tool.[47] The guild's benefit fund has partnered with the Black Car Fund to offer additional benefits, such as vision case, telemedicine, drug discounts and assistance in applying for Medicaid health insurance.

In Oregon the state Department of Administrative Services is currently partnering with a local union on a training program aimed at increasing state employee understanding of its retirement and health benefit plans and how to take advantage of them.[48] In this program, unions help workers navigate the state retirement and health benefits system to choose the appropriate plans for their situation, which participants believe will lead to savings for both workers and the state.

In addition to helping workers navigate public benefits, another Ghent-like model uses unions and worker organizations to help enforce workplace standards, as part of a co-enforcement strategy. There is a strong need for improved enforcement since evidence suggests that wage theft—or employers paying workers less than they are legally entitled to—and other violations of workplace standards are pervasive. A report by the Economic Policy Institute, for example, estimated that low-wage workers lost more than $50 billion to wage theft in 2016.[49]

The co-enforcement model helps improve enforcement of laws such as the minimum wage by recognizing what unions and worker centers can do that government cannot do on its own. These organizations are in contact with workers in more workplaces than government inspectors will ever be able to get to, and these groups have workers' trust. Thus, these organizations have information about what is happening to workers that government is not privy to—as vulnerable workers are often afraid to talk to government officials. As a result, these groups can serve as key intermediaries to bring workers and government together, both by informing workers of their rights and by helping workers take action to receive their earned pay and benefits.

Co-enforcement works for the public and unions. Co-enforcement initiatives, according to a study of them by professors Seema Patel and Catherine Fisk, improve "compliance and enforcement"; generate "professional development, sophistication, and commitment among enforcement officials"; and produce "modest revenue increases, better legitimacy, and strengthened institutional framework for groups working with, and composed of, low-wage workers most vulnerable to wage theft and other substandard working conditions."[50] Studies have also found that unions increase compliance with Fair Labor Standards Act overtime regulations.[51] For unions and worker organizations, the co-enforcement model can help increase access to workers, provide additional funding for some activities, and help them deliver real benefits to workers.[52]

One of the oldest and most successful co-enforcement programs is the Los Angeles Joint Labor Compliance Monitoring Program. Through it, the Los Angeles Unified School District (LAUSD) partners with trade unions to train volunteers to help identify violations of prevailing wage laws on district projects. The district authorizes these volunteers to conduct site visits and interview workers about compliance as well as help with audits, hearings, and review conferences.[53] The volunteers gather information and alert the city to problems, making it possible for city inspectors to determine penalties.[54] Professors Janice Fine and Jennifer Gordon noted that the program has expanded the city inspectorate's capacity and according to government officials helped identify more violations and improve compliance.[55] Similar programs exist across the city of Los Angeles as well as in Seattle and San Francisco.[56]

Another way to adapt the Ghent-like concept would be to bring unions more formally into the workforce training system. The current workforce training system in the United States is uneven, and outside of joint labor-management partnerships it is too often of low quality and fails to lead to good jobs.[57] For instance, studies find that while certificate and sub-baccalaureate programs generally yield some increase in earnings, returns vary significantly based on a student's field of study, race, and gender.[58] Moreover, a lot of training is firm-specific and leads to skills that are not transferable to other employers.[59] In addition, the United States spends less money on training than its competitors do, ranking at the bottom among OECD countries.[60] In other words, there is a large gap between the training that is needed and the training that is provided.

Involving worker organizations more robustly in the workforce training system could significantly improve training.[61] Unions already play a role in workforce training. They directly negotiate with employers to create labor-management training funds, and they participate in government-funded training in several roles, as both members of workforce boards and recipients of funding. But employers dominate the public system.[62] Rebalancing the workforce system to emphasize quality and ensure that unions and employers have equal power—as well as promoting joint labor-management programs—would help ensure that training leads to good jobs.

Research shows that when unions get involved, workers get more training, and this training leads to better results, including jobs with higher pay.[63] Furthermore, workers in labor-management programs are more likely to complete their training, and they drop out at lower rates during economic downturns.[64] Completion rates in labor-management construction apprenticeship programs in Ohio and Kentucky, for instance, are 21 percent and 35 percent higher, respectively, than in nonunion programs.[65] Union-sponsored training programs in the building trades also have higher enrollment rates and participation among women and people of color than training that is not sponsored by unions.[66] There is also strong evidence that workers highly value training and are willing to join unions because of it.[67]

Many states and the federal government have experience supporting training where unions play a key role.[68] A particularly strong version of using training to provide incentives for union membership is to ensure that the training necessary to enter into an occupation is provided by union-management partnerships. The best example of this comes from home care workers in Washington State (Montana has a similar system), as discussed previously. But New York State has had similar success with family child care providers; the workers' union, CSEA/ VOICE, helps ensure adherence to quality standards by providing training and technical assistance.[69] There is significant room to expand this required training model since there are hundreds of thousands of non-degree credentialing programs in the United States, and over one-quarter of workers are estimated to have certification or a license.[70]

Another way to increase the ability of unions to use training as a recruitment tool is to provide a dedicated funding stream for joint labor-management programs. One of the better-known labor-management training partnerships is the Las Vegas Culinary Academy, which provides preemployment training to people entering the hospitality industry, as well as advanced upgrade training to union members working for participating hotels on the Las Vegas Strip.[71] The academy arose out of a 1993 collective bargaining agreement between Las Vegas Strip properties and the two local unions—Culinary Workers Union Local 226 and Bartenders Union Local 165—that recognized the need to create a "reliable, trained" workforce, and it has since acquired its own building and become certified as a postsecondary institution by the State of Nevada.[72] Today the academy annually trains roughly sixteen hundred people—the majority of whom are Hispanic or African American.[73] Training is free for members from participating Las Vegas Strip properties, and nonunion entrants usually obtain funding from other federal, state, or nonprofit sources.[74] State funding helps the programs reach additional workers. By working with the industry's hiring hall to ensure that graduates are first in line for new job openings, the academy creates a clear path between training and existing jobs.[75]

The academy's unique structure gives the unions a role in structuring and regulating occupations, while also providing opportunities to extend union membership. Professors Mia Gray and James DeFilippis find that, "through the

Academy, many unemployed or underemployed local residents have trained . . . and have found their way into the industry and often, at the same time, into the union."[76] Providing a dedicated and adequate stream of public funding to similar joint labor-management training programs could help increase capacity.

Still, there are many other training models to build on, particularly in the public sector. For example, city employees in Toledo, Ohio, developed a program in which union members acted as peer trainers to promote safe work practices, leading to a decrease in employee injuries.[77] In California, public safety unions have partnered with the Office of the State Fire Marshal to create a joint apprenticeship committee that enables training consistency by having firefighters from different departments train under the same umbrella organization. This consistency was critical in 2015 when coordinating hundreds of firefighters across the state for a monthlong effort fighting wildfires.[78] The Washington State board that oversees the state's workforce development system is tripartite, with an equal number of representatives of workers, employers, and the public. Any or all of these policies could be expanded, such as by significantly increasing funding for training programs that involve unions, requiring employers to contribute to these funds, providing incentives to firms that involve unions in training programs, ensuring that mandated training is fulfilled by labor-management partnerships, and mandating that unions have equal representation with employers on governmental workforce training boards.[79]

It may take some experimentation to find the optimal mix of programs and union involvement for a Ghent-like system in the United States. But the goal is for unions to be involved in the navigation and delivery of the full range of governmental benefits that workers need—including health, retirement, and training—as well as enforcement of the law. As these examples demonstrate, there are opportunities across the federal, state, and local levels for policy makers to involve unions and worker organizations in training, navigation, and co-enforcement efforts. Doing so would help not only workers and their unions but also the government and the public.

In short, there are many existing models to build on and expand to create the new labor system. The United States has experience with prevailing wage extension, wage boards setting minimums across sectors, and Ghent-like policies in which unions help deliver public benefits. To be sure, none of the models have achieved the scale necessary, as they typically only apply in a limited area or to a specific industry or occupation. Still, they serve as proof of concept for local, state, and federal governments to build on. Policy clearly can seek to cover most workers with a collectively bargained contract and provide unions with a platform to recruit workers.

Union Power in the New System

In order for any labor system to succeed, workers need independent power as well as top-down power supported by government. Workers need bottom-up, grassroots, independent power so they can force recalcitrant employers to the bargaining table and because the politicians in control of government will not always support their goals. Yet maintaining high union density and high collective bargaining coverage over any length of time necessitates that government policy support unions and their bargaining. Workers need a supportive policy environment to help counterbalance the inherent power advantage of employers as well as market forces that often drive down wages. Only in rare cases can workers develop enough grassroots, independent power to succeed when employers and the market are aligned against them.

The new labor system is designed to increase workers' grassroots power as well as their top-down power. Bottom-up power would come from reforms that would, for example, improve strike rights, strengthen penalties on employers that violate the law, and get rid of exemptions in the law that deny rights to many categories of workers. Grassroots power would also be enhanced because the more novel elements in the new system, such as workers' boards and Ghent-like structures, would be designed to increase opportunities for member participation and recruitment.[80]

Still, the new labor system—especially broad-based bargaining and incentives for membership—is significantly about increasing labor's top-down, systemic power so that collective bargaining agreements cover far more workers and so that workers have stronger incentives to join unions. In any choice about labor's future there is an inherent tension between prioritizing bottom-up or top-down power. It is somewhat of a chicken-or-egg problem; workers need to pursue both.

The proposals advanced in this book cannot fully solve the problem of building grassroots power. They will help, but tremendous on-the-ground efforts are also required. More grassroots organizing and activism is needed, but this book emphasizes the importance of top-down power because bottom-up strategies are unlikely to succeed on their own, as subsequent chapters explain in more detail.

This top-down focus challenges an important strain of thought about labor unions. To some, unions should have relatively little to do with politics or policy—because whatever the state gives it can take away—and instead should focus on providing mutual aid and collective bargaining for a group of workers at a worksite. This view was strongly promoted by Samuel Gompers, the first president of the American Federation of Labor (AFL).[81] In views that emphasize voluntarism, power comes from the focused and independent actions of workers.

There is truth in the need for grassroots power, but in reality even those most dedicated to voluntarism have often also sought top-down power for workers. Samuel Gompers's views evolved over time so that he advocated for a wide range of measures to support unions and collective bargaining and for using policy to achieve these goals. Under Gompers, for example, the AFL worked to pass over one hundred pieces of legislation. Gompers also supported working very closely with the government on tripartite labor boards during World War I. According to the labor historian Joseph McCartin, Gompers was most successful in advancing labor's interest when voluntarism "was honored in the breach"—meaning that the use of top-down governmental power was critical to Gompers's successes.[82] Gompers even went so far as to argue that unions needed a formal role in government decision making, writing: "Labor has a right to representation on all agencies that control or determine public policies or matters of general concern."[83] Thus, even the leading proponent of "pure and simple" unionism also had a top-down view of how to exercise power.

Unions have always played a variety of roles in society and have practiced various tactics to build power for workers.[84] Though each union may have emphasized one tactic over another throughout the years, unions generally rely on a mixture of top-down and bottom-up power.

Indeed, one of the most iconic grassroots organizing campaigns in recent US history—Justice for Janitors—relied on a combination of top-down and bottom-up tactics and helps illustrate how the policies in this book could support systemic power as well as bottom-up power.[85] The Justice for Janitors campaign is most known for its innovative organizing activities and disruptive actions— including street protests, marches, rallies, picketing, and strikes—that built worker solidarity and applied pressure on building owners and the janitorial companies that directly employed the janitors. But top-down elements were also key to its success. A California law limiting court injunctions against strikes provided some protection and helped facilitate the protest activities. The union also sought to take wages out of competition by negotiating "trigger" agreements that were binding only when a majority of the industry unionized. These top-down elements were important for helping the campaign overcome some of the challenges it faced, including a vulnerable, largely immigrant workforce and widespread contracting out of janitorial services—which meant that labor costs were a large portion of firms' costs and low-wage competitors were ready to take over work if wages increased. Thus, the law helped protect workers' protest activities to build grassroots power, and broad-based bargaining was critical to facilitating agreements that could raise standards in the industry. Under the new labor system, campaigns like Justice for Janitors would be more common because workers would have even greater rights to strike, picket and protest, and broad-based bargaining would be easier to achieve.

Still, it is worth acknowledging that straying too far from workplace-based organization and working too closely with the government could potentially undermine union strength. At the extreme, unions could become creatures of the government with no independence, or mere service organizations that people only join for a specific perk without a strong core of committed members willing to take the risks and actions necessary to build real power.

While these are legitimate concerns, they should be seen as relatively remote. The proposals in this book would still leave unions with significant independent power and would enable unions to more effectively wield their grassroots power.

Enterprise-based collective bargaining is still a part of the vision for the future of labor—as Samuel Gompers was certainly right that there is power in workplace organization. In addition, to exercise power in the new system, unions will still need to organize workers. Under broader-based bargaining, unions will still need sufficient density to successfully make demands on employers and on the political system. Further, providing additional incentives for union membership does not get rid of the existing reasons workers join unions, nor does it automatically translate into increased membership. Unions will still need to do a good job delivering benefits and provide tangible improvements in workers' lives, and they will still need to work to recruit members. More generally, the new labor system would rely on unions organizing workers—it is just that unions would have more opportunities and more favorable conditions to do so than under the current system. The new system would recognize that workers need to feel some solidarity to join together in an organization and that the organization they join needs to be worker-led.

Moreover, the new system would merely formalize what unions are already doing, based on successful models used in the United States and abroad by organizations that are considered independent trade unions with grassroots power, even if they work closely with governments. Though American unions may not always publicly say so, they act in ways that show they understand that even the most independent collective bargaining relies on the underlying legal and political structure and that top-down power is essential to their success and that of workers. Beyond the specific state and local examples previously discussed, American unions frequently use a range of policy and political tools to support collective bargaining and advance the interests of all workers.

They commonly push for policies to ensure, for example, that government does not do business with companies that break workplace laws, as part of a strategy to put additional pressure on recalcitrant employers during organizing drives.[86] They have supported reforms, for example, to require fly-by-night car wash companies to post bonds to stabilize the industry so that it can be organized, and they commonly work with governments to use zoning, permitting, and even antitrust laws in ways that benefit organizing.[87] Unions frequently ask friendly politicians to march with them during strikes or other public events to encourage companies to settle a contract or recognize a union. Unions also seek top-down power to help all workers—not just their members—as they pursue policies to raise the minimum wage and promote universal health care, for example. While part of the reason unions support these kinds of policies is to raise the floor and ensure that unionized firms are at less of a disadvantage, much of the reason unions do so is because they recognize that to advance the interests of all workers requires the exercise of top-down power.

American unions even have a history of supporting laws to promote top-down, broad-based bargaining and standard setting, such as the National Industrial Recovery Act of 1933, which encouraged the creation of industry-wide codes that effectively set wages and prices, and the Bituminous Coal Conservation Act of 1935, which regulated prices and working conditions in the industry.[88] These laws were short-lived because of constitutional issues and thus may not serve as policy models, but they provide evidence that American unions and labor law have a more diverse history than is commonly recognized.

Thus, the tension between pursuing grassroots or top-down power is less than it seems. Unions usually pursue both types of power. This book focuses on top-down power because American unions have rarely had much of it, and creating structures that promote it is vital for achieving labor's goals, as subsequent chapters will make clear.

The Modernized System

The new labor system would strengthen unions and promote broader-based collective bargaining by increasing workers' rights, providing strong incentives for membership, creating processes that extend collective bargaining agreements to similarly placed workers, and forging bargaining processes where none exist. Workers would have greater ability to strike, the process for joining a union would be much easier, and collective rights would be afforded to all workers. Unions would play a vital role in delivering or helping workers navigate a range of public benefits. Unions would ensure high-quality workforce training and strict enforcement of workplace laws, and workers could access key public benefits and be able to use this platform to recruit members. Collective bargaining would largely occur above the level of the firm and seek to cover all workers in a labor market. Unions would have greater abilities to bring multiple employers to the bargaining table and seek sectoral bargaining, but extension laws and wage boards would broaden coverage where they lacked sufficient power to cover the labor market.

This would require a fundamental break from our current system. Yet the new labor system would be as much evolutionary as transformative. The changes would be quite bold but based on successful models. Policy at the local, state, and federal level already contains elements of the necessary changes. From co-enforcement models to wage boards and prevailing wage laws, the building blocks exist. And American unions currently perform, or have performed in the past, many of the roles that would be necessary in the new system. They have engaged in multi-employer bargaining and worked closely with government to achieve their goals.

Unions will need to change to take full advantage of a new labor system. Still, the kinds of changes imagined are well within the capabilities and experience of American unions. Current union leaders may not have worked under a system that strongly supports fostering union membership and enables unions to wield great top-down power, but their unions have experience with broader-based bargaining, delivering workforce training, ensuring laws are enforced, and even working closely with government to advance the interests of workers.

This framework understanding of a new American labor system will enable readers to follow the next several chapters, which explain why such a system is so necessary. Additional details about how the new labor system would work and how it could be achieved will be provided in the final chapters.

UNIONS AS THE SOLUTION

This chapter provides the theoretical and empirical basis for the book's claim that stronger unions operating under a new labor system would help solve America's economic and political challenges. Unions perform many different roles—from bargaining with employers over wages and benefits to mobilizing members and lobbying politicians. But, at the core, unions help bring people together to help address the inherent power imbalances at the worksite, in the larger economy, and in a democracy.

Unions help all workers—no matter their gender, race, ethnicity, skin color, or sexuality—negotiate for fair compensation on a more even playing field, and the gains they secure can spread throughout the economy. They also bring workers together to pressure elected officials, so that the will of the majority is more likely to be realized. And their efforts often do the most to help those who have traditionally been marginalized, including workers that are female, black, Hispanic, Asian, and LGBTQ. Simply put, employers and politicians are far more likely to listen to organized workers than they are to a lone, ordinary individual.

Simplistic theories of the economy assume that the magic of the market will automatically ensure that workers are paid what they are worth—ignoring that employers have numerous advantages in their dealings with employees and overlooking that worth is as much a social construct as an economic one.[1] Similarly, simplistic theories of democracy assume that politicians automatically give equal weight to all constituents—ignoring the numerous advantages the wealthy have. In the real world, most individuals acting on their own have little ability to influence employers or politicians. Unions organize people, bringing them together to provide a counterbalance to employers and the wealthy and make the market and democracy work properly.

This chapter provides a deeper investigation into what unions do in the economy and in a democracy to explain why organized labor is so important in addressing the country's challenges. It begins with a detailed review of the basic economic and political problems the United States faces. The middle class is withering away, government largely does the bidding of the wealthy, racism and sexism are widespread, and social cohesion is breaking down as people increasingly distrust trust others. It then explains what unions do. Unions help raise wages and reduce economic inequality by bringing up the bottom and the middle while restraining pay for the ultra-rich. Unions address democratic weakness by increasing political participation and making politicians more responsive to ordinary citizens. Unions can even help rebuild trust and reduce racial and gender discrimination.

The discussion will emphasize unions in the United States but will also bring in evidence from unions around the world, making comparisons to explain the functions unions serve and suggest reasons a new labor system would be so helpful. The bulk of the chapter will focus on the positive attributes of unions, but labor's flaws will also be discussed. Labor unions are not always right, and they should not always get what they seek. But not everything unions do needs to be unambiguously beneficial to society for them to have tremendous overall benefits. It would be incredibly shortsighted to call for the elimination of all business because one particular firm broke the law or because some of the things that businesses can do, such as pollute the environment, cause harm. Yet something akin to a standard of no harm is too often applied to unions. When great capitalist scandals occur, such as when the American energy company Enron Corporation went bankrupt and was found to be defrauding the public, few called for the elimination of capitalism. Yet most any time a union leader does something unsavory, critics are quick to seize on that as proof that unions are fatally flawed.

The right question to ask is whether the benefits of unions outweigh their costs. Unions help raise wages, reduce inequality, strengthen the middle class, and make democracy responsive to the masses while also helping reduce discrimination and social tensions. Strong labor unions help ensure that the perspective of workers is adequately considered and prevent employers and the wealthy from completely dominating workers, the economy, and government. Unions also cause far less economic harm that their opponents claim. As a result, unions clearly provide more benefits than costs. Furthermore, there are ways to maximize their benefits and minimize their costs.

American Troubles

Even before COVID-19 and the inadequate government response to it drove unemployment to double-digit rates, placed massive new strains on households, and made work much more dangerous, the US economy was not working for most people. Though the basic facts of the long-standing economic problems are relatively well known, they are still shocking. The percentage of jobs with good wages and benefits has been falling for decades.[2] Children can no longer count on doing better than their parents: the typical thirty-year-old today makes roughly the same as a thirty-year-old in the 1980s, adjusting for inflation, even though today's generation is much more highly educated, our economy more productive, and our country richer.[3] Workplace laws are routinely violated by some of the largest companies in the United States, with one estimate indicating that more than two-thirds of low-wage workers received less in pay than they were legally entitled to.[4]

About half of private-sector employers compel their workers to sign forced arbitration agreements, which prevent workers from going to court if their employer breaks the law and directs them into an arbitration process that heavily favors companies.[5] Roughly two in five workers have been forced to sign a non-compete agreement at some point in their career—meaning they cannot work for a competitor, even though many do not have any trade secrets—including low-wage workers doing things like making sandwiches at fast food franchises.[6] Workers increasingly are coerced into supporting their bosses' political agendas, with one in five workers having felt pressured to advocate for their employers' favored policies and politicians.[7]

Wages for the typical American worker, after adjusting for inflation, have hardly increased in over four and a half decades. In fact, wages for the median male worker are the same today as they were in 1973.[8] Women's wages have slightly increased since then, but they are still well below male wages, and the pay gap between black and white workers has actually grown over recent decades.[9] Wealth gaps are much bigger than pay gaps: compared to the median white family, the median black family has one-tenth the wealth and the median Hispanic family just 12 percent the wealth.[10]

Over the past four decades, the overall economy has grown significantly, and workers have become much more productive.[11] But most workers have received little of the gains they help create. Only the very rich have seen significant income gains over recent decades.[12] The share of the nation's income going to the top 1 percent is now near record highs, while the share that goes to the middle class is near record lows. The top 1 percent have more of the nation's wealth than the middle class, while the bottom 50 percent have virtually no wealth. Almost half of American households have less wealth now than the typical household did in 1970.[13]

Not so long ago—between World War II and the mid-1970s—economic inequality in the United States was much lower and shrinking as incomes for poor people and the middle class rose more rapidly than those of the rich. But now economic inequality has risen to such extreme levels that some comparisons are necessary to help put them in context. In the early 1970s, the typical CEO made about twenty-two times more than the typical worker did, while today CEOs make over three hundred times more than the typical worker.[14] To visualize this difference, imagine an apartment building with the CEO in the penthouse and the typical worker on the ground floor. In the 1970s this twenty-two-story building would not have been out of place in most US cities, but today it would be taller than three Empire State Buildings.

Not only is inequality extreme by US historical standards, inequality in the United States is much higher than in every other wealthy democracy. The wealthy democracy with the most similar levels of inequality to the United States is Great Britain, but in Britain the share of the nation's income going to the top 1 percent is still much less than that of the United States.[15] In other rich democracies, the share going to the top percent is well less than half that of the United States. In fact, the overall level of US inequality is most comparable to places like Saudi Arabia, Peru, Guyana, and Thailand.[16]

At some level, the United States is suffering from a basic problem of modern capitalism. Capitalism is extremely productive when it works well, promoting economic growth as well as freedom. But unless the market is properly managed it tends to destabilize and undermine the political and economic conditions necessary for its success. Poorly managed capitalism leads to great concentrations of power, leaves many people behind, and destabilizes communities, which ultimately undermines democracy, freedom, trust, and markets themselves. Unfortunately, the current version of US capitalism is not conducive to democracy.[17]

That the nearest inequality neighbors to the United States are not stable democracies is worrying, as are the patterns from US history showing how democracy suffered greatly during other extremely unequal eras. During the Gilded Age in the late 1800s and early 1900s, when inequality was very high, for instance, wealthy corporations controlled government actions to such a degree that former president Rutherford B. Hayes wrote in his diary, "This is a government of the people, by the people and for the people no longer. It is a government by the corporations, of the corporations, and for the corporations."[18] Similarly, the pre–Civil War South was one of the most unequal societies in the world, with less than 1 percent of slaveholders owning one-quarter of US enslaved people.[19] At the time, rich plantation owners used their wealth to dominate not only African Americans but also white citizens, doing things like requiring very high levels of property ownership to hold elected office, refusing to update state voter rolls to reflect the growing population areas, and changing state constitutions to lock in their power.[20] The majority of southern whites wanted things like "roads, schools, and other mundane public services," as the historian Robin Einhorn wrote, but "slaveholders simply would not allow nonslaveholding majorities decide how to tax."[21]

Similar trends of inequality undermining democracy are apparent in the United States today. Academic studies find that Congress generally ignores the desires of the middle class and the poor but is highly responsive to the interests of the rich.[22] Furthermore, nearly two-thirds of Americans now think that "quite a few" government officials are "crooked," while just one-third felt this way in the early 1970s.[23] The share of the public trusting government "most of the time" or "just about always" fell from 77 percent in 1964 to just 17 percent in 2019.[24] The number of corruption convictions have quadrupled over the past four decades, and the number of special-interest tax breaks have tripled. In contrast, public spending, as a share of the economy, on basic infrastructure that the public wants and needs, like roads and bridges, has fallen sharply.[25]

A big reason why high levels of economic inequality corrupt government is because the rich have so much more money to spend—and a strong desire to protect their wealth.[26] This is clearly happening in the United States. Campaign contributions come almost exclusively from the top 1 percent; large corporations spend over sixty times as much on lobbying as unions; most candidates are rich; and elected officials spend much of their time trying to raise money from rich people rather than meeting with constituents.[27] Some of the extremely wealthy even appear willing to subvert democracy to preserve their money and power, such as by pushing policies that limit citizen access to the ballot box, gerrymandering electoral districts to prevent voters from choosing their favored representatives, and using the courts to undermine the political process.

Yet extreme inequality harms democracy and society not just because the rich have more money and incentive to override the common good. Extreme inequality causes people to feel powerless and withdraw from the political process.[28] Occasionally their anger may lead them into action, such as voting in the 2020 presidential election, but mostly it causes them to participate in political activities less frequently and become less civic-minded.

The hollowing out of the middle class also undermines social trust, which has devastating consequences. As society divides into rich and poor, people become less trusting of others. Extreme inequality causes people to lead separate lives, to have fewer interactions, to feel they have less in common. Trusting others depends on thinking that people you do not know are like you. Inequality makes that feeling less likely. In fact, research finds that the level of inequality in society is the most important societal factor in the overall level of trust in a country.[29] Researchers have shown that inequality shapes trust in a variety of ways. Some studies compare the level of inequality across place and time with how people respond to surveys asking whether they trust strangers. Other studies use laboratory experiments that assess how willing strangers are to cooperate in various games when the level of inequality is varied, and still others perform real-world experiments such as leaving a wallet on the street and seeing if it is returned.[30] All these different methods find that inequality erodes trusting behaviors.

In the middle of the twentieth century, the United States was among the most trusting societies in the world. Americans often thought other people, even those they did not know, would act fairly and decently. But trust has declined precipitously over recent decades and is much lower than in most other advanced countries.[31] Growing racial and ethnic diversity has contributed to the decline in trust in the United States because it makes it easier for people to think that others are not like them. Increasing diversity and inequality are both important, but inequality appears to be particularly important. Many other countries have also seen large increases in racial and ethnic diversity over recent decades, but trust has dropped the most in those that have also had large increases in economic inequality, according to research by Professor Christian Larsen. He finds that increases in racial and ethnic diversity do not have very large effects on their own, rather "it is the interaction between ethnic divides and economic inequality that can lower trust levels."[32]

A lack of trust makes governing harder and more costly. As inequality rises, the public and their elected representatives become more polarized and less able to compromise.[33] They fight harder and longer and are willing to inflict more damage on the other side. Without trust, people are reluctant to work with others—especially other people who do not look like themselves. As a result, lack of trust also exacerbates underlying problems of racism and sexism, making it easier to stereotype and scapegoat. People who do not trust others have less favorable views of groups that are often discriminated against, including African Americans, religious minorities, women, immigrants, and gay people, and are less likely to support policies to help these groups.[34]

Extreme inequality not only exacerbates political and societal problems, it can also undermine the elements necessary for economic growth and make the economy more fragile and volatile. As inequality has risen, the government has invested less in social goods like infrastructure, people have become less trusting and more defensive in business arrangements, and it has become harder for ordinary people to start new businesses.[35] Likely in part because of these problems, economic growth has been slower over recent decades than it was in middle of the twentieth century. Worse, inequality helped contribute to the financial crisis and Great Recession of 2007–9 by providing Wall Street with the money and influence to get rid of government safeguards on banks and encourage regulators to ignore wild financial speculation, while stagnant wages pushed many Americans to borrow to maintain their standard of living.

All told, extreme inequality increases the power of the wealthy, fosters political polarization, degrades the quality of government, weakens social ties, exacerbates racism and sexism, and creates fertile conditions for financial crises and deep recessions.[36] Because these problems compound, they can lead to even more serious breakdowns of democracy and society.

In the long run, US democracy may not be able to survive if the hollowing out of the middle class continues. Scholars throughout history—from Aristotle to the framers of the US Constitution to modern political scientists—have observed that extreme class divisions destroy democracies.[37] Great class divisions have tended to lead to a takeover of government by the rich or a breakdown of government into a kind of mob role, but a strong middle class helps stabilize democracy by minimizing grievances and providing a buffer between rival camps and competing claims for power. As Aristotle wrote, "the best political community is formed by citizens of the middle class . . . for the addition of the middle class turns the scale, and prevents either of the extremes from being dominant."[38] Extreme inequality gives great wealth and power to the rich who will go to great lengths to keep their advantages while stoking great resentment in the masses, who have little to lose. Which is why James Madison wrote, "The most common and durable source of factions has been the various and unequal distributions of property."[39] Modern scholars echo this line of thinking. Indeed, law professor Ganesh Sitaraman argues the "number one threat to American constitutional government today is the collapse of the middle class."[40]

Though history and political theory suggest that democracies without a strong middle class do not last, the ultimate breaking point for the United States may never arrive or could be a long, long way off. Indeed, with its treatment of African Americans—from slavery to Jim Crow to racist policing—the United States has rarely been a model democracy. There may not be a clear point at which the United States slips into something much worse than an imperfect democracy. Modern democracies are thought to fail by suffering a gradual erosion of rules and norms, rather than through a violent coup. In modern democratic failures, deep political polarization in society enables elected autocrats to "subvert democracy," by weaponizing courts, government agencies, and the media.[41]

How far America lies along this process of democratic decline is debatable. The election of Donald Trump as president in 2016, his actions while in change, and his behavior after he lost the 2020 election presented clear threats to many democratic norms. Still, many problems predated him. Political and social polarization and the weaponization of government were significant problems for years before Trump was elected president. Indeed, for years the Republican Party has pushed policies that make it harder for people—particularly, young, black, and Hispanic citizens—to vote.[42]

But Trump's election in 2016 dramatically highlighted deep problems in the United States. Discriminatory attitudes are key to understanding Trump's popularity, but extreme inequality and wage stagnation also clearly helped bring Trump to power. Trump won in large part because he was able to activate a white group identity and play on their fears of nonwhites; and he also benefited from sexism against his opponent Hillary Clinton.[43] Still, it seems hard to believe that he would have been elected without stagnant wages and extreme inequality causing deep, underlying economic and political problems.

Most directly, some of his supporters were frustrated with typical politicians whom they felt did nothing to address the economic needs of regular Americans, and as a candidate Trump claimed he would address these problems—though his governing agenda largely did not, as he cut taxes for corporations, for example, while making it harder to join a union and receive overtime pay and easier for companies to misclassify employees as independent contractors with no rights.[44] Trump voters were more dissatisfied with the economy, more supportive of progressive economic policies such as a higher minimum wage and increasing taxes on the wealthy, more concerned about the inability of ordinary citizens to influence government, and more likely to live in economically distressed areas than were other Republican primary voters.[45]

Less directly, political polarization meant that some Republicans felt compelled to vote for the Republican Party candidate no matter who it was. They may not have liked Donald Trump, but they were not going to vote for the Democratic Party candidate.[46] Another group of Trump's supporters felt they had little to lose from the current system, so why not blow it up—echoing the ancient fear of anarchy caused by class conflict from those who have been left out. Indeed, almost 20 percent of Trump's own voters felt he was unqualified for office.[47] Most of the country felt a blend of somewhat related nihilism and apathy. In 2015 nearly two-thirds of Americans felt their vote didn't matter because of "the influence that wealthy individuals and big corporations have on the electoral process."[48]

The underlying economic conditions probably also contributed to some portion of the racist vote for Trump because scarcity and economic inequality lead to less-trusting attitudes and behaviors. Certainly, Trump's racism would have found a home no matter the state of the economy. Racist individuals come from rich, poor, and middle-class backgrounds. Economic scarcity does not need to result in racial scapegoating; historically it has led to many other political reactions, from withdrawal to support for social democracy or even communist revolution. But, when inequality is high, people are more likely to perceive others, especially those with visible differences—be it race, ethnicity, gender, nationality, or anything else—as a threat.[49] That does not excuse the racism, but it likely explains some portion of it. In other words, Trump's racism found more support because of underlying conditions. Trump helped racialize economic grievances, thereby gaining support from whites who believed minorities and immigrants were the cause of economic problems.[50]

As president, Donald Trump further degraded US democracy and increased the risk that it could potentially face a breakdown. Trump further divided an already divided society and dramatically exacerbated existing risks. He pushed the boundaries of rules and norms that were already beginning to fray. He abused power, broke the law, and engaged in self-dealing. He criticized the independent media, calling factual reporting "fake news," made up his own "alternative facts," and threatened to change libel laws and sue reporters who criticized him. He attacked the independence of judges and nonpartisan agencies and threatened to use government to jail his political opponents. He also stoked racial anger, scapegoating immigrants and communities of color for America's problems.

As much of a threat as Trump is, America's problems do not end with Trump. The 2020 election of Joe Biden as president is likely to stop the immediate danger to democratic laws and norms. Yet, the defeat of Donald Trump may provide only a brief respite. Joe Biden's electoral victory was convincing, but it wasn't so large as to provide a thorough repudiation of Trump. Further, the shameful rejection of legitimate election results by Trump, many of his supporters, and many leaders in the Republican party highlights how much of a problem Trumpism remains in the near future. Over the longer term, the kinds of problems that led to Trump's rise pose a continuing risk.

Wage stagnation, extreme inequality, and the lack of responsiveness of the political system to ordinary people are long-standing problems that predated Trump and will outlast him. Even more worrying is that the country's underlying economic, social, and political problems are likely to grow in severity—unless major new policies are put in place. Trump's actions exacerbated economic inequality, racism, political polarization, and low levels of social trust. Even worse, economic inequality creates a vicious cycle that tends to reinforce itself. The greater the level of economic inequality, the more power the rich have to further increase their wealth and the less trust there is for people to try to work together to combat this power. Without a strong set of political and economic structures, inequality will increase. And if inequality continues to increase, it will cause additional havoc.

Whether current trends will lead toward a truly undemocratic society may be unknowable, but these are clear warning signs of danger ahead. Because ordinary Americans have lost so much power in the economy and in democracy, the country faces problems that pose a serious threat to its future. The economy threatens to become even more unbalanced, subject to wild swings and catastrophic collapses. Economic grievances have become increasingly racialized, and communities of color—who are already worse off than most whites—are increasingly scapegoated for America's political and economic failures. The country is in danger of turning into an oligarchy—where the rich and powerful control virtually all elements of government and society—and of possibly slipping into fascism. Even basic rule of law is at risk, as Trump and his allies continually subverted legal requirements. The United States is in dire need of real solutions to these economic and political problems. Unions are an essential part of the solution because they can provide a democratic check on capitalism's worst tendencies to concentrate money and power and overrun society and democracy.

Economic Functions of Unions

In the economy, the most basic function labor performs is to bring workers together to bargain for higher wages and benefits. The standard and overly simplistic economic theory of labor markets maintains that employers and employees freely and fairly negotiate on equal footing. While something like this can occasionally happen, in most circumstances employers have far more information about the market and far more power than their workers. Employers know what they pay all their current employees, and they likely have surveyed competitors, information almost no individual worker has. Employers also generally have far more options and financial resources than do workers. Employers can usually hire any number of people to perform a particular job, while workers' options are usually limited, especially if they want to remain in a particular area. Workers also need an income more than an employer needs work from any particular worker.

For a number of reasons, workers do better when they bargain collectively—especially those who tend to have less power in society, such as those with less education, African Americans, and women. Compared to trying to negotiate on their own, unionized workers engaged in collective bargaining have better information about what colleagues and competitors earn as well as their employer's ability to pay. Most importantly, they have greater market power. Most individual workers are relatively easy for an employer to replace. But replacing a group of workers is harder—though not impossible, as will be discussed in more detail later. This means employers have a stronger incentive to negotiate with a group than they do with most individual workers. In addition, as part of a union, workers are better able to ensure that employers follow through on any promises to raise wages and benefits. Put differently, unions help workers negotiate and enforce contracts.

Unions also provide important services and benefits. For example, union training programs run jointly with employers help workers gain skills that lead to higher-wage jobs—and generally do this better than nonunion training programs, which do not always lead to a higher-paid job or even a job at all.[51] Finally, unionized workers also gain a greater voice on the job, which in addition to tangible gains for workers and sometimes firms can also lead to less easily measurable benefits such as feelings of greater agency and well-being.

All told, collective bargaining provides a way to discover a fair and economically sustainable price for work. It minimizes the distorting effects of employers' vastly superior power and generally leads to a compensation package that is acceptable to both workers and employers. One side may have had the upper hand in the negotiation, but both had some degree of influence to shape the outcome, and both prefer the outcome to the alternatives—the likes of strikes, lockouts, and closing plants.

Not surprisingly, unions produce significant economic benefits for their members. In the United States, unionized workers earn about 13 percent more than comparable nonunion workers and are much more likely to have health care, pensions, and paid leave and vacation days and to receive employer-provided training.[52] Research on other countries finds similar advantages to collective bargaining. Unionized workers also have much greater wealth—roughly twice as much—as comparable workers because of the cumulative effect of higher wages, better benefits, and increased job stability.[53] Unions even help the next generation do better: children raised in a union household earn significantly more than children raised in an otherwise similar, nonunion household, and the results are strongest for households with less education.[54]

The private contractual standards that unions help set often spread to the larger economy. When unions have sufficient strength in an industry or region, collective bargaining creates a set of high standards that most employers—even nonunion ones—have to follow.[55] As a result, unions and collective bargaining also tend to raise standards and improve working conditions for all workers, not just those that are unionized.

In the United States, with its worksite bargaining system—often known as enterprise-level bargaining—this spreading of standards generally happens through an informal process. When unions have high density, nonunion employers raise their wages and benefits to levels comparable to most other employers in the market in order to attract and retain employees and ward off potential unionization efforts. In most other economically advanced countries, as well as in a few limited policy areas in the United States, such as in prevailing wage laws for government contracts, there are more formal processes for extending the standards set by collective bargaining to other employers. These broad-based bargaining processes are actually much more effective at raising wages and reducing economic inequality than enterprise-based bargaining, as will be discussed in more detail later, but the point to remember now is that unions and collective bargaining play key roles in the larger economy—even when the role they are playing is more as a private actor than a political one. Thus, collective bargaining and union enforcement of contracts can be viewed as a way to privately regulate the market.

This private regulatory function is deeply intertwined with the more political functions that unions perform. As a result of their self-interest, as well as their broader mission to represent workers, unions often advocate to promote policies such as a strong government antipoverty programs and adequate investment in social goods like education and roads and full employment. They have been a major force behind the passage of laws, from ones establishing higher minimum wages and improved safety standards to ones expanding access to health care and ensuring civil rights.[56] Indeed, unions have been called "probably . . . the most effective advocate for public policies advantageous to the less affluent."[57]

Unions also ensure that companies and governments comply with legal standards. Unions help secure adequate funding for government enforcement agencies, educate workers about their rights, draw public and government attention to violations, and make it safer and easier for workers to stand up to rule-breaking employers.[58] Not surprisingly, research in the United States and around the world finds that union worksites are safer and that unionized workers are less likely to have their legal rights violated.[59]

All told, unions help regulate the economy and make it work better through private and public actions.

Indeed, the combined economic and political impact of unions is immense. Research by professors Bruce Western and Jake Rosenfeld finds that the decline of unions from 1973 to 2007 explains about one-third of rising wage inequality among men and one-fifth among women over that period.[60] Other studies from the United States and countries around the world similarly find that unions significantly reduce economic inequality, increase the share of income going to the middle class, and constrain incomes for CEOs and the top 1 percent.[61] Unions also reduce poverty rates, as studies in the United States and around the world have found.[62] Analysis of US states found that state-level unionization measures had a larger impact on poverty rates among workers than any other state-level economic or policy factor including unemployment, economic growth rates, and welfare spending.[63] Unions also boost economic mobility across society. One US study found that an area's union density was as strong a predictor of upward economic mobility for low-income children as the area's high school dropout rate.[64]

Democratic Role of Unions

The role unions play in democracy is vital to these achievements—at least as important as their role dealing with employers. The simplistic version of democracy holds that elected representatives automatically carry out the will of the people. In this view, candidates seek out positions that match the preferences of the majority of the public and then govern in ways that are responsive to the majority's preferences. While there is an element of truth to this story, this version of events is largely misguided.

Unfortunately, in the United States today politicians pay vastly more attention to the rich and the powerful than they do to ordinary citizens, and most citizens have basically no influence on what the government does. Though the government sometimes does what most citizens want, studies increasingly find that only happens when the rich or the powerful also want the same thing.[65] As the political scientists Martin Gilens and Benjamin Page explain based on their research on nearly two thousand public policy issues over recent decades, "economic elites and organized groups representing business interests have substantial independent impacts on US government policy . . . while average citizens have little or no influence."[66] As a result, theories of politics based on elites having great power and interest groups representing the already powerful wielding significant influence have been much better able to explain what has happened to US democracy over recent decades than the standard hopeful theories based solely on majority rule.

There are a number of reasons that the US government is no longer responsive to ordinary citizens. Supreme Court decisions like *Citizens United* are part of the issue, but the main story boils down to this: As inequality has risen to extreme levels, the wealthy have been able to use their money to exert great political influence. In contrast, most people need to act as part of a group to have much sway, but there are few groups representing ordinary citizens.

The money and standing of the wealthy commands great attention from elected officials. But the single vote of an ordinary citizen does not mean that much, nor does any modest financial contribution they may make. Moreover, it is difficult and time-consuming for an ordinary citizen to pay attention to everything elected officials are doing and communicate with them at important points in the policy process.

For a typical citizen, being part of an organized group is essential for them to have much political influence. Labor unions perform several important roles in the democratic process. First, they help mobilize individuals to participate in the political process, by voting, contacting their representative, and volunteering in campaign. Unions also educate their members about political issues and help them make connections between their lives and policy decisions—which is increasingly important as technology increasingly enables the spread of fake news. Unions even increase the effectiveness of political actions by bringing people together and making success more likely. Thus, unions reduce the costs of participating and increase the benefits of doing so.[67]

Because of union efforts inside and outside the workplace, union members are much more politically active than comparable nonunion workers, but union efforts also increase political participation by nonunion workers. Participation increases are most pronounced for those with less education and income.[68] Research shows that union members are much more likely to vote, take political action, join other kinds of membership groups, and contribute more to charities compared to otherwise similar people.[69] Overall, these effects are quite large. According to analysis by political scientists Benjamin Radcliff and Patricia Davis each percentage point increase in union density in a state increases voter turnout rates by about a quarter of a percent.[70]

In addition, unions, like other civil society organizations, can act as mini schools of democracy. Internally, unions have regular elections for leadership positions that provide firsthand experience in small-scale democracy; opportunities for ordinary Americans to witness and participate in elections as both voters and leaders. Unions also help shift the nature of the workplace into something more resembling the give and take of a democracy, where employers must at least discuss certain workplace changes with a union representative elected by workers.[71] A number of researchers and political theorists believe that the degree of democracy in a workplace—where citizens spend more time than anywhere else except home—can make them more likely to be either passive followers of authoritarian leaders or active democratic citizens.[72]

Unions can also help solicit small political contributions from their members and aggregate them into more meaningful contributions. Money that is concentrated in the hands of a few wealthy people is not subject to collective action problems, but workers' money is spread out among many individuals and must be coordinated in order for it be meaningful.

Just as importantly, unions also serve a critical representative function, advocating on behalf of members who often do not have the time or knowledge to closely follow every political detail. Unions monitor votes, highlight issues for the media, draft legislation, figure out which politicians merit campaign contributions, lobby, work behind the scenes with policy makers, and even create opportunities for citizens to hold elected officials accountable.

In a large, diverse country like the United States, this representative function is particularly important. Most people cannot be super-citizens and do not want to be, but rather they want their interests represented.[73] A well-functioning democracy requires a reasonable balance of power and that all major political interests are adequately represented. This encourages negotiation and compromise and helps ensure that there is a fair political fight. But when huge groups of people are not represented, or are only weakly represented, there is not really a fair fight, and one side governs at the expense of the other. This is especially true because research shows that politicians are even more likely to favor wealthy campaign contributors when there is less attention paid to their actions.[74]

With labor in sharp decline, there has been virtually no organization helping the poor and the middle class have a strong political voice on most issues.[75] Most organized groups represent powerful special interests, particularly business interests.[76] And as labor unions have declined, business and the wealthy have increasingly dominated politics. Campaign contributions from the wealthy and business outweighed those from labor unions by fourteen to one in 2018, more than twice as much as roughly two decades ago.[77] Spending on lobbying is even more uneven—with business lobbying more than sixty times higher than lobbying by labor.[78]

Labor is just about the only organized interest group that represents the public will on a wide range of issues. Indeed, studies of the positions taken by leading interest groups matched up with the preferences of the public on poll questions find that most interest groups—especially those that represent business interests—take positions that the public opposes. Only a handful of reasonably large organizations actually represent the interest of the middle class and the poor, and almost all of those are labor unions.[79] The few nonlabor groups that have been shown to take positions the public agrees with have narrower agendas, such as universities pushing for increased education spending or AARP to preserve Social Security and other retirement programs. Certainly not every issue that labor gets behind will be broadly in the public interest, but most are. As a result, labor unions have proven to do quite a good job representing the interests of workers. Indeed, research shows that in districts where unions are stronger, members of Congress are much more likely to respond to the preferences of the poor and middle class.[80]

This means that Americans have been suffering from a double whammy of democratic unresponsiveness. The rich have independent political power, and they are getting richer and more powerful. The middle class and poor need to be organized to have political influence, yet most interest groups now represent the wealthy.

While representation of all interests is central to any notion of democracy, some scholars argue that the goal of democracy is also to ensure "non-domination"— the idea that individuals should have the actual freedom to pursue their interests without the potential for others to exert arbitrary influence over them. Critically, unions are also essential to this more expansive definition of democracy in that they help ordinary citizens have agency and provide a check on the potential for employers and the wealthy to dominate workers.[81]

All told, unions are vital to ensuring that democracy works properly.[82] They advocate for workers and help workers advocate for themselves. And the decline of unions has created a political vacuum that has led the wealthy to capture significant control of government, as the political scientists Jacob Hacker and Paul Pierson explain in the book *Winner-Take-All Politics*.[83]

Beyond the contemporary United States, unions and democracy also tend to go together. Research finds that government is more transparent, more effective, and more responsive to its citizens when unions are strong and well connected with other civil society organizations.[84] Not surprisingly, countries that score highest on international rankings of democratic quality by academics and journalists generally have strong unions, while those that rank at the bottom tend to have weak or nonexistent labor movements.[85]

Unions often stand up to dictators and push for greater openness and have been a driving force in the democratization of countries around the world—from Poland to South Korea.[86] When dictators seize power, from Hitler in the 1930s to Pinochet in the 1970s to Viktor Orbán today, one of the first things they usually do is seek to weaken or outlaw labor unions so their agenda faces less opposition.[87] (Even in cases where dictators claim to promote workers and unions—as in China today or Argentina under Peron or Egypt under Nasser—the autocrats prevent unions from being independent organizations and make them an arm of the state, with their views and actions screened for political loyalty.)[88] And countries like Germany after World War II and more recently South Africa in the aftermath of apartheid have sought to strengthen their labor movements as part of a process to rebuild democracy.[89]

Minimal Economic Harm

A skeptic might question whether unions impose a significant burden on the economy. Critics often drag out stories of unions negotiating for "unreasonable" benefits, like the ability to get paid even if there is no work available or trying to ensure that a light bulb is changed by a union member rather than the person who could most easily do it.

Closer investigation often reveals that these criticisms are overblown, but unions, like any other institution, have flaws and can do things that cause some economic harm. But their flaws are much smaller than opponents claim. Indeed, the overall impact of unions on economic growth is negligible and sometimes positive. Moreover, the US system of firm-based bargaining arguably encourages some of the behaviors that critics dislike because it often requires unions to focus on narrow interests and limits their ability to advocate for the broad needs of all workers. Thus, the economic impact of unions could be even more positive if labor policies were reformed.

To free-market conservatives, anything that raises the cost of workers above what employers would pay on their own will cause economic harm. According to this logic, employers already pay workers what they are worth—their marginal product. "Artificially" increasing pay through union negotiations will supposedly reduce employment or make companies less able to afford other needed investments and thus become less efficient and less competitive in the economy. Labor unions in this view are merely dead weights for employers and the economy.

Of course, the economy does not actually attain the perfectly competitive conditions that free-market conservatives and too many economists assume. Employers and society at large can place barriers to advancement in front of women and people of color. Employers can also make it hard for workers to earn what they are worth with another employer by, for example, forcing employees to sign noncompete agreements. Firms can earn monopolistic "rents" over and above what they would make in a competitive market.

Employers also have what is known as monopsony power, which can enable them to pay workers less than they are worth because it is time-consuming and costly for workers to change jobs.[90] Workers can face large transaction costs in finding out what their value is in the market. It takes time and effort to get another job. Workers do not have perfect information about what their colleagues make, let alone what other firms pay. Workers do not always know what skills employers really want—and they may not be able to trust employers' promises that they will get a higher wage if they get more training. Changing employers means potentially altering commute routines and even friendships and creates the worry that the new job may be an even worse fit. The list of market failures could go on and on.

Moreover, the labor market is different than other markets. People are not widgets. If the price of a commodity, like oil, goes up, the commodity still performs the same. But, if a worker's pay increases, something different happens. Some workers value their job more and are less likely to leave—which reduces turnover, and turnover is quite costly to employers. Some workers may increase their effort because they feel they are being paid what they are worth. Some employers restructure processes to help make workers more productive and promote additional training to help workers become more efficient. Workers can also have good ideas to improve productivity and may be more likely to offer them when they feel they are being fairly compensated and feel their voice is heard.

Further, higher wages also enable workers to purchase more goods and services. Increased consumer demand gives firms an incentive to invest in new factories and products, which can create additional jobs. Put another way—the ability to pay low wages may be helpful for a particular firm, but low wages are not necessarily good for the broader economy. The growing economy relies on growing consumer demand.

In a similar vein, employers also often underinvest in training—relative to both their needs and the best interest of society. This occurs in part because employers fear their competitors will hire away workers they have spent money to train before they are able to recoup their investment. A related reason is that turnover is very high in some jobs—in large part because pay is low—so employers do not want to train workers that are just going to leave the job. As a result, it may be rational for an individual firm to avoid training investments and instead hire trained workers from another company or just let workers leave the industry. But this can lead to a problem for the overall economy. Unions can negotiate for greater investments in training and can create the structures to deliver it in ways that benefit workers and employers.

All of this means that in the real world there is plenty of opportunity for labor unions to raise wages and not hurt, and perhaps even help, economic growth. Which is why decades of research has shown that unions and collective bargaining do not lead to economic ruin. The research is very clear that unions raise wages and reduce inequality, but their effect on other economic outcomes such as productivity, economic growth, employment, and firm profitability depends heavily on the context, especially the response of management but also the specific firm, region, and time period under study.

The classic work on the economic impacts of unions was written in 1984 by Harvard economists Richard Freeman and James Medoff, and more than three decades of subsequent research has largely verified their findings.[91] Freeman and Medoff explained that unions have "two faces." In one, collective voice acts as an accountability check on management, helps workers' preferences be accurately communicated to management, and ensures that gains from productivity are equally shared. The other, a monopoly face, can be used to "raise wages above competitive levels" and promote "restrictive work practices." The collective face boosts productivity by "open[ing] an important communication channel between workers and management," bringing out the best in workers and management to solve problems collaboratively that could not be solved by individuals working alone. The monopoly face, Freeman and Medoff argue, can produce uncompetitive pay and inefficiencies that "lower the productivity of labor and capital," such as through "restrictions on tasks performed."[92]

Both faces exist simultaneously, but Freeman and Medoff argue that, on balance, the impact of the positive face dominates, even in the United States, which has a less-than-optimal system. There has been an enormous amount of research building on and supporting the two-faces argument, looking into economic outcomes such as productivity, employment, profitability, and physical and human capital investments. Some studies find that the negative face is more prevalent, while others find that the positive face is more prevalent, but most find that the impact of unions on economic growth or the competitiveness of an economy is roughly a wash—often boosting productivity while slightly reducing corporate profits.[93]

For some people it may be helpful to reference the research on minimum wages to round out the research on unions, as the minimum wage has been the subject of frequent debate. Unions do a lot more than help set minimum compensation standards, but, to economists, raising wages above what employers would pay on their own is analogous to raising the minimum wage. And fortunately there has been much recent and important research on the minimum wage. For decades economists assumed that the minimum wage must have significant harmful effects, but once they really began studying minimum wage increases in detail, they began to understand that the minimum wage significantly increased the earnings of low-wage workers without much or any reduction in employment.[94]

As with the minimum wage research, there is a growing understanding that unions do not do dramatic harm to the economy. Unions can in fact help the market function properly, balancing the power of employers and workers, helping workers earn a share of the "rents" that powerful companies get, limiting discrimination, reducing transaction costs so workers can understand their options, providing incentives for training programs, reducing turnover, and helping workers gain leverage that can improve not only working conditions but also the efficiency of production processes.

All of these good economic effects can and do happen under the current US labor system. But the US system is not set up to maximize their occurrence. Rather, in some ways the current system is set up to hinder them because it emphasizes enterprise-level bargaining that exacerbates conflict between workers and owners, encourages low-road companies to compete based on squeezing wages rather than increasing productivity, and fails to foster industry-wide training systems—indicating that there are ways to further improve the economic impact of unions by moving toward sectoral bargaining, as will be discussed in the next chapter.

Critically, the economic impacts of unions are even more positive when their broader consequences are considered. Unions also help make government work in ways that are better for the economy. Because unions help balance political and economic power, government is less likely to be captured and used to protect the interests of the rich, the rule of law is stronger, and investments in social goods like education and infrastructure are greater—all of which are good for the economy.[95] Unfortunately, the vast majority of research on the economic impact of unions "ignores politics," as the economist Daron Acemoglu and the political scientist James Robinson write—meaning that it misses perhaps the most important way that unions help make the economy function.[96] As a result, unions have a far more positive economic impact than most economic studies are able to show.

Of course, the role of a well-functioning democracy is not simply to make the economy work better. Rather democracy is an end in and of itself, a way to govern that allows for the dignity of every human to be expressed, that has proven to be more responsive to the public's will and more protective of individual rights than any other system of government. Still, the fact is that, even focusing on narrow questions of economic growth, unions do not cause the harm their critics claim but rather can help make the market work better.

Race and Gender

A new labor system would help all workers but would be particularly important for women, African Americans, Hispanic, Asians, and other people of color, as well as LGBTQ people. Unions reduce the pay gaps between women and men and between communities of color and whites and dramatically shrink wealth gaps.[97] They can also help limit the abuses of power that fuel harassment, and they can even help create a broader social environment that is more open, tolerant, and trusting. Unions could do even more of this if they were stronger and operating in a new system.

To be sure, the labor movement is far from perfect in promoting equality. Overall, the racial and gender history of unions in America is somewhat like the history of the country as a whole but generally better than that, with a mixture of discriminatory and egalitarian actions.

From the beginning, many union leaders and members were openly racist and sexist. And the law often promoted or reinforced discrimination and stymied inclusive impulses in labor unions. The National Labor Relations Act of 1935 excluded domestic and agricultural workers—occupations that were predominantly black—and initially failed to legally prevent unions from discriminating.[98] The 1947 Taft-Hartley amendments to weaken unions were designed in part to keep unions from organizing black workers in the South.[99]

Still, unions have generally been better than the rest of the country in promoting equal treatment for all workers. The president of the AFL-CIO maintains, "[The] labor movement—imperfect as we are—is the most integrated institution in American life"; and there is good justification to think his description is accurate.[100] In fact, it is fair to argue that today unions are one of the most important and powerful organizations for full social inclusion, if not the most important.

Unions and collective bargaining do a lot to reduce gender and racial pay and wealth gaps. Collective bargaining directly raises wages for workers who are covered by union contracts—especially for lower- and middle-income workers. Because women, Hispanics, blacks, and many Asian workers are disproportionately represented in lower-wage groups, higher wages for low- and middle-income workers decreases pay gaps. In addition, some groups, such as blacks and Hispanics, tend to get a higher union wage premium than the average.[101]

Collective bargaining also more directly addresses discrimination by changing how workplaces are run. It helps workers set their pay based on objective standards, such as skills and education, creates rules for management to follow, makes salaries more visible, and establishes enforcement mechanisms for workers to ensure that these standards and rules are followed. These effects leave less room for pay discrimination and help to secure equal pay for equal work. Collective bargaining also leads to greater job stability, especially for vulnerable workers, which is critical to enabling workers to continue earning and saving and thus building wealth. In addition, collective bargaining can and should be designed to secure worklife supports such as paid leave policies, the lack of which can contribute to the gender pay gap.[102]

As a result, unions make a big difference addressing pay and wealth gaps. One study found that a country moving from the 25th percentile of union coverage to the 75th percentile was associated with a 10 percentage point decrease in that country's gender pay gap—or about half of the pay gap in the United States.[103] In the United States, the gender pay gap among full-time workers—controlling for variables including education, experience, and geographic division—falls by about one-fifth when comparing unionized women to nonunion women.[104]

Black workers who are unionized in the United States are paid about 15 percent more than similar nonunion workers, while Hispanic union members are paid about 22 percent more than their nonunion counterparts.[105] Unions can be particularly helpful for women of color. Estimates suggest that had union membership remained at its 1979 levels, the weekly wage gaps between black and white women workers in the United States would be up to 30 percent lower.[106]

The impact unions have on closing the racial wealth gap is even more dramatic than on pay gaps. Because unionized workers receive higher incomes, better benefits, and have greater job security, workers covered by a union contract—whether white, black, or Hispanic—generally have significantly more wealth than workers who are not covered by a union contract. But union coverage provides the greatest boost to the wealth of African Americans and Hispanics. As a result, the racial wealth gap is three times as big when comparing nonunion workers to unionized workers. In other words, the ratio between the median wealth of whites and communities of color is nearly three times larger for nonunion members compared to union members.[107]

Unions also help to reduce less easily measurable forms of mistreatment such as harassment and discrimination. Unions create standard processes and enforce them, which reduces opportunities for harassment and discrimination against all workers—including women and people of color, LBGTQ people, and even straight white men. Unionized hotel workers have, for example, pushed to ensure that housekeepers have panic buttons and to create trainings to limit harassment, while unionized actors have been seeking to block one-on-one meetings in hotel rooms, to prevent the kinds of sexually exploitative meetings that some producers are alleged to have engaged in.[108] Unions also bargain to prevent discrimination based on sexual orientation and decades ago created a pathway to domestic partner benefits by extending health plans to "spousal equivalents."[109] Indeed, unions commonly lead the way in bargaining for equalizing benefits—from domestic partner benefits to paid maternity leave to greater job flexibility—that eventually spread to other employers.[110]

Unions promote messages of interracial solidarity that resonate with workers, and research finds that joining a union leads to lower levels of racial resentment among whites.[111] Unionized workers also have a greater collective voice to push for policies that further reduce gender and racial wage gaps such as civil rights and equal pay legislation, pay transparency, and paid leave—and unions have long championed these equalizing policies.

In addition to the direct impact that unions and collective bargaining have on promoting equal treatment of all workers, they also provide significant indirect help toward achieving these goals by reducing economic inequality. A more compressed economy-wide pay structure, especially where the lowest-paid workers are closer in pay to those at the median, reduces gaps between different industries and firms that can lead to gender and racial wage gaps.[112] It also means that even if employers unfairly view the qualifications of women or workers of color as lower than comparable men or white workers, the resulting gaps in pay are smaller. Research has found, for example, that that the widening of the black-white wage gap in the United States over recent years is in part due to growing overall inequality.[113]

Even less directly, but perhaps most importantly, by reducing economic inequality unions help create a more tolerant and trusting society, which makes it easier to promote racial and gender equity.[114] When people trust others, they are more likely to have more favorable views of groups that are frequently discriminated against and are more willing to work with people who they do not think are like themselves. Thus, trust minimizes underlying problems of racisms and sexism and makes addressing them easier.

It is important to note that unions are able to achieve these impressive results, even under the current system that makes it harder than necessary for unions to promote equality. Not only are certain occupations excluded from being afforded basic rights, but also the current law with its emphasis on workplace-level bargaining makes it particularly difficult for the least powerful workers—often women of color—to organize and collectively bargain. Further, workplace-level bargaining provides less opportunity than does broader-based bargaining to address systemic racism and sexism. Not surprisingly, research finds that industry-wide bargaining is even more effective than worksite-level bargaining at reducing racial and gender inequities—as will be discussed at greater length in subsequent chapters.[115] As a result, strengthening unions and modernizing the labor system would create a major opportunity to make significant advancements against discrimination.[116]

Despite these achievements and the potential to do even more in a new system, unions are nowhere near perfect on race and gender. Looking back at the history of labor in the United States, racism and sexism are easy to spot. In the mid- to late 1800s, as some of the first unions in the United States were being formed, a number of them, particularly those that organized by the craft of the work rather than across an entire industry, excluded blacks and women from their ranks and fought to prevent employers from hiring these groups, and this open racism and sexism continued throughout the nineteenth and early twentieth century. In 1894, for example, the American Railway Union voted to exclude African Americans from their membership; in 1909 unionized white employees of the Georgia Railroad struck to demand that black firemen be replaced by higher-paid whites; and in 1941 unionized male workers at Kelsey-Hays Wheel Corporation struck to get rid of women who were doing work they considered theirs.[117] A less public version of racism and sexism continues to this day with some union members and some local unions.[118] And sometimes this racism becomes very public, such as with the Minneapolis police union, after the police killed George Floyd in 2020.[119]

Still, even in some of the most resistant sectors and local unions there has been significant progress. For example, much of the labor movement—including the AFL-CIO, many large international unions, regional labor councils, local unions, and even a number of police unions—took action in response to the police killing George Floyd and other black men and women, including calling for the leadership of the Minneapolis police union to resign, demanding antiracist reforms from the police union, supporting changes to policing in the United States, embracing the Black Lives Matter movement, and supporting walkouts for black lives.[120] A 2017 study of construction in New York—where discriminatory practices had been particularly notable and recent—found that unionized black construction workers were more likely to be employed (and paid more) than nonunion black workers.[121] Similarly, a study of apprenticeship programs, which were once viewed as notoriously closed, has shown that participation and completion rates for women and people of color are higher in union programs than in nonunion programs—though they still have a long way to go (for example, women made up just 4 percent of union construction apprentices in the study).[122] Further, as bad as union racism and sexism was and is, it should be put in the context of a larger society where racism and sexism were and are still common, especially because research suggests that mistreatment is often worse at nonunion worksites.[123]

More than just having a history of being slightly better than the rest of society, unions in general, especially certain ones, also have a long tradition of respect for all workers. Since the 1800s, some unions have encouraged women and people of color to join. Indeed, from its 1890 founding, the United Mine Workers has been open to all workers and actively fought for the rights of African Americans to join a biracial union—even when it cost the union dearly in lives and organizing strength.[124] Overall, industrial unions have a more positive history than craft unions, as they have long sought to organize all workers at a factory regardless of demographics, rather than just a particular occupational group. But even the more restrictive craft unions can point to their long-standing efforts for equality on at least some matters. Indeed, as early as the 1890s the craft union–based American Federation of Labor supported equal pay for women and women's right to join a union—though this was often a separate women's union.[125]

Here are but a few examples of long-standing union efforts to create an inclusive society for African Americans: In Birmingham, Alabama, during World War I, unionists trying to organize black steelworkers faced off with the Ku Klux Klan, which marched through the streets with over one hundred robed horsemen calling the strikers "disloyalists."[126] In the 1950s and 1960s, the United Auto Workers was one of the driving forces (and funders) behind the civil rights movement.[127] Similarly, when Martin Luther King was assassinated he was marching to support AFSCME's efforts to stop the mistreatment of African American sanitation workers.[128] Not only do a number of unions have a long-standing tradition of fighting for the rights of African American workers, several also have had African Americans in leadership positions for nearly one hundred years.[129]

Similarly, some unions have long fought for gender equality. The Knights of Labor supported equal pay for women in the 1800s.[130] In the early 1900s, the International Ladies' Garment Workers' Union was an important force in the American labor movement, pushing not just for better labor standards but also for arts and education, health care, housing, and recreation opportunities.[131] Organized labor supported the Equal Pay Act of 1963 to make gender pay discrimination illegal.[132] Unions have even gone on strike over equal pay, with an important 1981 strike in San Jose, California, leading to $1.5 million in adjustments to equalize pay between men and women.[133]

Today this more inclusive orientation has come to dominate most union actions. For a mixture of reasons—including an altruistic mission to raise standards for all workers, the increased diversity of the workforce, a pragmatic understanding that employers can more easily exploit workers if they are divided by race and gender, and legal changes that have required unions to be more inclusive—unions have become a strong advocate for all workers.[134]

As early as the 1940s, African Americans were joining unions at roughly the same rate as the underlying population—which is remarkable given that the National Labor Relations Act excludes occupations that were primarily done by black workers at the time, such as farm labor and domestic work—and for decades African Americans have been more likely to be union members than whites.[135] Today more than a third (35.8 percent) of union members are black, Hispanic, Asian, or other nonwhite workers.[136] Similarly, as women increasingly entered the workforce throughout the twentieth century, they poured into unions.[137] Today nearly half—about 46 percent—of union members are women. All told, about two-thirds of workers covered by a union contract are women or people of color (or both).[138]

As the workforce has become much more diverse, unions have changed to reflect this diversity so much so that union members today look remarkably like the workforce today. About 11 percent of male workers are unionized, while 10 percent of women are; roughly 10 percent of whites are unionized, while the figures are 11 percent for blacks, 9 percent for Asians, and 9 percent for Hispanics.[139] Compared to most other organizations, union membership is remarkably diverse. According to professor Kate Bronfenbrenner, and Dorian Warren, president of the Center for Community Change: "The labor movement is the largest mass membership organization of women, African Americans, Latinos, and Asians in the country (larger than the NAACP, NOW, La Raza, and LULAC combined)."[140]

The leadership and staff of unions are also quite diverse. Though union leadership may not be perfectly representative of their membership, it is particularly diverse when compared to the boards of US corporations: nearly 70 percent of board members of Fortune 500 companies are white men.[141] For example, in 2020 the leaders of many the largest US unions were often women and people of color. Lee Saunders, an African American male, is the president of the American Federation of State, County and Municipal Employees, which represents 1,600,000 members.[142] Mary Kay Henry, the president of the Service Employees International Union, with two million members, is a lesbian.[143] So too is Randi Weingarten, president of the American Federation of Teachers, with 1,700,000 members.[144] The president of the National Education Association (three million members), Becky Pringle, is an African American woman, and her predecessor was a Latina.[145] And at the AFL-CIO, the confederation of most American unions, the number two person in the hierarchy is a woman, and number three is a black man and immigrant.[146] The second layer of leadership at national and international unions is also diverse, with women, for example, making up 40 percent or more of the vice presidents and executive council members at several large unions.[147]

All told, unions are a major force for fair treatment of workers, helpful for all workers but particularly helpful for women, people of color, and groups such as LGBTQ people. Strengthening the labor movement would reduce gender and racial pay gaps and wealth gaps, help address harassment and discrimination, and indirectly improve societal trust. As a result, a renewed labor movement would provide significant help addressing major racial and gender fault lines our country faces. Unions still have a ways to go, but they are clearly part of the solution to racial and gender inequity, and a new labor system would better enable them to promote equality.

Summary

The United States faces deep economic, political, and cultural challenges. Wages are stagnant, inequality has risen to near record levels, and government has become increasingly polarized and corrupt. Women and communities of color often have worse economic outcomes than white men even as they are scapegoated for problems they have little to do with. Worse, these problems could signal the beginning of a more severe democratic breakdown.

Yet, as bad as Americans' problems are, a stronger labor movement operating under a new labor system could help solve them. This would make a major difference in raising wages, reducing inequality, making government responsive to ordinary people, and helping address racial and gender challenges in society. At bottom, many problems in the United States stem from a great shift in power to wealthy individuals and businesses and away from ordinary people. A new labor system would give ordinary people the power to negotiate for a fair deal from employers and politicians and fundamentally transform the way America's economy and democracy work.

THE CONTOURS OF A MODERN LABOR SYSTEM

Organized labor plays a vital role in making the economy and democracy work for regular people, but unfortunately America's problems cannot be solved with the country's current labor system. Unions represent too few people, and the law undercuts their ability to recruit new members, while the way collective bargaining is structured leaves out most workers and is ill-suited for today's economy. In the new labor system, public policy needs to actively support unions and encourage broader-based collective bargaining.

Research in the United States and across countries clearly shows that unions are much stronger and can successfully recruit members and fund their activities when they operate in a favorable legal environment. Unfortunately, US law is stacked against unions in numerous ways. Current law provides only very limited strike rights and incredibly weak penalties for employers that violate the law, for example. But, critically, it also fails to provide a structure that facilitates union recruitment. Virtually the only places in the world where unions are currently able to thrive have laws that strongly favor union recruitment. Unions are struggling in most countries because their laws are hostile or only mildly favorable toward unions.

Research also shows that higher-level bargaining raises wages for more people and also does more to reduce overall economic inequality than does enterprise bargaining. It enables and encourages unions to look out for all workers and is particularly effective at promoting racial and gender equality. Higher-level bargaining also minimizes employer opposition to unions, helps high-road firms compete on an even playing field, and is likely to lead to greater economy-wide productivity. It is much better suited to today's economy because it can cover all workers, no matter how firms are structured or how much they contract out. Enterprise bargaining, in contrast, becomes less and less workable as firms increasingly shift work around.

This chapter will develop these claims about the need to reform the US labor system with policy that supports union recruitment and promotes broad-based bargaining. Based on economic and political science theory as well as evidence from US history and states and countries around the world, it will show why labor has been in decline in the United States but has been able to maintain strength in a few countries. It will clarify why a supportive policy environment is so important and explain what types of policies are most helpful to strengthen unions. The Ghent system, in which unions help deliver a public benefit like unemployment insurance, is particularly effective but no single policy is a silver bullet. Rather, a broadly supportive environment—one that facilitates recruitment and enables unions to deliver for their members—is critical.

The chapter will then discuss why bargaining does not work very well in the United States but could be much improved. It will show, based on international comparisons as well as before-and-after research on countries that have changed their bargaining systems, that broad-based bargaining covers far more workers and is better at raising wages and reducing inequality. Higher-level bargaining helps facilitate bargaining for those in difficult economic environments and helps spread the gains of more powerful workers to the majority of workers, those with less market power. Higher-level bargaining also leads to greater productivity because it facilitates better training, leads to less workplace conflict, and encourages innovative competition.

All told, the chapter will explain how these two fundamental changes—a favorable policy environment that actively encourages union membership and broad-based bargaining—would enable labor to deliver much more for the economy and democracy while minimizing any harm unions may do. It provides the theoretical and empirical background for the policies of the new labor system. In short, it explains why the policies described in chapter 1 are so vital.

Unions Decline without Active Support

If unions do so much good—strengthening the middle class, reducing inequality, and making democracy work—why are they in such sharp decline in the United States and much of the world? Why have US unions gone from representing roughly one-third of all workers in the 1950s to just 10 percent in 2019 and only 6 percent in the private sector? Why have unions suffered major decreases in countries ranging from Britain and Australia to Germany and the Netherlands?

The main answer is that in recent decades government policies have made it difficult for unions, particularly in the United States but in many other countries too. Because of the nature of what unions provide (a public service that benefits society) and what they do (challenge employer power), unions need a supportive policy environment. If public policy is merely indifferent to unions, they will struggle. When public policy places barriers in front of unions, sharp decline is almost inevitable. This is especially true as the economy has changed in ways that make organizing and bargaining collectively more difficult.

Unions can be thought of as what economists refer to as a public good—which means a good or service that does not get depleted if more people use it and whose benefits are not exclusive.[1] Public goods have "positive externalities," meaning that many people benefit from their provision, not just those directly paying or providing the service. As a result, public goods suffer from a collective action problem—where people can free ride and benefit from the efforts of others to provide the public good.[2] When a group needs to act collectively to provide a public good, individuals have an incentive to free ride on the efforts of others in the group.

The classic examples of public goods are things like lighthouses, clean air, and official statistics. Public goods are inherently under-provided by the market because it is difficult to privately charge everyone in society who benefits from them. In order for a society to have the optimal amount of a public good, the government usually must directly provide it or else provide incentives for others to provide it.

Unions have many attributes of public goods. The standards unions set do not get used up if additional people benefit from them but rather remain available for others to use—just as official statistics can be used at the same time by academics and businesses. It is also difficult to exclude people from all of the societal benefits unions provide, such as higher wages, lower economic inequality, and political empowerment and advocacy for workers.

With unions, sometimes people think only about part of the free-rider problem—and worry that, for example, under "right-to-work" laws, workers who work at a particular worksite can directly benefit from a particular contract without paying for the costs of negotiating and enforcing it. Getting rid of right-to-work laws by requiring that all workers at a worksite covered by a collective bargaining agreement pay "fair share fees" can address a component of the free-rider problem. But it would be virtually impossible, as well as counterproductive, to exclude people from other benefits that unions provide, such as a stronger democracy and higher standards for workers at nonunion firms.

When thought of in the broadest terms, the free-rider problem, the collective action problem, and the public good problem are the same. All get at the idea that unions and collective bargaining provide services that have wide benefits, yet many workers and members of the public can receive these benefits without paying for them. This means that unless public policy promotes unions and collective bargaining, there will inherently be less of them than is optimal.

In addition, unions—unlike many other public interest organizations—are built to challenge the power of employers, which means unions often face strong opposition that can limit their ability to recruit members. Unions challenge employers' ability to pay whatever the market will let them, to exert unquestioned authority about how to run a workplace, and to have their preferred policies enacted without opposition. As a result, employers have incentives to oppose unions, and, in a capitalist society, they have significant power to do so. Employers often pressure workers to not join a union at their workplace, and they commonly seek to turn public opinion against unions as well as work to change laws to make unionization more difficult. Certainly, unions can provide benefits to employers, and some employers are quite supportive of labor unions and collective bargaining.[3] But employers do not like their power to be challenged and thus generally oppose unions unless they are forced to deal with them. As Walmart's former CEO once said about his opposition to unions, "We like driving the car and we're not going to give the steering wheel to anyone but us."[4]

In recent decades, the economic environment has become more difficult for unions, compounding the permanent problems that unions face delivering a public good that challenges the power of employers. Increased global trade places US workers in more direct competition with workers in other countries, including those with minimal or no labor standards, and allows employers greater power to move work or threaten to exit and avoid dealing with a union. Rapid technology change has also facilitated outsourcing and restructuring even of white-collar jobs, which further strengthens the hand of large businesses and undermines the power of unions.[5] In addition, increased financialization has created an even greater focus on short-term results. All these changes have helped capital become increasingly mobile and powerful, and they have further tilted the playing field against unions.[6]

As a result of all these challenges—the public goods problem and the disproportionate and growing power of employers—unions will struggle to achieve their optimal societal levels without well-crafted public policies that encourage workers to join them. Unfortunately, US labor policy is not well-crafted but rather is structured in ways that are designed to weaken unions. This structural tilt against unions has occurred because of active policy choices and what political scientists call "drift"—the failure to update policy to reflect new realities, such as increased employer opposition and contracting out.[7]

US law makes it very hard for workers to form a union if management resists. If workers want to join a union, they first have to sign a card. If a majority of workers at a worksite sign cards, their employer can choose to recognize the union. More likely, the employer will require an election process that resembles that of sham elections in less democratic countries.[8] The process allows employers to, among other things, force workers to attend antiunion meetings and subject workers to one-on-one discussions about the union with their direct supervisor.[9] Penalties for employers that break the law and, for example, fire a worker who supports the union are laughably weak. There are no fines; only back pay minus interim earnings is required. In fact, owners sometimes refer to these meager payments as the cost of their "hunting license."[10] Employers illegally fire workers in about one-third of union organizing efforts, and over half of employers threaten to close the worksite if workers unionize.[11] The potential costs to workers under the current system are great, and many are simply unwilling to take the risk, especially because in the United States workers rely on their employers not just for wages but also for health and retirement benefits to a far greater degree than workers in most other countries.

When a company violates the law, less than one-tenth of organizing drives achieve a first contract.[12] If workers are able to make it through the gauntlet and unionize and sign a contract with an employer, in more than half of US states that are "right-to-work," unions face the narrow free-rider problem described above, in which workers can benefit from the contract without paying for the costs of negotiating and enforcing it.[13] Because the law is so stacked against workers forming a union, organized labor has increasingly tried to avoid the existing legal framework—for example, using economic pressure to encourage firms to allow workers to join unions through "card check" sign-up or other more favorable processes than guaranteed by law, though unions rarely have the power to achieve this goal.[14]

Enterprise-level collective bargaining also exacerbates employer opposition. Under enterprise bargaining, if a firm or unit in a firm is unionized, employers will face increased labor costs compared to their nonunion competitors, which creates a strong incentive to oppose unions. Higher-level bargaining tends to equalize labor costs across competitors and thus lessens incentives for employer opposition.

Compounding the problem of increased employer opposition due to higher labor costs, employers under worksite-by-worksite bargaining have additional opportunities to resist union efforts. Enterprise bargaining allows employers ways to avoid unions and collective bargaining by outsourcing and shifting their business strategy. Employers can, for example, contract out a line of work to another firm, close an entire worksite or line of business (possibly restarting something similar without unionized workers), or restructure work so that it is done by independent contractors without union rights.[15] Indeed, enterprise bargaining provides financial incentives for firms to take these actions. Even when these actions are done for reasons that have nothing to do with union avoidance, the impact can still undermine unions and collective bargaining. Unions are either outright prevented from operating or have little ability to improve working conditions because they are now bargaining with a very small employer with no market power and have a hard time bargaining with the dominant players. In contrast, higher-level collective bargaining takes away the incentive and limits the opportunities for employer exit from collective bargaining—since, for example, all workers in an industry are covered, no matter who their employer is or how the firm is structured.

Finally, workers' right to strike and picket in the United State are quite limited, which further fuels employer opposition and weakens unions. Strikes are a critical source of power for unions because they have the potential to disrupt the regular activities of an employer or group of employers.[16] This potential for disruption enables unions to have a seat at the table and is the ultimate backup when negotiations fail. Indeed, the 2018 teacher strikes in several US states clearly show the importance of the strike, since they led to pay increases and increased funding for education after years of cuts and failed negotiations.[17]

Strikes may not always achieve their immediate aims, but, without a credible threat to use them, workers and unions have less power, and employers are more emboldened to oppose unions.

Unlike workers in many other countries, US workers can be permanently replaced if they strike.[18] Further, US unions can legally strike only against their direct employer.[19] They are prevented from participating in "secondary boycotts"—activities against other employers that may be able to influence industry standards—and cannot legally engage in general or political strikes or mass picketing to try to change policy in a direction more favorable to workers. These activities are allowed in many other countries.[20] And many public-sector workers, including many teachers, have almost no right to strike. Indeed, many of the recent teacher strikes were illegal.

All told, the current US policy environment makes it very difficult for unions and subverts the ability of workers to join organizations they want to join. Indeed, US labor policy violates a number of basic international standards, including the Universal Declaration of Human Rights.[21] US policy is so hostile to unions that Human Rights Watch—an international nonprofit that normally focuses on abuses in less democratic countries—wrote a report finding that "workers' freedom of association is under sustained attack in the United States."[22]

The close correlation between union density and policy environment can be seen in the figure below that charts union density in the United States from

1880 to the present. The figure shows clearly that unions have been able to succeed when policy is favorable but have struggled when policies have not actively supported them in significant ways.

In the late 1800s and early 1900s, before legislation was passed directly relating to unions, judge-made common law was largely hostile to labor unions, with judges often issuing injunctions to break up strikes, and the government sometimes actively cracked down on unions by sending police or the army to break up strikes.[23] Not surprisingly, union density was very low in this period. A few very slight and brief increases in density are visible as in the late 1880s—when, for example, the Knights of Labor was created and the American Federation of Labor was founded—but even creative organizing was not particularly successful in this environment. In the early 1900s, legislated policy on unions moved a bit away from outright hostility and toward a kind of neutrality. In 1914, for example, Congress passed a law declaring that union actions were exempt from antitrust laws, and then in 1932 it passed another law that further restricted court injunctions.[24] Still, neutrality did relatively little for growth. Between the early 1900s until 1935, unions only grew significantly during World War I, when the government actively sided with unions to prevent strikes that could potentially limit war production.[25]

Immediately after the passage of the National Labor Relations Act (NLRA) in 1935 and during World War II, US policy was most favorable to private-sector

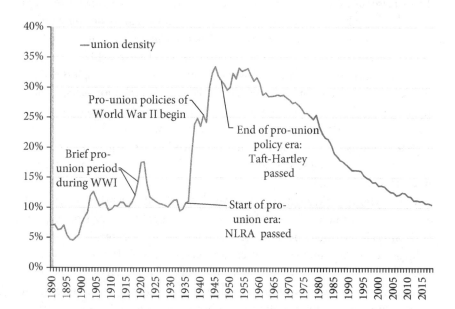

FIGURE 1. Union density varies with the favorability of government policy.
Source: Historical Statistics of the United States, unionstats.com, cited in Colin Gordon, "State of the Unions," *Dissent*, February 13, 2019, https://www.dissentmagazine.org/blog/state-of-the-unions.

unions. Unsurprisingly, unions grew rapidly during this period. Indeed, almost all of the growth, as a percentage of the total workforce, unions experienced in the twentieth century came in these few short years when policies actively encouraged unionization. The NLRA declared that it was "the policy of the United States to . . . encourag[e] the practice and procedure of collective bargaining" and gave workers new rights to join together and compel employers to recognize their unions and bargain, and during these years employers followed the law.[26] World War II supported union growth through the National War Labor Board that, among other things, gave organized labor an institutionalized seat at the table, actively promoted collective bargaining, and facilitated new workers to join existing unions.[27]

To be sure, increased worker activism and union organizing were an important part of the reason why union density increased sharply in the late 1930s and early 1940s. There is ample evidence that workers took many bold and brave actions to demand that employers recognize their unions during this period.[28] Grassroots efforts were critical. But the favorable legal environment made it safer and more fruitful for workers to act on their long-standing grievances. Worker activism coupled with a favorable legal environment from the NLRA and World War II policy led to a dramatic increase in union density—a far sharper and longer increase than the United States has ever experienced. Some accounts maintain that worker action was the sole or most important factor in the increase, but these bottom-up accounts at odds with the general research on social movements, which finds that protest actions require not only means and motive but also political opportunity.[29] Bottom-up only accounts also have trouble explaining why density did not increase much before 1937, when the Supreme Court decided the NLRA was constitutional—even though the kinds of grievances that led workers to demand unions had existed for years.[30] These accounts cannot explain why previous worker activism did not lead to such dramatic increases in density. Nor can they fully explain why union density was able to increase for many years although all prior spurts in growth quickly faded. This activism-only account also has trouble explaining why density began to stagnate and decline when it did.

Union density peaked not long after World War II and then plateaued through the mid-1960s as policy became less favorable for private-sector workers. The 1947 Taft-Hartley amendments to the NLRA significantly weakened union strike rights as well as their abilities to collect membership dues, and important administrative and Supreme Court decisions in this period favored employers over unions.[31] These changes started to cause difficulties for private-sector unions, but struggles were largely masked during this period because public-sector workers began to win state-level union rights in the late 1950s and 1960s, which helped overall union density remain relatively stable.

The underlying weakness of the private-sector law became more apparent in the 1970s and especially in the 1980s, as employers increased the intensity of their opposition to unions, which continues to this day.[32] Hiring "union-avoidance" consultants became standard, and violations of the law increased rapidly.[33] Because the underlying law was quite weak, employer opposition was often successful at preventing unionization or breaking unions. As the law was shown to be ineffective, Congress failed on a number of occasions to make even modest reforms—to strengthen penalties for violations of the law, for example.[34]

Legal changes in recent years have made it even more difficult for workers to unionize. Since 2011, five states have passed right-to-work laws, so that now more than half of all states ban fair share fees for private-sector workers.[35] The Supreme Court effectively made the entire public sector "right to work" in 2018 with the *Janus* decision. Efforts to weaken public-sector unions have been particularly aggressive—and creative—at the state level, where governors and state legislatures have the authority to set union rules for their workers. The classic example is the State of Wisconsin, which in 2011 virtually eliminated collective bargaining rights for most public-sector workers, required unions to be recertified every year, and prevented unions from collecting money through the efficient method of payroll deduction, among other things.[36] Other states, such as Iowa, have passed similar legislation.[37]

Compounding the problem of antagonistic labor policy is that other policies that structure the labor market have also indirectly weakened unions in recent decades—for example, by failing to promote full employment and allowing employers to misclassify employees as independent contractors without union rights. As labor historian Nelson Lichtenstein explains, the story of unions in America shows that "even the most creative forms of rank-and-file militancy could but rarely triumph against a free market–oriented neoliberal legal and financial regime."[38]

It is also important to note that the policy environment has not only reduced overall union density but has also affected the type of worker that unions have been able to represent. When policy is less favorable to unions, workers generally need more independent, market power—such as by having a college degree or particularly valuable skills—to be able to form a union and deal with employer opposition. But when policy is most favorable and union density the highest, workers with less education and less power are more able to join unions.[39]

Even though US history is quite clear that policy plays a critical role in shaping union density, there are several other sources of data to consider. First, there are studies that look at the success unions have had organizing workers under different presidential administrations; these find unsurprisingly that unions do worse when labor law is interpreted in less favorable ways.[40] Presidential administrations can take actions that set the broad approach toward unions—such as President Reagan firing striking air traffic controllers—as well as appoint agency officials that, for example, delay union elections to give employers more time to oppose unionization or rule that certain employees are not eligible to vote.

More broadly, polling on public support for unions and comparisons of union density across US states and countries around the world all indicate that policy is of the upmost importance. Polls show that about half of US workers would like to join a union.[41] But, despite the public's strong desire to join, relatively few workers are members today. Today just more than 6 percent of private-sector workers are union members, which is about as low as union density has been in one hundred years. What's more, public approval of unions is currently as high or higher than it was in the 1970s and 80s, when private-sector density was two to three times higher.[42] All of which strongly suggests that the policy environment today, rather than a lack of interest, has made it hard for workers to get what they want.

Another way to see how government support or opposition shapes union density is by looking at union membership in the public sector. From the 1930s until the early 1960s, when collective bargaining in virtually all parts of the public sector was banned, public sector union density hovered around 10 percent; however, once public sector workers gained rights in a number of states density shot up and has remained above one-third.[43] Labor historian Joseph E. Slater explains that before the 1960s, "public sector unions often failed to accomplish moderate goals or even to survive, largely because of the legal climate and the attitudes of employers," but were much more successful once laws were changed.[44] Examining public-sector density at the level of states, where law varies dramatically, is also revealing. It is true that public-sector union density is generally higher than in the private sector because the economic constraints are different—governments are not going to pick up and move to get lower labor costs, and they generally do not go out of business. Still, states can create a more or less supportive climate for public-sector unions. These policy differences explain much of the variation in public-sector density across states. In South Carolina, for example, where collective bargaining for public-sector workers is outlawed and other restrictive measures are in place, union membership in the public sector was just 7 percent in 2017, while in New York, with more supportive policies, it was over 67 percent in 2017.[45] Certainly other factors, such as social customs and worker attitudes, matter.[46] But the structure of the law is determinative. In Wisconsin, before Act 10 limited union rights in 2011, public-sector density was about 50 percent, but by 2017 this had fallen to less than 19 percent.[47]

Similarly, the percentage of workers who are members of unions varies widely across the world—from nearly all workers in Iceland to around two-thirds in

Sweden and Demark, half in Belgium, about a quarter in Britain and Canada, around 17 percent in Germany and the Netherlands, less than 15 percent in Australia, and barely 10 percent in the United States.[48] Research comparing countries finds that a supportive policy environment largely explains the huge differences in union density as well as why unions, on the decline in recent decades, have not declined in all countries. One key study of western European countries over more than four decades found that changes in the economy or society did not explain the level of union density, rather that only the level and type of state support could account for the variation over time and across countries—a result that several other studies have corroborated.[49]

The main point that all this research highlights is that societies have stronger unions because they want to. When policy makers want unions, they set up rules that make it possible for them to survive. When policy makers do not want unions, they neglect them or are hostile.

A related point to consider is that governments frequently provide support for various organizations, from Mothers Against Drunk Driving, Planned Parenthood, to even chambers of commerce.[50] In fact, the US government provides a wide range of support for small businesses, including through grants and loans, antitrust laws, and favorable access to government contracts. Small businesses face a tough environment competing against large firms, and the government has taken a number of steps to help. In 2019 the federal government estimated it would support over $42 billion in loans to small businesses, provide training to one million small business owners, and ensure that 23 percent of all federal contracting dollars went to small businesses.[51]

Organizations such as Mothers Against Drunk Driving and Planned Parenthood are independent of the state, but the state encourages their activities. When the government supports an organization's mission or a particular activity the organization is engaged in, it finds ways to provide support. The state could do the same for unions.

Policies to Support Unions

There are almost an infinite number of things governments can do to support or hinder unions. A vast range of policies around the world have been used to support unions and collective bargaining.[52] Indeed, the imagination of policy makers and their publics seems to be the most important limit on how policy can relate to unions. Still, research shows that there is no single policy that will create a vibrant labor movement by itself. Rather, policy makers need to create a broadly supportive environment that ensures workers have the ability to take independent activities that can improve working conditions as well as take more proactive measures to promote union membership. In other words, policy should ensure that workers have real rights, unions can deliver for workers, and there are individual incentives for joining a union.[53]

In studying what leads to higher union density across countries, the main factors that researchers have focused on are worksite access, the ability to charge fair share fees, sectoral bargaining, and the Ghent system.[54] Other researchers have focused on workers' rights, such as their ability to strike. All of these policies provide some degree of support for unions. Still, as stand-alone policies, they have typically not been enough. When several powerful policies are combined together, however, labor unions are often able to thrive.

The Ghent system has been perhaps the most important policy to maintain high and stable membership, especially over recent decades as the economy has shifted in ways that make organizing workers especially difficult. While the Ghent system provides a strong incentive for membership, it is not enough to renew unions by itself. Under the Ghent system, unions help deliver unemployment insurance, a benefit that is subsidized by the government, as is done in countries such as Belgium, Denmark, Sweden, and Iceland. This increases membership for a number of reasons: workers have an incentive to join unions to receive the benefit, unions have regular access to workers outside the conflictual workplace, and unions are seen as helping workers and sanctioned by government to do so.[55] Research shows that the Ghent system is essential to obtaining very high union density, and countries with the Ghent system, particularly Belgium and Iceland, have been virtually alone in maintaining density over recent years.[56] Estimates suggest that the Ghent system boosts union density by around 20 percentage points—or roughly the typical difference in density between Sweden, which has Ghent, and its neighbor Norway, which does not, and much of the difference between Belgium, which has Ghent, and the Netherlands, which does not.[57] Further evidence of the value of providing incentives for membership through the Ghent system is that some countries with the system, such as Sweden and Finland, have recently taken steps to make union-provided unemployment insurance more expensive and thus less attractive, which has slightly reduced density.[58]

Still, the Ghent system is not a panacea. Even in Ghent countries, the level of union density at a worksite is important in determining whether workers join.[59] This strongly suggests that workers need to feel a social connection to their union as well as have a financial incentive to join. In addition, countries with the Ghent system and strong unions also have numerous other policies that support unions. In Belgium, for example, the government provides strong supports for centralized collective bargaining, individual worksites have works councils, and unions have important rights in working with works councils.[60] Swedish unions have strong strike rights, rights to information, and the ability to get leave time from their employer, and legislated workplace standards provide the unions flexibility for negotiation.[61]

The ability of unions to access workers and have a presence in the workplace provides them with critical opportunities to recruit potential members, but again this is insufficient as a stand-alone policy. The workplace is where people think most about work issues, it is where the culture of unionism often takes hold, and access here can provide additional legitimacy to unions. Policy can provide worksite access to unions directly as a matter of right, as is done in New Zealand, for example, or indirectly through organizations like works councils—which are worker-led organizations that discuss a range of workplace issues other than wages and benefits—as in Germany and the Netherlands.[62] Unions can also gain access to the workplace through collective bargaining agreements, as in the United States. While there is little doubt that strong worksite access helps, access alone is not enough. Unions in Germany and the Netherlands both have significant workplace access through works councils (and they also have sectoral bargaining), yet density has declined quite a bit over recent decades, as access by itself does not provide enough of an incentive for workers to join.[63]

Unions' ability to charge fees to workers covered by a contract, as is done in much of the United States and Canada, has unsurprisingly been found to be helpful for supporting union density. Still, union density has been in decline Canada as well as in US states where fair share fees are allowed. Further, even when unions were at their strongest in the United States and Canada, fair share fees led to only relatively modest levels of union density compared to much of Europe. Indeed, most of Europe is effectively right to work—meaning fair share fees are not allowed—yet many countries there have managed to achieve much higher densities than the United States or even Canada. Researchers using more advanced analysis have made similar findings and concluded that fair share fees or even a closed union shop are not enough to "stave off decline."[64]

Bargaining that occurs above the firm level also helps support union membership, but by itself it is clearly not enough for high and stable membership.[65] As discussed previously, this type of bargaining reduces employer opposition, which makes it easier for unions to organize workers. Yet, because all workers in a sector are covered whether they are members or not, bargaining above firm level also increases the incentive for workers to free ride and benefit from union membership without paying for it. Thus, sectoral bargaining exerts mixed pressures on union membership. So even though countries with sectoral bargaining generally have higher membership than enterprise countries, they can still struggle for membership. Indeed, over recent decades, union density has declined

significantly in countries like Germany and the Netherlands, where there is sectoral bargaining, and in France union density is even lower than it is in the United
States.

Whether workers have the right to strike is also essential for the strength of any
union movement, but, as with the other policies, the ability to strike is not a sufficient condition for high membership. Strikes are a vital basis of power for unions
and thus affect whether workers think joining could actually help improve conditions. Indeed, the ability for workers to use a wide variety of economic weapons
undergirds the impressive union achievements in places like Scandinavia. Strike
rights are also a basic human right in international conventions.[66] Still, some
countries with relatively strong strike rights have relatively modest union density, such as the Netherlands, with 17 percent density, and some countries where
strikes are frequent have very low density, such France, at around 8 percent.[67]
Further, countries like Australia in the mid-twentieth century had high union
membership of roughly 50 percent with limited strike rights.[68]

All told, there are a range of policies that can help support unions. The Ghent
system, worksite access, the ability to charge agency fees, higher-level collective
bargaining, and having basic rights all help unions. The Ghent system is critical to sustaining high union density with the incentives, access, and stamp of
approval it provides unions, but no single policy, not even Ghent, is enough to
overcome the structural disadvantages unions face. A combination of policies
is required to really strengthen labor. Policy must provide multiple ways and
multiple reasons for workers to join unions. Workers join unions for selective
benefits and because of cultural norms and solidarity, as well as because they
have frequent contact with the union inside and outside the workplace and see
it delivering benefits. Policies that provide a broadly supportive environment are
necessary to strengthen unions because they give workers more reasons to join
and make unions less reliant on any one motivation. Labor policies that seek to
provide a "mix of social norms and individual benefits provide the incentives
for individuals to incur the costs of providing public goods," as law professors
Catherine Fisk and Martin Malin, professors explain.[69]

In summary, unions face a number of structural disadvantages to achieving
adequate membership and require a favorable policy environment that provides
workers with multiple reasons to join unions in order to thrive.

The Importance of Higher-Level Bargaining

While it is important to have policies that support union membership, it is also
critical for policy to support broad-based bargaining, as can be seen in table 1
presented later in this chapter. Enterprise bargaining does many things to help

workers. But workplace-level bargaining works best in a system that emphasizes higher-level bargaining. As this section will explain, broad-based bargaining, compared to workplace bargaining alone, leads to much greater coverage, significantly lower inequality, and higher productivity. Broad-based bargaining is also particularly well suited to the modern economy.

The simplest reason that a system with higher-level bargaining is better than one with only enterprise bargaining is because it leads to more workers being covered by the terms of a union contract.[70] With higher-level bargaining, most or all workers in an industry or sector are covered, not merely those who work in an enterprise or division of an enterprise that is unionized. Greater coverage by union contracts in turn means that wages are higher for more workers and economic inequality lower. When coverage is widespread, high standards can be maintained and improved upon, rather than continually undercut by low-road competitors.

The basic logic of higher-level bargaining leading to greater coverage and thus higher wages and less inequality is pretty simple. Still, explaining a bit more of the mechanisms at work can help clarify why higher-level bargaining would be so valuable in the United States. Higher-level bargaining helps spread the gains of more powerful workers to those with less market power. All types of collective bargaining increase the power of workers, but enterprise bargaining does less to broaden the achievements of powerful workers to include others. Workplace-level bargaining can help spread gains to other workers, but this is largely through an indirect "threat" effect of other employers weighing whether they should raise wages in order to limit their workers' interest in forming a union. In contrast, higher-level bargaining spreads bargaining coverage more evenly and completely. Higher-level bargaining can also provide a way to cover workers who would otherwise struggle to bargain with their employers—while enterprise bargaining often leaves little recourse for workers without much market power. Finally, higher-level bargaining can help give unions a structural kind of power to bargain that complements the market power unions derive from density. In this way, higher-level bargaining can help compensate for any modest declines in union density and market power and maintain relatively stable coverage.

Workers can have some degree of market power for a number of reasons—for example, when they are particularly skilled and hard to replace; working on a time-sensitive, highly profitable or capital-intensive project, in which any kind of disruption would be very costly; or from a favored demographic group, such as white men. Similarly, the ability of workers to collectively negotiate with their employer is affected by a number of factors, including the capacity of the direct employer to pay, whether the industry is comprised of stable employers or small, fly-by-night operations, and whether workers are classified as independent contractors and legally barred from collective bargaining.

Enterprise bargaining can and often does work quite well for certain types of workers, particularly those who can potentially disrupt employer profits and are employed in a manner that is conducive to bargaining.[71] A group of workers at a massive, capital-intensive factory, for example, would have the potential to cause costly delays if they went on strike and thus often have the necessary leverage to bring their employer to the bargaining table. In addition, at factories and other capital-intensive worksites, labor is a relatively small portion of the cost of overall production and thus employer opposition to increased labor costs is diminished, making organizing somewhat easier. In cases where workers have power at a particular worksite, enterprise bargaining can provide significant benefits to workers—possibly even greater benefits than these workers would achieve under higher-level bargaining. Indeed, for some workers who currently have great influence at their worksite, sectoral bargaining can lead to less power and smaller wage increases. Under broad-based bargaining, these powerful workers' gains are constrained by what other workers can obtain and what the broader economy can sustain.

But enterprise bargaining does not work very well for those with less power and a less favorable industry structure. And even workers with greater worksite power need to worry that their employer can find ways to escape enterprise-level bargaining.

Indeed, in today's economy, enterprise bargaining does not work well for most workers. Many workers are essentially interchangeable. In addition, as service employment increasingly dominates the economy, worksites are smaller and less capital-intensive. Some firms may have gotten much larger over recent decades, but the actual worksites where workers spend their days have gotten smaller and more fungible.[72] The work of call center workers, building janitors, fast food workers, gig workers, truck drivers, and most types of workers today can be easily moved or replaced with minimal disruption to the firm. Moreover, even if the workers are not easily replaced, they are often subcontractors of subcontractors and thus struggle to negotiate with the person who actually has the ability to increase their wages. Even the prototypical powerful factory worker discussed above often has far less power today than one did several decades ago. Globalization, technological change, and corporate organization has made it easier for companies to move factories, spread out their supply chains so they are less reliant on one factory, and even staff the factory with temp workers who are designed to be easily replaceable.

Broader-based bargaining would help ensure that all workers could be covered by collectively bargained agreements and that those with similar skills would receive similar pay. Not only would the same construction worker using similar skills receive similar pay no matter the type of project they were working on, but also janitors, home care workers, and other similarly disadvantaged workers would actually have a forum in which to bargain collectively. Not surprisingly, research shows that higher-level bargaining leads to much greater coverage for people employed by small firms and who work part-time or have other kinds of nonstandard employment.[73]

The classic examples of countries with higher-level bargaining include Sweden, Denmark, and to a lesser extent Germany, but most advanced countries have had significant experience with this kind of bargaining at some point in their history, including the United States, as well as other English-speaking countries such as Britain and Australia. There are many reasons that some countries have broad-based bargaining and others rely heavily on worksite bargaining. The choices of unions and employers are important, but policy plays a vital role.[74] Indeed, the degree of higher-level bargaining a country engages in is often the direct result of policy choices, as in the decisions of a number of countries, including Portugal, Spain, Israel, Australia, and Britain to move away from higher-level bargaining, and in the decisions of Norway and Uruguay to increase the centralization of bargaining.[75] It is also important to note that countries that have broad-based bargaining tend to do most of their bargaining at this level, but they also often engage in some bargaining that happens at the firm level or below, and there is usually some give and take between the levels of bargaining.[76]

The basic results of higher-level bargaining leading to greater coverage can be seen in a variety of ways. At the simplest level, a quick look at the bargaining coverage of countries around the world shows that value of higher-level bargaining. All of the countries with near universal coverage, including not just Scandinavian countries but also places like Austria and Belgium, engage in multi-employer bargaining. Further, with higher-level bargaining and structures that effectively extend union contracts to similarly placed workers, extremely high union density is not always required to achieve relatively high coverage rates. Germany, with less than 20 percent union membership, covers roughly half of workers, and the Netherlands covers around three-fourths of workers with density that is even lower than in Germany.[77]

More sophisticated analysis leads to the same conclusion that higher-level bargaining produces higher coverage by collectively bargained agreements.[78] While enterprise bargaining can occasionally lead to high coverage when density is very high, research shows that most of the time enterprise bargaining leads to low coverage. Only broader-based bargaining consistently produces high levels of coverage by union agreements. As the researchers at the OECD explain, "collective bargaining coverage is high and stable only in countries where multi-employer agreements (i.e. at sector or national level) are negotiated."[79]

Critically, higher-level bargaining coverage leads to better results for workers. Indeed, the importance of sectoral bargaining for reducing inequality is hard to overstate.

TABLE 1 Broad-based bargaining and incentives for membership are necessary to achieve high union density and high collective bargaining coverage

COUNTRIES WITH LOW UNION DENSITY AND LOW COLLECTIVE BARGAINING COVERAGE

	UNION DENSITY (PERCENT)	COLLECTIVE BARGAINING COVERAGE (PERCENT)	EMPLOYEES COVERED BY MULTI-EMPLOYER AGREEMENTS (PERCENT)	GHENT SYSTEM
Australia	14	36*	low	No
Canada	28	30	very low	No
Japan	17	17	very low	No
United Kingdom	23	26	very low	No
United States	10	12	very low	No

COUNTRIES WITH HIGH COLLECTIVE BARGAINING COVERAGE BUT LOW UNION DENSITY

	UNION DENSITY (PERCENT)	COLLECTIVE BARGAINING COVERAGE (PERCENT)	EMPLOYEES COVERED BY MULTI-EMPLOYER AGREEMENTS (PERCENT)	GHENT SYSTEM
Austria	27	98	95	No
France	9	98	96	No
Germany	17	56	50	No
Netherlands	17	79	76	No
Switzerland	16	58	41	No

COUNTRIES WITH HIGH UNION DENSITY AND HIGH COLLECTIVE BARGAINING COVERAGE

	UNION DENSITY (PERCENT)	COLLECTIVE BARGAINING COVERAGE (PERCENT)	EMPLOYEES COVERED BY MULTI-EMPLOYER AGREEMENTS (PERCENT)	GHENT SYSTEM
Belgium	50	96	86	Yes
Denmark	67	82	63	Yes
Finland	60	89	80	Yes
Sweden	66	90	75	Yes

Sources: Australia density: "Trends in Union Membership in Australia," Parliament of Australia, October 15, 2018. Coverage: Tess Hardy and Andrew Stewart, "What's Causing the Wages Slowdown?," in *The Wages Crisis in Australia*, ed. Andrew Stewart, Jim Stanford, and Tess Hardy (South Australia: University of Adelaide Press, 2018), table 4.1. Note that coverage in Australia is likely overstated, as explained in chapter 4. Canada density and coverage: Statistics Canada, "Union Status by Industry;" United Kingdom density and coverage: "Trade Union Statistics 2017: Tables," table 1.10. US density and coverage: Barry Hirsch and David Macpherson, "Union Membership and Coverage Database from the CPS," Unionstats.com. All other countries: for union density and collective bargaining coverage, see OECD.Stat; for percent of employees covered by multi-employer agreements, see Jelle Visser, "ICTWSS: Database on Institutional Characteristics of Trade Unions, Wage Setting, State Intervention, and Social Pacts in 51 Counties between 1960 and 2014," University of Amsterdam, 2016. For all sources, most recent year data used; accessed May 4, 2019.

It is pretty easy to see that countries with higher-level bargaining and high coverage—such as Denmark, Sweden, Belgium, France, and the Netherlands—tend to have relatively low levels of inequality. But research that compares countries over time and controls for a variety of other economic and political factors also finds that higher-level bargaining leads to lower economic inequality. As one study put it, "the most important factor in explaining pay dispersion is the level of wage-setting."[80] In fact, a review of more than a hundred different studies concluded that "the most robust result is that countries with a high level of bargaining coordination tend to have a more compressed wage distribution."[81]

Studies with different approaches also come to the same conclusion. Only a few countries have moved toward higher-level bargaining in recent decades, but those that did saw significant reductions in inequality.[82] When Norway, for example, moved to a more centralized bargaining system in the late 1980s, pay distribution became more equal, even though other economic trends were pushing toward greater inequality.[83] Similarly, in the early 2000s Uruguay reinstituted a wage board system to negotiate industry-wide standards, and it took steps to increase union density, which helped lead to significant wage increases and reductions in inequality.[84] In contrast, a number of countries, including Australia, New Zealand, Britain, and Israel, moved toward lower-level bargaining. Before-and-after studies of these countries show that moving from higher-level bargaining toward more enterprise-level bargaining increased inequality.[85] Indeed, even Germany, with its strong tradition of unions as well as works councils and workers on corporate boards, has struggled with wage stagnation and rising inequality over the past two decades as its sectoral bargaining system has weakened.[86] Compared to the United States, Germany's sectoral bargaining is still quite strong and its inequality low. But as Germany has moved away from sectoral bargaining, inequality has risen sharply, and wage growth has been quite slow, despite productivity gains. Germany's neighbor France has had productivity growth over recent decades similar to Germany but much higher wage growth and lower inequality, in part because it has maintained a more centralized bargaining structure.[87]

Research on higher-level bargaining in the United States also indicates that it was helpful in reducing earnings inequality, especially when it was more widespread.[88] A telling US research project found that various forms of higher-level bargaining (including multi-firm bargaining, region-wide pattern bargaining, and industry-wide pattern bargaining) were able to raise wages and spread the gains throughout local labor markets and industries from 1957 to 1979 but had far less ability to do so after 1980, as unions weakened and broader-based bargaining became rarer. The authors of the study, professors Thomas Kochan and Christine Riordan, explain that the weakening of broad-based bargaining structures were at the "root" of the increase in inequality.[89]

Broader-based bargaining also tends to provide significant benefits to women and people of color. Because higher-level bargaining leads to a greater percentage of workers being covered by a collective bargaining agreement, more workers get pay raises and have their pay set based on measurable standards, which limits the opportunity for discrimination. Broad-based bargaining also structures negotiations to be about all workers, not just unionized workers at a particular worksite, which makes bargaining more inclusive and more able to tackle issues of racism and sexism. It can also provide greater opportunity to address leave policy and less obvious drivers of pay gaps. And, critically, broad-based bargaining helps workers in jobs with the least market power get covered by a union contract.[90] These workers are often women and people of color. Finally, higher-level bargaining reduces economic inequality in society more than enterprise bargaining, and the smaller the overall pay distribution in society, the smaller the pay differences tend to be between men and women and between whites and other races.[91]

Unsurprisingly, the international research finds that bargaining at higher levels generally reduces pay gaps more than firm-level bargaining does.[92] Similarly, the more limited evidence on wage setting that occurs above the firm level in the United States also shows that it is quite effective at reducing gender and racial pay gaps. For example, one analysis found that the income gap between white and black construction workers would be roughly 7 percentage points smaller if a state without a prevailing wage law instituted such a law.[93] As discussed previously, prevailing wage laws require that government contractors pay the wage that prevails in the market—often set by unionized firms—and are analogous to laws in other countries that extend the pay scales of union contracts to non-union firms. Research also shows that US public-sector pay scales and bargaining as well as minimum wage laws lead to smaller gender and racial pay gaps.[94] Public-sector wage setting and minimum wage laws are methods of pay setting that occur above the workplace level and are therefore somewhat analogous to broad-based collective bargaining.

While the research suggests that bargaining above firm level is particularly effective at reducing gender and racial pay gaps, it is important to note that it is not a panacea. Some counties with sectoral bargaining, such as Austria, still have relatively high pay gaps, indicating that bargaining partners must consider gender and racial equity at the bargaining table and take care not to extend preexisting societal inequities by setting compensation standards that disadvantage industries and occupations where women and racial minorities are overrepresented.[95]

Boosting Productivity

Not only does broad-based bargaining lead to greater coverage, and thus higher wages for most workers, as well as less economic inequality and smaller pay gaps, these gains do not cause significant economic harm. Indeed, the more unions are able to represent all workers, the more positive their overall economic impact is likely to be.

There are a number of theoretical reasons to expect that higher-level bargaining would increase productivity and thus help the overall economy. First, broad-based bargaining would raise wages for more workers, and higher wages help reduce turnover and encourage innovation.[96] Moreover, similar pay for similar work—a key goal of higher-level bargaining—enables a more efficient allocation of resources, which speeds up the movement of labor and capital from low- to high-productivity activities.[97] Put another way, similar pay for similar work forces companies to compete based on productivity improvements, not squeezing workers. By making the rationale for pay increases clearer and more transparent—such as by identifying measurable skills—higher-level bargaining may be particularly motivational for workers who seek to advance their careers and can reduce discrimination even more than firm-level bargaining. Further, broad-based bargaining also creates an opportunity for workplace organizations like works councils, which provide a forum to discuss work processes and have been shown to increase productivity.[98] In addition, by elevating some conflict about pay scales to outside the firm, higher-level collective bargaining can enable greater collaboration in the workplace.[99] Collaboration between workers and management is often key to improving production processes. Finally, broad-based bargaining can also promote worker training by minimizing the employees' financial incentives to leave firms once they are trained and creating an opportunity for well-designed training systems.[100] These latter two—reducing conflict and promoting training—merit additional explanation.

One of the most important factors in determining the economic impact of unions is the quality of the relationship between labor and management—whether it is collaborative or conflictual.[101] Unfortunately, the US system is geared toward producing more conflict than it needs to. The highly conflictual and deeply flawed union election process is one important reason why the US labor relations system is so conflictual. But even more critical is that enterprise bargaining creates additional incentives for managers to oppose unions and can push unions and managers to act in ways that may not be in the best interests of the firm or all its workers.

From the management perspective, enterprise bargaining means that if a firm or unit in a firm is unionized, employers will face higher labor costs than their nonunion competitors. Moreover, managers have to negotiate over the way work is conducted in this unit, while their competitors will not. This makes many managers view unions as a threat to their company and ability to manage and feel that nonunion firms have cost and discretionary advantages. Given these incentives and beliefs, it is not surprising that many US firms vigorously oppose their workers unionizing and retain an adversarial approach if their workers do unionize.[102]

From the worker perspective, enterprise bargaining means that although unions may care about a broad group of workers, the law pushes them to bargain for only the particular group of workers they represent rather than negotiating to improve conditions for all workers in an industry or a region.[103] The ability of unions to represent a broad group of workers is further limited because current law prevents many kinds of workers from joining unions and allows employers to evade unions by shifting the form of their business.

When unions had high membership rates, they could indirectly raise wages for workers outside a particular unit, but, as they weaken, they have far less ability to do so. Now every wage increase or benefit improvement that a small group of unionized workers in a particular unit in a particular firm achieves makes them more and more different from the nonunion workers around them. This means that unions must worry constantly that management will seek other, cheaper workers to work for them. As a result, unions have incentives to create rules that ensure that work is done by their members rather than in the manner that makes the most economic sense, as well as to approach management in a defensive posture, fearful that business decisions have nefarious motivations.

Of course, there are many exceptions to this negative picture. High-road productive labor-management relationships are clearly possible in our current system—think Costco, Southwest Airlines, and Kaiser Permanente, among many others.[104] But they are the exception, not the rule, because the incentives are stacked against collaborative relationships.

Enterprise-level bargaining also makes it hard to develop a top-notch workforce training system. The United States does too little workforce training, and the training we do is often not very good and does not always lead to a good job. Employers, who pay for the majority of workforce training, spend significantly less than they used to and have pared back internal career ladders.[105] Governments have also pulled back, mirroring broader trends of disinvestment in public goods like infrastructure.[106] As a result, the United States spends less on workforce training than other rich countries—and the gap is growing as other countries increase their investments.[107] Too often training is firm-specific, fostering skills that are not necessarily valuable to other employers. Worse, some training that individuals seek on their own produces credentials that are not particularly valuable to any employer. One need not look further than the for-profit college industry for countless examples of programs that produce little labor market value but put students deep into debt.[108] All told, the average skills of the US workforce are in the middle of the pack of economically advanced countries and well below those of the highest-ranking countries.[109]

Enterprise-level bargaining contributes to problems in the US training system in several ways.[110] It helps lead to widely varying labor costs across firms, which means that executives at firms that train workers worry that they will fail to recoup productivity gains because their newly trained workers will be hired away by higher-paying competitors. This leads to less investment than is optimal because employers have an incentive to poach workers from other firms rather than train their own. In other words, under enterprise bargaining, firms have an incentive to underinvest in training. This is especially true as jobs that once were part of a central firm are increasingly contracted out, outsourced, franchised, or reclassified to independent contractor status.

Further, the enterprise-level bargaining structure is not well suited to providing a forum to discuss regional or industry training needs. In contrast, broader-based bargaining naturally brings together groups of employers and workers, providing an opportunity to discuss the broader needs of the industry. This is especially important for small- and medium-sized employers that may not be large enough to create training programs on their own. The training programs in the United States that that operate on a sectoral level or across several sectors lead to good results for participants.[111] But this kind of training—where training is broad-based and leads to a good job—is relatively rare in the United States and quite hard to create without broad-based bargaining.

Macroeconomic research also suggests that broad-based bargaining and greater union density would increase productivity. For example, research on Organisation for Economic Co-operation and Development (OECD) countries by the British economists Guy Vernon and Mark Rogers find that greater union density promotes productivity growth in those countries with higher-level bargaining.[112] Similarly, a review of the literature by the economists Toke Aidt and Zafiris Tzannatos found support for the assertion that countries with "coordinated bargaining systems," similar to those proposed in this book, "on average, achieve better economic outcomes."[113] In addition, there is a host of research finding that higher-level bargaining generally does not lead to harmful macroeconomic impacts, such as higher unemployment. If anything, higher-level bargaining reduces unemployment.[114]

Another way to understand the broad economic impacts of labor policy is to look at trade data, which can provide some insight into the overall competitiveness of an economy. Of the OECD countries that have large trade surpluses—such as Germany, the Netherlands, Sweden, and Denmark—the majority have higher-level bargaining and relatively strong labor movements, while those with trade deficits, including the United States and Britain, tend to have enterprise-based bargaining systems and weaker labor movements.[115] While many factors affect trade and overall economic performance, and thus simple cross-country comparisons deserve healthy skepticism, it is clear that countries with higher-level bargaining are among the most internationally competitive, while countries with policies like those of the United States are currently struggling. The fact that countries with sectoral bargaining are among the most competitive in the world suggests at the least that higher-level bargaining is compatible with a highly competitive economy. These comparisons also show that broad-based bargaining is unlikely to prevent good trade performance.

That higher-level bargaining is likely to promote higher productivity across the economy is important because, in the long run, higher standards of living for workers depend on higher productivity. Productivity gains by themselves do not automatically translate into higher wages, as the United States has experienced. For decades, workers' wages have lagged far behind productivity gains, indicating that economy can support significantly higher compensation for workers even without additional productivity gains. Still, over any significant length of time, higher productivity is a necessary condition for higher wages. Making more with the same or less is what enables material conditions to improve.

Higher-level bargaining has several other positive attributes worth noting. It is cheaper and easier to administer for unions and employers because similar contracts cover a range of employers, and thus fewer lawyers are needed to negotiate and enforce them. Higher-level bargaining can also help bring out the most public-spirited elements in unions. Representing most or all workers encourages unions to see themselves as acting for the welfare of all workers and helps others to seem them in this light, while enterprise bargaining gives more fodder to detractors dismissing unions as just another interest group.

Summary

This chapter has explained why the new labor system needs to provide a supportive environment for union recruitment and higher-level bargaining. A supportive policy environment that provides workers with multiple reasons to join unions—incentives and solidarity—is necessary to produce high and stable membership and overcome powerful forces working against high union membership. Unions are a public good that all workers can benefit from without paying their full costs, and they challenge powerful business interests, which means society will have less of them than optimal unless policy support is provided. Broad-based bargaining is necessary to provide consistently high collective bargaining coverage in the modern economy. Under enterprise bargaining, coverage is too hard to achieve for workers with little power and is relatively easy for businesses to evade through strategies such as contracting out.

To be sure, policies that support recruitment and broad-based bargaining work best when supported by many other factors, including the strategies and tactics of union leaders, the grassroots efforts of workers, and a host of other economic policies and the larger political environment. Broad-based bargaining also relies on some degree of worksite bargaining to address issues at individual worksites and maintain a grassroots connection to workers. Similarly, incentives for membership require workplace organizing to ensure high union density.

But the evidence from around the world, as well as across the United States and throughout US history, shows that a supportive policy environment for union recruitment and broad-based bargaining are of the utmost importance. No matter what other factors are also at play, incentives for membership and higher-level bargaining are critical to the success of the labor movement. They lead to higher union density, greater collective bargaining coverage, wage increases for more workers, lower inequality, smaller racial and gender pay gaps, and higher productivity in the economy.

4

LESSONS FROM CANADA, BRITAIN, AND AUSTRALIA

Previous chapters have highlighted the weaknesses of current US labor law and the importance of moving toward broad-based bargaining and promoting policies that encourage union membership. Though some of the evidence for this argument was based on the US experience, much was based on general comparisons across wealthy democracies, including European countries like Sweden, Denmark, Belgium, Germany, France, and the Netherlands. Because these countries have historical, cultural, and legal backgrounds quite different from the American tradition, skeptics might question their relevance. These countries also in many cases were industrialized and democratized later than the United States, which helped create different kinds of labor policies and unions.[1] But, as this chapter will explain, these lessons also hold true in the countries more like the United States—Canada, Britain and Australia. The story of labor policy in Canada, Britain, and Australia shows that US-style labor law does not work very well in today's economy and suggests that broad-based bargaining and stronger incentives for union membership would lead to better results.

While there are many differences between the United States and Canada, Britain, and Australia, the United States shares a fair amount of history, culture, and law with the other three countries. All are relatively wealthy, English-speaking democracies. Britain and the United States were among the first countries to industrialize, and both became democracies before most of the rest of Europe. Canada and Australia are, like the United States, former British colonies and quite geographically large. Canada is a neighbor of the United States, and Australians often express a fondness for rugged, frontier individualism like Americans do. In addition, all have recent experience with American-style labor law. As a result, the lessons from these three countries are especially relevant to the United States.

The Canadian experience highlights that strengthening unions will require a much more supportive policy environment than traditional reforms would provide. Unions are in decline in Canada even though the country's laws provide for the kinds of recruitment tools that US unions have historically sought, such as the ability to recruit members through "card check" sign-up instead of elections and the ability to charge fair share fees. Relatedly, the British example shows that even the most voluntaristic unions rely on government policies for much of their strength. Historically, British unions felt that much of their power came from independent activities that had very little to do with the government, but union density in Britain plummeted after Thatcher-era "reforms" undercut unions. Australia most clearly illustrates the difficulties of enterprise bargaining and the value of bargaining and setting standards at a higher level. As Australia began to promote enterprise bargaining instead of higher-level bargaining, coverage fell sharply and inequality increased. The British case tells a similar story about the benefits of broad-based bargaining and the harm done by moving toward enterprise bargaining. Canada, which has much less experience with higher-level bargaining than the other two countries, also highlights the weaknesses of enterprise bargaining in the modern economy.

Moreover, the failures of American-style labor law in Canada, Britain, and Australia have prompted academics, unions, and elected officials in these countries to argue for bold changes that promote sectoral bargaining and support union membership. In short, in the countries most like the United States, independent scholars as well as much of the political left have realized that the kinds of changes proposed in this book are necessary for unions and collective bargaining to succeed in today's economy. All told, the examples of Canada, Britain, and Australia, combined with prior evidence from US history and countries around the world, provide strong evidence that policy reforms to support broad-based bargaining and encourage workers to join unions are needed.

Canada

To a greater degree than any other country, Canada's labor system is similar to that of the United States. In fact, Canada largely copied US law when legislators wrote its labor laws after the Second World War. Because union density is significantly higher in Canada and economic inequality much lower, some think that the United States could just adopt Canada's more labor-friendly version of US law and that would be enough to revitalize labor and address many US economic problems. While moving toward the labor policies of Canada would certainly help improve conditions in the United States, it would not be enough. The real lesson from Canada is that US-style labor law does not work very well in today's economy. Unions are struggling in Canada too, and significant parts of the labor movement now think broader reforms, such as higher-level bargaining, are necessary.

Unlike labor law in most other countries, labor law in Canada and the United States is based on the idea that once a group of workers demonstrate that they represent a majority they gain the right to collectively bargain with their employer, primarily at the enterprise level. One difference in Canada, however, is that unions have the right to charge dues or agency fees to prevent free riding, so there is no such thing as "right to work." Unions can also engage in a number of activities at secondary worksites, and there are limits on employers' abilities to permanently replace striking workers. In addition, provinces have much greater ability to set labor policy than do US states, which has led to even more favorable policies in a number of provinces. Some provinces (and the federal government, which sets labor rules for about 10 percent of Canadian workers) allow card check sign-up instead of requiring elections; several also provide for first contract arbitration and other supports to help get collective bargaining established; and two provinces even have anti-scab laws that prevent striker replacements from being used at all. But most other elements are quite similar or identical to the United States. In short, Canadian labor law is similar to that of the United States but more favorable, especially when compared to so-called right-to-work states.[2] Indeed, the Canadian provinces with the most favorable labor policies have a structure that is roughly equivalent to the National Labor Relations Act before the Taft-Hartley Act severely limited strike rights and allowed states to enact right-to-work laws.

Trends in union membership in the two countries were quite similar until the 1970s. In the 1920s and early 1930s, union density was virtually identical in both countries. For the next several decades density in Canada lagged behind as the United States passed the National Labor Relations Act in 1935, while Canada did not pass its version until 1944. In the 1950s, union density in Canada caught up to the United States and then stayed even for the next decade. In the 1970s, unions in Canada pulled ahead, and density remains much higher than in the United States, at 28 percent in 2018.[3] Bargaining coverage in Canada, like in the United States, has largely tracked union density, because both rely almost exclusively on enterprise bargaining. (Quebec has a procedure that extends collective bargaining agreements in some industries, and there are some other examples of policies that promote broader-based bargaining, but these are exceptions.)[4]

Researchers find that the legal differences between Canada and the United States explain much of the difference in union density between the two countries.[5] While there are a number of other potential reasons for unequal density, such as differently structured economies, employer attitudes, and political culture, these do not account for much of the difference. Both economies are relatively open to trade, with similar industry and occupation mixes, though Canada does have a larger public sector, which increases its overall union density.[6] Employer attitudes toward labor are similar in the two countries—which makes sense since both countries have enterprise bargaining and the union wage premium employers pay in both countries is similar.[7] Some surveys suggest that employer attitudes toward unions may even be more hostile in Canada, though other research suggests employers there have slightly less antagonistic attitudes.[8] Similarly, public opinion about labor unions is comparable in both countries, with opinion perhaps slightly more favorable in the United States.[9]

To get a more precise estimate of the impact of favorable Canadian policies like card check—that allow unions to sign up enough members to unionize a worksite without going through a full election process—researchers have compared density across Canadian provinces that have slightly different labor laws and looked at density before and after provinces made various changes. Estimates indicate that union density would increase by 7 percentage points if all Canadian provinces adopted the most union-friendly policies possible out of twelve labor law policies that exist in provinces, including card check and first contract arbitration.[10] Gains in density were predicted to be biggest for primary industries, public services, and manufacturing, with little to no effect in private services. The study also suggested that relatively skilled workers would be the most likely to unionize under the changes.

Translating those results to the United States is not an exact science, but it is probably a fair guess that adopting Canada's most favorable policies—basically the legislative wish list that US labor has developed over recent decades—could lead to a doubling of private-sector union density from 6 to 12 percent. This would be a significant achievement and would clearly help workers. Yet the importance of this kind of increase should not be overstated. It is but a first step, as far bolder policies would be needed to make a more significant impact.

If similar policies were enacted in the United States, nearly nine out of ten private-sector workers would not be unionized or covered by collective bargaining agreements. In addition, the Canadian studies suggest that the types of workers that would remain uncovered are likely to be the most in need of a union.

Further, the bump in density might erode over time: density and coverage have continued to shrink in Canada even in places with such favorable policies, indicating that a similar outcome is likely in the United States. Though Canada currently has a greater percentage of union members than the United States, the trends in unions density in Canada over recent decades are not that much different than in the United States. Union density in Canada hit as high as 38 percent in 1985 but has been declining since and was 28 percent in 2018.[11] While nearly 30 percent density may on first glance seem pretty good, these overall figures paint much too rosy a picture because they include public-sector workers. Canada has a larger public sector than the United States, and about three-quarters of public-sector workers there are unionized. The private sector is a critical measure of union strength; private-sector density in Canada has been in sharper decline and was just 14 percent in 2018.[12]

Worse is that union density has declined in most private-sector industries, not just traditional strongholds like manufacturing.[13] Not even the most favorable provincial policies have been able to stop decline. Since the 1980s, union density has decreased in every Canadian province.[14] Density has fallen even in provinces with the full wish list of policies that American unions typically advocate for in the United States, such as card check and fare share fees. (Quebec, which has a limited form of broad-based bargaining as well as other favorable policies such as card check, has the highest coverage of any province and just about the highest density.)[15] It is true that over the past five years the decline in union density has been smaller than in most other countries—but decline in Canada still continues.[16] All told, unions in Canada have been weakening for decades, and, though the pace of their decline has been relatively slow, if trends continue they could eventually reach US levels.

The long decline in Canadian union density coincided with predictable problems. Wages have grown much more slowly than productivity over the past three decades, and for a number of groups, such as young workers and mid-career men, have actually declined.[17] Over the past several decades there has been a sharp increase in income inequality in Canada, with the top pulling away from the middle and bottom.[18] Between the early 1980s and 2010, incomes for the bottom 90 percent of income earners grew by only 2 percent, while over this period the incomes of the top 10 percent increased by more than 75 percent, and those of the top 0.01 percent grew by 160 percent.[19] The share of the nation's income going to the top 1 percent roughly doubled.[20] The share of the nation's income going to workers has declined sharply.[21] Wage theft is now a common problem.[22] Not surprisingly, research finds that a significant portion of the rise in inequality in Canada is due to the decline of unions.[23]

Compared to the United States, inequality in Canada is significantly lower, and far more of the increase in inequality of market incomes has been offset by government supports.[24] Still, many economic trends in Canada are not great and closely resemble those in the United States, with perhaps a lag of a decade or two.

Because of results like this, several recent academic appraisals argue that union density and coverage in Canada will continue to decline without more dramatic changes that move away from the Canadian and US model.[25] David Doorey, industrial relations professor, bluntly argues that Canadian labor law is outdated, writing: "A giant corporation that operates through dozens of small stores, franchises, or branches is mostly impenetrable for unions under existing laws, which were designed to facilitate collective bargaining in giant car plants, steel mills, and mines."[26] Joseph Rose, human resources professor, and Gary Chaison, industrial relations professor, explain in more academic terms, "Significant gains in union membership and density levels will require nothing less than a paradigm shift in the industrial relations systems."[27]

Similarly, some Canadian unions have begun to recognize that smaller-scale reforms won't cut it and have begun to call for more far-reaching changes. Unifor, Canada's largest private-sector union, for example, argues that "fundamental changes in the economy and labour market" require "collective bargaining to apply on a sectoral basis, in addition to on an enterprise or workplace basis."[28] Marty Warren, director of the United Steelworkers in Ontario, argues, "Our current system of labour relations was designed in the 1930s and '40s when workplaces were very different—and it is profoundly ill-suited to accommodate collective bargaining at thousands of retail franchises across the province."[29]

In recent years, policy makers in several provinces, most notably Ontario, British Columbia, and Alberta, have undertaken systematic evaluations to consider how their labor and employment laws should be adapted to economic changes and new workplace realities and considered detailed proposals to support broad-based bargaining.[30] Though bold steps toward sectoral bargaining had not passed as of 2019, some minor reforms in this direction had, and these efforts have significantly increased discussion and awareness of these issues among unionists, academics, business executives, and policy makers.[31] Indeed, during these processes, the Ontario Federation of Labor, representing fifty-four affiliate unions, and the Alberta Federation of Labor, with sixty-four affiliates, came out publicly in support of policies to promote higher-level bargaining.[32] While Canada has not fully embraced the need for bold reforms that move beyond the US model of labor law, a growing segment of the country's leaders have.

Importantly, union supporters in Canada have thought deeply about how to move from a US-style enterprise bargaining system toward a sectoral system. One of the more notable proposals is the Baigent-Ready sectoral certification model, named after two advisers to a governmental committee that considered possible labor law reforms in British Columbia.[33] Under the Baigent-Ready proposal, if a union is able to organize a majority of the workers at two or more different worksites in certain types of fragmented industries, this would trigger a multi-employer bargaining process with the employers of the organized worksites. Any subsequent worksites the union organized would be covered by the same contract terms. For example, if a union organized a majority of workers at two coffee shops in the same region, they would bargain a contract for these worksites with the two firms. Any additional coffee shops in the region where the union was able to sign up a majority of workers would automatically be covered by the master, multi-employer contract. Thus, the policy seeks to maintain the existing worksite majority rule but makes broader-based coverage easier to attain. This model is particularly relevant for the United States, as discussed in chapter 1.

In sum, unions in Canada are stronger than those in the United States, and the economic and political conditions significantly better, but unions in Canada are also on a downward trajectory, and economic inequality is rising. While adopting Canadian labor policies would certainly help the United States, the evidence suggests that they are not a silver bullet and would fall short of getting unions and the country back on track. The lesson from Canada is that conventional reforms as well as more ambitious labor policies are needed.

Britain

The story of unions in Britain, as we shall see, very clearly highlights how much unions—even the most fiercely autonomous and independent ones—are dependent on government policy to operate effectively. Historically, British labor policy was seen as among the most voluntaristic in the world, and British labor unions themselves supported the concept of voluntarism—a belief that the appropriate role for unions is self-help and free collective bargaining without government support or interference. While British labor policy was never really as hands-off as most people claimed, the British case shows that even supposedly voluntaristic unions require a supportive policy environment to succeed.

The British example also illustrates the value of broad-based bargaining and the weaknesses of enterprise bargaining. Under broad-based bargaining, Britain was able to maintain high levels of coverage and high levels of union density, but coverage as well as density declined significantly once the country shifted to enterprise bargaining.

As such, Britain helps illuminate the flaws of the US model and the need for bolder action. While British labor policy is quite different from US law, by international standards the countries' policies are relatively close and becoming ever more so. As Britain has increasingly adopted US-style labor law, unions and coverage have continued to decline, even though in many ways British law is more favorable to unions than US law. Now British academics as well as labor unions and Labour Party politicians increasingly recognize the need for a bold shift in direction toward policies that help increase union membership and support sectoral bargaining.

In 1979, British unions were quite strong, representing 55 percent of workers, and collective bargaining coverage was 70 percent, with most bargaining done with multiple employers.[34] Including all types of collective pay-setting institutions, such as wages councils that set wages in nonunion industry based in part on union pay scales, coverage was over 80 percent—very close to the level it had been after World War II.[35] It is important to note that there were multiple levels of bargaining activity, with enterprise bargaining operating alongside and often in conjunction with sectoral bargaining, as is common in other countries with higher-level bargaining.

But then Margaret Thatcher came to power and gradually but decisively changed a number of policies so that union density and coverage dropped precipitously, and they have continued to decline since. By 1990, density had fallen to 40 percent, coverage had dropped to 47 percent, and only a minority of bargaining was multi-employer.[36] In 2000, density was 30 percent and coverage was 36 percent, and in 2017 density was around 20 percent and coverage only slightly above that.[37] Today Britain has among the lowest levels of collective bargaining coverage in the European Union.[38] That such a sharp drop could occur in Britain is puzzling for those who think unions can go it alone and organize in such a way that they can have significant power even without a supportive policy environment.

If any unions around the world would have been able to maintain strength in the face of policy changes it should have been the British.[39] In the late 1970s, unions were quite strong—with among the highest density of any large, rich country, a decentralized structure, and a strong presence in many workplaces. Critically, union power was based in significant part on their market strength and the interests of employers. Indeed, the British system was generally thought of as the "classic example of the abstentionist state and the voluntarist industrial relations system."[40]

Claims that the British system was purely voluntary were always a bit of an exaggeration—especially after legal changes in the 1970s. But historically British law provided little, if any, direct regulation of unions and collective bargaining and gave unions few, if any, positive rights. For much of British history, there were no laws determining what constituted union membership, obligating employers to bargain, making collective bargaining agreements legally enforceable, or determining how collective bargaining should take place. Rather, long-standing British policy toward unions was largely based on giving unions immunities from common law, so that, for example, strikes would not be subject to restraint by injunction.[41] The protection was wide and enabled unions to engage in solidarity action and secondary boycotts. In short, unions were subject to few legal restraints. Union leaders generally liked this voluntaristic emphasis because they felt it meant the government could not take away what it had not given. The British system became significantly more legalistic in the 1970s. First the Conservative government provided more formal regulation of unions, and then the Labour government granted some affirmative rights to unions such as requiring employers to disclose certain information for collective bargaining and protecting workers for union activities as well as creating a union recognition procedure and fostering arbitration.[42] Still, British labor policy has long been considered hands-off, and even the 1970s changes did not provide a level of positive union rights comparable to those in most other countries.

Yet in Britain, as elsewhere, the state plays a central role in the success or failure of the union movement. The state can give and take away supportive policies, and it can even take away things it has not given by creating additional restrictions on unions. The state made "voluntarism" possible.

While historically British policy did not directly legislate labor union policy, it has strongly impacted unions and collective bargaining through many other mechanisms.[43] Prior to the start of the Thatcher government in 1979, Britain maintained a relatively large public sector, and the British public sector supported collective bargaining, which meant that privatization policy reduced unionization. Similarly, Keynesian economic policy promoting full employment was crucial in defining the union role and legitimizing the role of unions in their efforts for higher wages.[44]

On occasion the British government has made more direct efforts to support unions, especially during wartime. For example, during World War II a tribunal had the power to impose union working conditions on nonunion firms, which encouraged firms to recognize unions, otherwise wages would be set without the firm's input.[45] Not surprisingly, unions grew most when the state was most supportive. In the period around World War I, union membership doubled, and similarly in the period around World War II, from 1940 to 1950, coverage grew by 20 percentage points.[46] These spurts in growth mattered greatly for overall union strength and had lasting legacies.

British policy also strongly supported collective bargaining, especially multi-employer bargaining. The Ministry of Labour made clear that part of its mission was to promote collective bargaining, and active steps were taken to support it through the establishment of joint industrial councils for multi-employer bargaining.[47] Where this was not possible, wages councils operated in a number of sectors to establish minimum terms and conditions for each sector. Wages councils were tripartite in structure (business, labor, and government nominees), often set pay based on collective agreements, and sometimes operated as a de facto collective bargaining forum.[48] (Wages councils share a number of similarities with US workers' boards as well as to the award system in Australia, discussed later in this chapter.) Government purchasing policies also provided support for unions and collective bargaining. "The 'system' in place in the post-war era was thus one of sectoral bargaining underpinning establishment level negotiation," write the law professor Keith Ewing and labor lawyer John Hendy. "It was built mainly by bureaucratic power, underwritten by statutory bodies in the form of wages councils and reinforced by ad hoc extension mechanisms and other indirect props."[49]

The Thatcher government gradually but decisively shifted the legal balance against unions and away from sectoral bargaining. Among other things, the Thatcher government undermined union organizing activities by prohibiting closed and union shop arrangements; removed state support for collective bargaining; encouraged the breakup of sectoral bargaining machinery (though some of it still exists); abolished wages council regulation; imposed tight restrictions on the right to strike; introduced restraints on the right to peacefully picket; and introduced a "scabs" charter whereby union members could not be disciplined by their union for failing to observe a strike call.[50] These legal changes, when coupled with economic changes such as increased global trade and a growing desire by business to avoid unions, proved deeply harmful to unions.

Indeed, the legal changes were likely central to the decline of British unions, as a number of reviews have found.[51] Public opinion actually became more supportive of unions as they began their decline.[52] Union density fell across virtually all groups of workers and in most sectors, not just those that were exposed to trade, indicating that globalization or structural changes in the economy were not the full story.[53] The poor state of the British economy around the Thatcher years certainly mattered, but it does not explain why unions continued to decline even in good times nor why they grew in the early 1970s before antiunion policies were enacted.[54] It also does not explain why Ireland—which did not change its laws—maintained union density despite a worse economy.[55] As economist Richard Freeman and coauthor Jeffrey Pelletier state plainly, "The Thatcher government's labor laws caused much of the . . . fall in British union density" in the 1980s.[56]

The end of Thatcher-era rule did not end union decline. Labor unions continued to struggle even after the New Labour government took power in the late 1990s and ended nearly twenty years of Conservative rule—in large part because the Labour government did not markedly alter Thatcher's changes but rather mostly accepted the new order.[57] Still, the New Labour government did make some modest efforts to help unions, passing policies that created some rights for unions that made British labor law a bit more like that of the United States. Legislation in 1999, for example, created a system for union recognition similar to US labor law, where if unions show 10 percent support at a workplace they can trigger a process designed to encourage collective bargaining.[58] A union passing the 10 percent admissibility threshold may secure bargaining rights in a bargaining unit if it can then demonstrate either majority membership (usually without a ballot) or majority support (after a ballot). This process is more favorable to unions than US law because it allows for demonstration of majority support through membership rather than requiring an election.

Unfortunately, the new legal process for organizing workers has not worked very well, though it may have helped provide a small, temporary bump in union density. Not only has it been used less frequently as time has gone by, but density and coverage are far lower now than they were when the US-style policies were first enacted in Britain. As one study of British labor policy put it, these changes are "not promising as a way of reversing" union decline.[59] Or as professor Keith Ewing puts it: "Even a better version of US-style bargaining doesn't work."[60]

British unions have also tried a variety of new organizing techniques to recruit new members—often based on the grassroots organizing efforts of US unions. But these had had only limited success and have failed to reverse the basic trends, further emphasizing the importance of a supportive policy environment.[61]

All told, the fate of British labor has always been intimately tied to state policy, even though historically unions and government policy emphasized voluntarism.[62]

As unions and collective bargaining have declined, workers have suffered. Workers' earnings once closely tracked GDP growth, but in the 1990s these began to decouple, and over the past decade they have become completely detached. Between 2008 and 2018, real average weekly earnings declined, even though the economy grew significantly over this period.[63] Wage stagnation is so bad that it is estimated that wages will not to return to 2008 levels until 2025, which would be the longest period without wage growth since the Napoleonic Wars of the early nineteenth century.[64] The share of income going to labor has declined sharply.[65] Poverty for a number of types of working households has increased over recent decades.[66] Estimates suggest that wage theft has roughly doubled from prior levels, and now about one in five low-wage workers over age twenty-five is paid less than they are legally entitled to.[67]

In contrast to most workers, rich people have seen significant income gains. The share of the nation's income going to the top 1 percent has roughly doubled since 1980, making Britain about the most unequal wealthy democracy outside of the United States.[68] Over the past four decades, the top 10 percent of earners received almost 40 percent of the economy's gains while the bottom half of income earners saw very little increase in earnings (and the bottom third experienced virtually no increase at all).[69] Study after study finds that a significant share of the rise in inequality and stagnation of wages for many workers are due to decline of unions.[70]

British trade unions have come to recognize the importance of supportive policy, and many unions now reject voluntarism after over one hundred years of belief in its effectiveness. Union leaders have realized that, in today's economy, unions' market power alone is insufficient to effectively recruit members or compel employers to collectively bargain and that they need government to help equalize power. Indeed, the Trades Union Congress—the main federation of trade unions in Britain—began arguing in 1991 that legislation "supporting and underpinning" collective bargaining was required.[71] Chris Howell, a political science professor explains that British unions have "finally acknowledged their dependence on political resources and sought a political settlement that embeds a set of positive rights . . . in labor law."[72]

What's more is that, in recent years, key think tank members, academics, labor unions, and leaders of the Labour Party have all realized that much bigger and bolder policy changes are necessary to boost union membership and make collective bargaining work properly.[73] Policy ideas that are drawing increased support among the left include boosting union density by increasing union access to workers at worksites and online as well as creating new structures to foster sectoral bargaining.[74] This agenda now enjoys widespread support across the labor movement and has been the official agenda of the Labour Party since 2017. Indeed, party leaders have indicated that they will push this agenda if they regain power.[75]

Australia

A close look at industrial relations in Australia illustrates the advantages of higher-level bargaining and the weaknesses of relying solely on worksite bargaining. The Australian story shows that broader-based labor systems lead to greater coverage, increase wages, reduce inequality, promote more and better training, and may help increase productivity. The Australian example also helps show how countries can come up with labor policies that may on first glance seem quite different from US law but at the bottom are simply varieties of some common strategies to either help or hurt unions and workers. Finally, Australia highlights how even a very strong minimum wage policy is no substitute for unions and collective bargaining.

The basic story of Australian labor law is that from the early 1900s through the 1980s, Australia had a unique labor system based largely on a model of industry-wide arbitration. Unions were strong and afforded a central place in the economy, most workers were covered by a collective bargaining agreement—or at least something analogous to a collective bargaining agreement, and the middle class was among the strongest in the world. GDP growth was strong as well. In some ways, Australia could have been considered the Sweden of the South.

Then, in the 1980s and especially in the 1990s, Australia began dismantling its unique labor system and weakening unions to create something a bit closer to the US system. Under its more American-style, enterprise bargaining system, labor union density has been in steep decline, bargaining coverage has fallen, inequality has risen sharply, wage growth has begun to stagnate, the middle class has weakened, and economic growth has lessened.

Australia still has some structures that provide real help to workers. Indeed, Australia's governmental wage-setting process works relatively well and in some ways is a model system, with among the highest minimums in the world and the ability to set industry-wide standards. Yet even the process of setting a minimum wage is showing signs of weakness. Without strong unions, the standards are often evaded and there is less of a push to increase minimum wages. Indeed, some question whether the high minimum standards can continue to exist without strong unions.[76] As a result, the Australian experience also highlights the limits of a policy strategy that focuses on relatively strong statutory workplace standards but weakens unions and collective bargaining—institutions that are necessary to continuously enforce, defend, and improve those statutory standards.

There are some nuances that complicate the story. The dismantling has gone in fits and starts, with some slight reversals, and there have been some periods of wage growth even as the system was weakened. But the larger story is quite clear: strong unions and broad-based bargaining and arbitration led to positive results, while changes that weakened unions and promoted firm-based bargaining led to worse outcomes. Inequality is now greater in Australia, on average, than other industrial countries, and the gap is getting wider. In short, Australia is no longer close to being the Sweden of the South; in fact, unless it changes course, it could turn into the US of the South.

Because the Australian system is so different from those of most other countries, it is worth providing a relatively long explanation of its labor policy. The story of Australian industrial relations often starts in 1907—the year of the "Harvester Judgement," the first real-world application of a labor policy based on having a tribunal weigh in on labor disputes as an arbitrator.[77] A few years earlier, Australia had passed the Commonwealth Conciliation and Arbitration Act of 1904 to minimize the strikes, lockouts, and occasional violence that had marred industrial relations in prior decades. The law aimed to encourage collective bargaining and sought to do so through tribunal-mandated decisions on the terms of a contract, if necessary.

Specifically, the 1904 act sought "to provide for the making and enforcement of industrial agreements between employers and employees in relation to industrial disputes," and it created an arbitral body that could encourage agreement between the parties by conciliating disputes, but if unions and employers couldn't agree, the tribunal would "provide for . . . equitable award."[78] In 1906, Australia increased the power of this special labor tribunal by imposing a tariff that could be avoided if wages were considered "fair and reasonable."[79]

Possibly because of Australia's unique history as a penal colony, where poor, petty criminals were shipped across the world as part of a harsh British legal system, the country thought it could do better than allowing pure economic power to determine wages and benefits and the outcomes of labor disputes. Australia wanted the "rule of law" to prevail. Compared to most other countries at the same time, when unions were often banned or harshly dealt with and violence between employers and workers was relatively common, Australia was charting a very different course.

The justice in the *Harvester* case, Henry Bourne Higgins, was a strong supporter of creating the special labor body when he was a legislator and in 1907 as a justice was keen on setting an important precedent. He wanted the right case to determine what a "fair and reasonable" wage was. The Sunshine Harvester Company was a large, successful manufacturer of farm equipment, owned by a man with a track record of opposing unions and government wage decisions. Indeed, the company's owner had previously closed a factory to avoid a local wage board's decision.[80] Out of more than a hundred applications, the justice specifically picked the application by Sunshine Harvester's owner for an exception from the tariff because the "factory was one of the largest, and had the greatest numbers and variety of employees; and because his application was to be keenly fought."[81]

The *Harvester* decision is rightly famous in Australian history as the arbitral tribunal's first arbitrated wage decision—but it was much more than that as it helped establish the basic framework of Australian labor policy that would dominate for eighty years. The decision set wages for unskilled male laborers at seven shillings a day and provided overtime rates—creating a standard that provided a living wage for a male worker, his wife, and three kids, not just a minimum wage, well before most other countries were even thinking about doing so.[82] It also set higher rates for skilled workers such as machinists, carpenters, and blacksmiths. Later, the justice wrote that he sought to set wages based on "the normal needs of the average employee, regarded as a human being living in a civilised community."[83]

Beyond setting the actual standards at a living wage, the case helped establish most of the elements of the unique Australian model of labor relations. In the decision, Higgins rejected the ideas that "fair and reasonable" was whatever the employer wanted to pay or could afford or whatever an employee could negotiate for on his own. The tribunal was "not going to accept as final the employer's unchecked opinion as to an employee's worth in wages." Rather, "fair and reasonable" meant something employees "[could not] get by the ordinary system of individual bargaining with employers." The tribunal also noted the value of collective bargaining and setting standards across workplaces. "Instead of individual bargaining," the justice wrote, "one can conceive of a collective agreement—an agreement between all the employers in a given trade on the one side, and all the employees on the other." Elsewhere in the decision, Higgins explained that he was "impressed with the importance and the justice of uniformity as between manufacturers." In short, the 1904 law and the 1907 *Harvester* decision helped set up the Australian system of labor relations as a sort of hybrid between collective bargaining and governmental wage setting that occurred largely at the industry level—a structure unlike most others in the world, though New Zealand also created a similar system.

Under the Australian system that was set in motion by the *Harvester* decision, the tribunal weighed in on all manner of labor disputes, bringing parties together to negotiate, and making binding decisions if there was an unresolved dispute, as well as deciding whether strikes and lockouts were authorized. The idea was that the tribunal could help mitigate and even avoid unproductive labor disputes by helping set and spread fair standards to most workers. This gave employers and unions an incentive to come to an agreement, because otherwise the tribunal would decide for them. It may also have provided an incentive for one party to create a disagreement if they thought the tribunals' judgement would be favorable. Thus, there were effectively two types of standard setting: a more traditional collective bargaining directly between employers and unions, and a newer form that occurred through conciliation and arbitration. Bargaining, as academics often put it, took place under the shadow of the law.[84] As the system matured, manufacturing industry awards often set the national standards that flowed through to other industries.

Unions were at the heart of this system and were afforded the means to build membership and power. The system was "based on unionism," as the justice in the *Harvester* case wrote.[85] Only unions and employers, not individual workers, were a party to the tribunal decisions, and unions had a primary role in enforcing the decisions. Unions were allowed to negotiate closed shop or required dues payments from covered employees and often received tribunal support for these efforts.[86] In addition, union officials had broad rights to enter workplaces to inspect payroll records and ensure compliance as well as to recruit members.[87] Not surprisingly, unions did well in the system, with density hitting 27 percent in 1911 and 53 percent in 1920, the highest in the world at that time.[88] There were some ebbs and flows in the system, but the basic arrangement held for decades.[89] In 1980, labor union density was roughly 50 percent, and coverage was nearly 85 percent.[90]

This system that encouraged unions and collective bargaining and spread the gains to other workers was remarkably successful, though it was not perfect or necessarily replicable in another setting.[91] Indeed, in 1980, income inequality was so low that the bottom 99 percent received 95.4 percent of the nation's income, almost the level in Sweden and slightly better than in Norway.[92]

But Australia has a very different system now. Cracks in the old system began to show during the 1980s as Australia wrestled with stagflation, but the big breaks from the old system started in the 1990s when Australia began a series of neoliberal, free market–oriented labor reforms. These reforms emphasized firm-level bargaining instead of industry-wide bargaining, weakened unions in a variety of ways, and ended the arbitration system and replaced it with a commission that sets the minimum wage and minimum awards for industries, among other activities.

While some of the most decisive breaks from the old system were led by conservative politicians and their business allies, the general direction of most of these changes was supported by much of the left—including the Labor Party and a number of labor unions.[93] In fact, the initial push for enterprise bargaining came from labor unions. Some union leaders thought their workers could do better if they got out from the centralized system, which had been used to limit wage increases as part of a compromise effort to reduce inflation in the late 1980s and early 1990s.[94] A Labor government passed legislation in 1993 that facilitated firm-level bargaining and opened the door to a host of other policies that would be used to undermine unions and collective bargaining.[95]

Supporters of the changes maintained that they would encourage flexibility and unleash the dynamism of Australia's economy by giving employers greater ability to set the terms of employment and tailor contracts to the needs of their particular firm rather than the needs of the larger industry or economy. But the public was not always sold on gutting the old system. In fact, a conservative government was voted out of office in 2007 largely because of public opposition to its extreme labor reforms, such as a policy that allowed employers to encourage individual workers to sign contracts that contained weaker standards than the collective agreement they were covered by.[96] But even when the Labor Party was put into office because of the public's rejection of anti-worker changes, the legislation it ultimately passed largely reaffirmed the direction of those changes, only slightly rolling back some of the most heavy-handed attempts to increase the power of business.[97]

The current industrial relations system largely reflects the 2009 law passed by the Labor Party. The party's political opponents have been in charge of government in recent years but have mostly left in place the basic framework they inherited and have sought to further weaken unions through investigations of union finances rather than legislation.[98]

Australia's system can now be thought of as a strong workplace safety net that is starting to show some cracks, with a broken collective bargaining system on top of it. The system still delivers relatively high minimums for workers but is no longer able to push higher standards throughout the broader labor market.

The government—now through an independent agency (the Fair Work Commission) rather than an arbitral system—sets the overall minimum wage as well as industry and occupational awards, with generally higher minimum rates and pay scales. Individual or collective agreements must improve upon the awards. The minimum wage is adjusted annually, with similar increases flowing through the other awards. The Fair Work Commission also sets several other employment standards, such as additional payments required for overtime, irregular hours, and work on weekends and holidays, which are on top of ten legislated national employment standards, such as guaranteed annual leave. The awards have become more streamlined, and there are far fewer awards than there used to be—122 compared to well over a thousand under the old system.[99]

Australian laws regarding collective bargaining and unions have become much less favorable.[100] The supposed aim of current laws is to foster firm-level collective bargaining, but they severely limit what unions can bargain for. Strikes for firm-level bargaining are heavily regulated and permitted only in limited circumstances.[101] Multi-employer or industry-wide bargaining is even more heavily restricted than firm-level bargaining. Striking for multi-employer bargaining is illegal, and unions are prevented from negotiating an identical contract with several firms as part of pattern bargaining; these provisions effectively prohibit multi-employer or sector-wide agreements. The government no longer arbitrates labor disputes and does not engage in any kind of de facto extension to spread the benefits of collective bargaining. Further undermining collective bargaining, employers are allowed to negotiate a "collective agreement" with no involvement by a union at all and even deviate from those statutory minimums set in the awards—so long as workers are judged to be better off overall than they would be under the awards.

Union funding streams—such as the one that comes with the ability to charge fees to all workers covered by an agreement—have been closed off, and union access to worksites is more limited. Unions no longer play a special role in the process of setting and enforcing awards but rather are now just one of many "interested parties" allowed to submit their views (but not to negotiate the terms). Unions get very little in return for all the limitations on their activities: the government can help mediate disputes and under certain circumstances require "good faith bargaining," but this has done little to encourage recalcitrant employers to do anything more than show up at the table.[102] Some Labor Party leaders hoped, and some employers feared, that adopting some elements of the US labor system, such as good faith bargaining, would strengthen unions and enable firm-based collective bargaining to thrive. Unsurprisingly, the adoption of some modest US-style policies as part of a slight adjustment to improve enterprise bargaining did not increase collective bargaining or strengthen unions in a measurable way.[103] Indeed, union density has continued to decline since these changes were passed.[104]

All told, the new system has some strengths and some weaknesses, which can help shed light on potential US reforms. In some ways, the minimum employment standards of Australia's system are quite strong, perhaps even stronger than those of the old system. Many of the minimum standards, such as for vacation and sick days, are now required by legislation rather than arbitral awards, so their coverage is broader. There are also are new employment benefits, such as a retirement fund that employers are required to pay into (part of a deal unions struck with a Labor government in exchange for wage restraint). In addition, the system is still adaptable enough that it can set standards for new types of occupations and industries. Further, the standards are quite high compared to the rest of the world.[105] The federal minimum wage in 2018 was $18.93 in Australian dollar per hour or roughly US$15. Award rates for most industries and occupations are even higher. Most of the minimums range between AU$20 and AU$30, and in some special cases minimums for particular occupations are well over AU$60 per hour.[106] About one-fifth of all employees have their pay set directly by an award or the national minimum wage, and many other employees have their compensation levels set in some relation to the awards.[107] Importantly, research has shown that Australia's system of industry and skill-specific minimum wages boosts worker wages without harmful employment effects.[108]

But the workplace safety net is fraying. The minimum rates have not increased much in several decades. After adjusting for inflation, the minimum wage is worth only slightly more today than it was in 1983, and it has declined notably relative to the overall level of wages across the labor market.[109] With unions losing strength, there is less pressure to drive the safety-net standards higher. As a result, the bottom end of the labor market is falling further behind the middle, even as the middle is stagnating, with the ratio of the minimum wage to the median wage falling from almost 70 percent in 1983 to roughly 55 percent in 2017.[110]

Even worse for the outcomes of the overall system, neither the minimum standard-setting process nor collective bargaining does much to raise wages for the broad middle class. Collective bargaining has been in decline, with both fewer agreements being made and the agreements leading to much smaller increases than they previously did.[111] For workers not covered by collective agreements, the outcomes are often even worse, as the government no longer spreads the benefits of collective bargaining to other workers, and these workers are increasingly reliant on the award minimums.

The numerical results of this new system are as follows. Union density has fallen sharply from the 50 percent levels in 1980 and is now around 14 percent— and even lower in the private sector.[112] Density is lowest for those with the lowest incomes, indicating that workers with little power have an especially hard time unionizing.[113] Over the past four decades, coverage by collective agreements has fallen sharply, from covering nearly all workers to covering 36 percent today.[114] These statistics probably overstate coverage because they include the public sector as well as the strange category, unique to Australia, of collective agreements that do not include unions and unsurprisingly do little to raise wages.[115] A truer reflection of the weak state of collective bargaining coverage may be that current enterprise agreements covered just 12 percent of private-sector workers in 2017.[116]

The results of the decline of Australian unions and collective bargaining have been predictable—though the award system has helped mitigate some of the expected harms. Since 1980, wages have grown more slowly than the overall economy and much more slowly than they grew in prior decades. Since 2013, real wages have been nearly flat despite sustained economic growth and higher labor productivity.[117] The share of the nation's income going to labor has reached its lowest point since Australia began publishing quarterly GDP data in the late 1950s.[118] Inequality has risen rapidly, with the share of income going to the top 1 percent roughly doubling from 1981 to 2014, rising from under 5 percent, to nearly 10 percent, much closer to the median of countries in the OECD—though still lower than most countries and well below the level of the United States.[119] Measures of relative poverty have gotten worse, with the share of the population earning less than half of the median rising by a few percentage points, as the poor fall further behind the middle, who in turn are falling much further behind the wealthy.[120]

Australia's labor system changes have also led to more subtle but entirely expected harms. Australia's training system was built up during the industry-wide award era but has begun to weaken under firm-level bargaining, as theory would suggest, because there is less of a way to coordinate training efforts and because the incentives of firms encourage poaching rather than investment. Research has found that individual employers, under firm-level bargaining, have not maintained strong connections between additional training leading to better pay and employment.[121] Similarly, another study finds that workers are less likely to get paid for their additional training or skills under enterprise agreements than they are under industry-wide awards.[122] Finally, over recent decades, Australia has reduced public spending as a share of GDP on active labor market policies, including workforce training.[123]

Another predictable outcome from Australia's policy changes is that the minimum standards are now frequently violated. Government and academic studies show that wage theft and other workplace violations have become common in.[124] Australian government reports indicate, for example, that roughly half of restaurants violated at least one wage standard. Investigations of large franchising retailers have found that between 70 and 80 percent had violations.[125] Even large, well-recognized employers commonly violate employment standards.[126] Research on Australian workplaces finds that violations—particularly on safety standards—are lower at unionized worksites.[127] The problem is that too few worksites have union representation to ensure that workplace standards are followed.

Compounding the problems workers now face is that the labor policy changes did not unleash the productivity gains that supporters claimed would result. An analysis of fifty years of economic data found that large productivity gains did not transpire; if anything, productivity gains were slightly slower in recent years compared to the arbitration era—a result consistent with a large body of research showing that unions do not harm the economy and that stronger unions and broad-based bargaining can boost productivity.[128]

While there are many domestic and international factors that affect these economic statistics, including technology, trade, and interest rates, to name just a few, the evidence suggests that the labor system is central. Policy changes to weaken unions and collective bargaining, especially sectoral bargaining, lead to bad results for workers, not to predicted booms in investment, productivity, and growth.

First, there is direct evidence of harm to workers from the Australian policy change. An important study by five Australian academics compared employment contracts in the retail and hospitality industries immediately before and after one of the key legislative changes that weakened the old system. This study found that, in the year after the change, employee earnings were typically reduced by 10 percent—and up to 30 percent. Put another way, the policy change allowed employers to immediately and significantly cut wages. The study also noted that these cuts occurred "under the best macro-economic conditions in a generation," suggesting that the pay cuts were due to the increased powers employers had acquired, rather than economic duress.[129]

What's more, the study found that most of the new contracts were virtually identical—even among different firms—indicating that employers wanted to get out from old collective bargaining agreements largely for the ability to reduce wages, not for the flexibility to tailor contracts to their unique circumstances, as many claimed. While some of the specific elements of the policy studied were later reversed, the overall direction it represented was not, nor were many of the economic losses that workers experienced.

Second, there is the sequence of events that happened after labor policy was weakened. As policy changed, there were fewer worksites where unions had sufficient membership to effectively bargain, and there was also less ability to extend collectively bargained rates to other similarly placed workers.[130] In addition, under enterprise bargaining, employers have had greater opportunity to avoid coverage by contracting out and creating layers of separation between many workers and the firm that actually has ultimate control over their working conditions.[131]

Third, study after study of Australian industrial relations finds that union density fell in large part because of the policy changes.[132] As one academic paper put it: "the reorientation of the state has been the most important factor in union decline."[133] And not surprisingly, studies also find that the decline in union density has led to greater inequality. Indeed, a 2018 estimate by a University of Melbourne economist suggests that the decline in union density "appears to explain a large fraction of the increase in inequality" in earnings.[134]

Finally, there is the comparison with New Zealand, which underwent a very similar chain of events. Like Australia, New Zealand used to have an industry-wide arbitration system that led to wage growth and low inequality. But New Zealand ended its compulsory arbitration system in 1987 and subsequently made a series of other changes to weaken collective bargaining and unions—getting rid of its old system more rapidly and completely than Australia. After these changes were made, coverage fell dramatically—falling by half in just five years and continuing to erode over time.[135] Union density also fell by a similar amount, inequality rose sharply, and wages stagnated. Estimates by the International Monetary Fund suggest that the decline of collective bargaining and de-unionization have been responsible for a greater share of the increase in inequality in New Zealand than in any other advanced economy.[136] After it had decimated its old system, New Zealand also made some modest efforts to strengthen unions—such as through the promotion of good faith bargaining—which as in Australia was not enough to reverse the damage to unions or collective bargaining. Since 2018, New Zealand has begun promoting bolder labor reforms to restore unions, broad-based bargaining, and tripartite institutions, and there are some signs that these changes may be starting to reverse trends, but it is too early for a thorough evaluation.[137]

A number of Australians have become quite concerned about economic trends in the country. Even the chair of Australia's Reserve Bank, who was appointed by the conservative Liberal Party, argues that wage stagnation is a big problem, stating in a 2018 speech that generated significant press attention, "It is clear that the slow growth in wages is affecting our economy."[138] Academics, labor leaders, and Labor Party politicians have increasingly been discussing the need to rebuild Australia's labor system into something like what it used to be, with a return to industry-wide bargaining and stronger unions.[139]

Big reforms are required, according to many Australian experts, not just the kind of tinkering that previously occurred—such as good faith bargaining and improved minimum standards—that some dismissively refer to as "neoliberalism with a human face."[140] Academics have been writing journal articles and popular articles debating how to make the kinds of major changes necessary, and even columnists are calling for fundamental reform.[141] The main Australian union federation ran a large organizing and advertising campaign to "change the rules," to garner public support for major legislative reforms that would encourage industry-wide bargaining, among other things.[142] Leading Labor politicians talked and wrote about the need for significant reforms, many of which are consistent with the union movement's major push.[143]

Business groups and the Liberal-National Coalition, the alliance of conservative parties that controlled government in 2019, wants to keep things roughly as they are.[144] In the May 2019 election, labor policy was one of the main themes as the Labor Party tried unsuccessfully to regain control of government. It remains to be seen whether the Labor Party will continue to advocate for such bold changes. But the fact of the debate in 2019 is remarkable in comparison to the United States. A critical mass of Australians were deeply worried about five years of wage stagnation and recognized that major labor policy changes are necessary to address this stagnation, while the United States is just now starting to have a debate after forty-five years of stagnation.

The Inadequacy of US Labor Law

A closer look at the labor systems in Australia, Britain, and Canada has helped clarify the inadequacy of US-style labor law. US-style law, with weak support for union membership and an emphasis on enterprise bargaining, is failing everywhere—even under the most favorable version of the policy. Even in Canada, which has a dream version of US law, union density and coverage have been in decline. Britain and Australia have also tried versions of US law, with little success. Union density and coverage in these countries are low and getting even lower. In addition, both Britain and Australia had much better results for workers under systems that supported unions in additional ways and promoted broad-based bargaining and wage setting.

Most importantly, the case studies have highlighted what is necessary for unions to succeed in the modern economy. Even though Canada, Britain, and Australia have different histories, cultures, and experiences with unions, in all three countries academics, labor unions, and politicians have come to realize that bold changes to labor policy are necessary and that the way forward is based on policies that help build union density and foster higher-level bargaining. The exact way advocates in each country would structure these changes differs based on their legal and cultural history, but the visions for the future in all of these countries share common elements.

In short, there is a growing recognition in the countries most like the United States that raising wages and reducing inequality requires state support for union recruitment and broad-based bargaining.

5

ANSWERING SKEPTICS

Previous chapters have explained what a new labor system would look like and why it would be vital in addressing America's problems with wage stagnation, extreme economic inequality, and a government beholden to the interests of those with the most money. Yet skeptical readers may still have questions. How exactly would the new labor system work? How would sectors be determined? What about alternative ways to strengthen the labor movement, such as increased grassroots organizing or proposals to increase workers' rights? Could policies that do not directly relate to labor unions—from a higher minimum wage to a universal basic income—address America's underlying economic and political problems?

Answering these questions shows that a new labor system could work in the United States. While there would be implementation challenges, they would be manageable, akin to those overcome in use of broad-based bargaining in the United States and elsewhere.

Further, the proposed new labor system compares favorably to other pro-union reforms, from increasing penalties on companies that violate the law to getting rid of right to work to increased organizing. These other methods for strengthening unions would help increase union density and are part of necessary reforms, but on their own would not increase density to high levels and would still leave the vast majority of workers without collective bargaining coverage.

Given the scale of the country's problems, many reforms are necessary beyond those of a new labor system, from increasing the minimum wage to limiting campaign contributions, but reform legislation would stand a better chance of being passed (and would work better) if workers gained power in a new labor system. Further, these types of nonunion reforms are not a substitute for bold labor reforms. Alternatives simply do not do enough to build power for workers—and a lack of power for workers underlies many of American's economic and political problems.

This chapter provides evidence to support these assertions. It first addresses some likely implementation challenges and how they might be resolved based in large part on a historical review of broad-based bargaining in the United States. It then discusses other pro-labor strategies, including improved organizing, more conventional labor policy reforms (like improved strike rights and stronger penalties for law-breaking employers), and bold ideas like placing workers on corporate boards. It shows that all of these changes would be helpful—perhaps even necessary, but they are not a substitute for policies that promote broad-based bargaining and provide incentives for union membership. Finally, the chapter examines how changes to tax law, education reforms, and even more radical policies like a jobs guarantee could help—but would do less in this regard than a new labor system. They would work best in conjunction with a stronger labor movement and thus should be viewed as complements to a new labor system rather than substitutes.

Implementation Challenges

Implementing the new system would create technical challenges for governments, employers, and unions to address. But a brief discussion of these challenges, followed by detailed case studies of broad-based bargaining from recent US history, will show how it can be done.

One of the challenges in any collective bargaining regime is determining the appropriate bargaining unit. In the current worksite-level system, the National Labor Relations Board must determine whether the appropriate community of interest for workers means, for example, that clerks at a supermarket location should be a single unit or whether they should be combined with baggers and stockers at the store into a larger unit. While there are inherent challenges in this process and significant debates about particular choices, the NLRB has proven over the years that it is has been able to make these decisions and that they are workable.

A related challenge exists in broader-based bargaining. A primary goal of the proposed new system is coverage for most workers with some sort of collective agreement, and this would mean arguments about whether some workers ought to be covered by a different agreement. The boundaries of any sector or region are imperfect; they can also change, and new sectors can be created. Boundaries can be debated, perhaps endlessly, especially when it is in the interests of employers or unions to support a particular decision. As a result, there are no perfect answers to boundary questions. But the boundary decisions in the new system do not need to be perfect, they just need to be workable. And that is a standard that the new system is very likely to meet.

In the ideal case, unions will decide the boundaries of broad bargaining units in the new system, and the government will not need to be directly involved. Unions will simply organize workers in their preferred bargaining unit and then attempt to negotiate with employers. Unions could combine previously certified units into broader-based bargaining units as well as choose the boundaries of a new unit they want to organize. Still, inevitably the government will need to make some boundary decisions, particularly in determining where the prevailing wage applies and in setting up wage or workers' boards. In addition, the NLRB will also have a role certifying the appropriate, broader-based unit that unions have chosen. Union decisions on the appropriate bargaining unit would be given great deference, but still there will likely need to be some governmental role in certification. While these decisions may present some challenges, similar boundary decisions are quite common in US policy, which strongly suggests that the boundary challenge would not be a big problem.

Though current law generally encourages fragmented units, the NLRB has some experience determining relatively broad units.[1] Cities, states, and the federal government also regularly make decisions on who is covered by prevailing wages—evaluating whether a particular job belongs in one occupational wage category or another. Sometimes employers or workers contest these decisions, but the capacity of the government to make these decisions is well-established. Several states even have experience determining the boundaries of industries for wage boards. California's wage board, for example, has historically categorized work into seventeen individual industrial or occupational wage orders.[2] New York, in contrast, determines industries on a case-by-case basis, and, for example, in 2015 decided that the fast food industry consisted of "limited service restaurants, where customers order at the counter and pay in advance, which are large chains with multiple locations nationally."[3] It is possible to quibble over whether an individual business is appropriately categorized, but the wage board system has proven workable. Similarly, government statistical agencies have a long record of classifying industries and occupations for data collection purposes. Classifications may not perfectly capture every industry or occupation, but they do a reasonable job so that employers and researchers have come to rely on them.

Another concern is that, under broad-based bargaining, employers typically join together for bargaining purposes in an association or committee, yet few of these employer bargaining committees currently exist. Some elements of the new system would actively encourage employers to organize together. The selection process for members of the workers' boards, would, for example, select organizations that represent the most workers in the sector.[4] And extension policies might encourage employers to bargain—possibly through an association—so that they have some influence on standards. But the main impetus to encourage employers to form bargaining committees is that unions would be more powerful and broad-based bargaining would be encouraged. Employers are good at responding to financial incentives, and their financial incentive would be in organizing together to more effectively bargain in the new system. On the occasions when unions have had significant power in certain sectors in the United States, employers have often formed bargaining committees or associations, as will be discussed later in this chapter. Further, broad-based bargaining can also work with a less than ideal level of employer associations. Pattern bargaining—negotiations with individual firms based on a similar contract—can lead to broad-based coverage. Similarly, extension policies can spread the terms of contracts to similarly placed workers—whether those contracts were negotiated with an employer association or not.

A somewhat related set of challenges surrounds union behaviors. Some may worry that the new labor system could create unions that have far more power than employers. In this scenario, there would not be give and take with employers, but rather unions would simply use their vastly greater power to get what they want and behave irresponsibly to the detriment of society—a bit like employers do in the current system. While this possibility may seem far-fetched given today's reality, it is worth considering because successful bargaining takes relatively evenly matched participants.

The first thing to note about this possibility is that it is relatively unlikely, given the forces that undermine worker power in the modern economy. From the extreme mobility of capital, to technological change, to the legacy of decades of extreme "free-market" policies, labor unions face a number of headwinds. In addition, private-sector union density is about as low as it has ever been. Policy would need to very supportive of labor unions to blow past these forces.

Second, this scenario assumes that unions would be irresponsible if they were to achieve great power. Some likely would be, but the successful experiences in the few sectors in US history in which unions have had very high density—such as in auto assembly, where density approached 100 percent in the mid-twentieth century—suggests that many would not be irresponsible. So too does the experience in other countries with extremely high union density. Indeed, the labor systems in a number of European countries create a check on how much compensation can increase by starting bargaining with tradeable sectors that are heavily exposed to foreign competition and are likely to suffer greatly if compensation vastly outstrips productivity.[5] In these models, increases in other sectors are tied the tradeable sector and thus restrained by this process—which is sometimes done through formal channels and other times through informal collaboration. Another method to limit the ability of powerful unions to extract too much from overmatched employers would be to encourage stronger employer associations—so the employers in a sector can better work together and match union tactics.[6] The goal of the new system would be to develop similar types of restraints if they become necessary as the system matures. This means that adjustments to broader-based bargaining would have the capacity to provide a check on even very powerful unions.

Finally, even if unions ultimately overwhelm constraints, it would likely take a long period of time for this to happen and especially for any harm to occur. Even if density grows quickly under the new system, it would likely take a decade or more to attain previous highs. Further, wages have grown much more slowly than productivity for over four decades, so there is a significant amount of room for compensation to increase until it outstrips productivity. This means that if unions somehow do get so much power in the new system and use their power irresponsibly, there is time to tweak the system to equalize power without doing much harm. There is no proximate worry that compensation levels will increase above productivity levels and stay there for a significant period of time.

A more immediate concern is that not every union is structured in ways that are best suited to broader-based bargaining. Unions won't necessarily have to change their structures to bargain in the new system, but they will be better able to engage in broad-based bargaining if they are more centralized and coordinated than some unions are today. As a result, some unions will feel pressured to create formal structures that match broader-based bargaining units or even merge—and they may be reluctant to do so, because, for example, a particular local union could lose some power in the process. In other words, there are likely to be conflicts between local and international unions and between international unions that represent somewhat overlapping workers.

While the new system might create tension between local and national unions and between various national unions, they are analogous to the kinds of challenges that unions have managed to make work under the current system. Unions have long had fights over jurisdiction, and locals commonly wrestle with internationals for power. Disputes happen, but unions generally find ways to deal with them. Unions have found ways to coordinate activities between locals and internationals as well as across international unions. To deal with these kinds of issues, unions sometimes even create formally interdependent structures or even merge. All of which suggests that in a new US labor system, unions might be able to structure themselves and coordinate activities to better match broader-based bargaining structures.

But even if unions are able to only imperfectly align with new bargaining structures, collective bargaining at a higher level can still occur. Imperfect union coordination might mean less than the ideal—pure multi-employer bargaining that covers an entire sector—but there would still be much more broad-based bargaining than under the current system. Critically, prevailing wage-style extensions would help ensure that the terms of union contracts spread to the entire sector. That is, even if several unions are fighting within a single sector and cannot coordinate to achieve multi-employer bargaining that covers the entire sector, the basic terms of the average union contract could still extend to other workers in the sector, so long as the combined union density was over the prevailing wage threshold.

Broad-Based Bargaining in the United States

A closer look at some examples of broader-based bargaining from recent US history helps provide additional evidence that the new system is workable. Indeed, the examples of broad-based bargaining in the United States help highlight how ordinary this type of bargaining can be.

In the mid-twentieth century, broad-based bargaining occurred in a variety of industries with a number of unions—providing evidence that boundary problems were not insurmountable, that local and national unions could coordinate, and that very powerful unions were not the problem that detractors asserted. Indeed, workers and employers often thrived under broad-based bargaining. In addition, the history suggests that the new system would be better than the old because it would make broader-based bargaining more achievable for unions as well as limit the ability of firms to escape coverage. Under the old system, unions often had to fight for decades to get something approaching sectoral bargaining, and then, once they did, the higher-level bargaining was quite fragile.

Perhaps the most well-known example of broader-based bargaining in the United States comes from the auto industry. Famously, broader-based bargaining, or indeed any kind of bargaining in the auto industry, was extremely difficult to achieve since employers fought unions with harsh measures. Ultimately, the historic sit-down strikes of 1936 and 1937 produced a great victory for workers and enabled General Motors to be organized, and then, soon after, Chrysler—with Ford not successfully unionized until 1941.[7] Direct action by workers was essential in forcing automakers to sign contracts with the United Auto Workers (UAW). Still, government action was also helpful in supporting union efforts—including the passage of the National Labor Relations Act, the pro-union governor of Michigan's helpful use of the National Guard as a peace-keeping force that protected workers from GM security officers, President Franklin Roosevelt's encouragement of GM to negotiate with the union, and World War II labor boards.[8]

Virtually all hourly paid auto assembly workers were organized by the late 1940s.[9] With union density approaching nearly 100 percent of auto workers and the Big Three automakers—GM, Ford and Chrysler—producing the vast majority of autos in the United States, conditions were ripe for broader-based bargaining, as unions covered virtually all workers and a few employers dominated the industry. Though the auto industry did not have true multi-employer sectoral bargaining, where a group of employers negotiated with unions for workers across the sector, from the 1940s up until the early 1980s the UAW set broad-based standards through pattern-setting arrangements. Under a pattern-setting arrangement, the UAW first negotiated a national contract with one of the Big Three and then negotiated virtually identical agreements with the other automakers. These national contracts set wages and benefits and prevented locals from negotiating over these, though they allowed some degree of local union bargaining at individual plants over plant-specific work rules, such as the form of the seniority ladder.[10] Thus, local UAW unions had some powers, but most of the power resided at the top, which inevitably created some conflict, although this was largely contained.

The pattern agreements in the auto industry influenced many other industries, with the standards spreading out to similar work in almost concentric circles. The UAW used the auto assembly contract as their template for negotiations with auto parts manufacturers. In addition, agricultural machinery manufacturing also typically followed the patterns set in auto, as did the rubber industry.[11] Ultimately, the auto industry influenced most of US manufacturing and industries well beyond. Autoworker compensation was typically higher than in most other manufacturing and other private-sector work, but autoworkers pulled others along with them. (Note that, in an ideal world, some of these categories—such as auto assembly and auto parts—probably should have been combined in a single sector. Bargaining as a single sector would have been more robust in the face of changes in the industry and produced a more even spread of standards, instead of the case where auto assembly compensation was higher than parts. But even imperfect boundaries proved workable for several decades.)

The benefits of the UAW's near-sectoral bargaining are well known. Wages and benefits for autoworkers were high and increased quickly—and the gains these workers achieved spread to many other workers in other parts of the economy, largely through informal processes. It is not too much of an exaggeration to say that pattern bargaining in the auto industry created the American middle class.[12]

Automakers also benefited. They were able to obtain predictable labor costs—which was important because of the long time required to take a car from concept to production. Automakers were also able to limit overt conflict, including strikes, that could reduce profits. National bargaining was important to achieving this goal because it reduced the ability of any particular local union to disrupt production.[13] Automakers also largely succeeded through these negotiations in keeping control of matters they cared deeply about and prevented workers from having a say about company profits or management decisions such as investment planning.[14] For decades under these nationwide contracts auto firms were able to increase output and generate high profits. From 1946 until 1979, the US auto industry experienced, as one study put it, "consistent growth and prosperity, even in the face of the industry's periodically sharp cyclical swings."[15]

But, under the US labor system, pattern bargaining in the auto industry and similar arrangements in other industries were dependent on a number of factors that were relatively hard to maintain. In the auto industry, the success of broad-based bargaining was dependent on low levels of imports, continued growth in domestic auto sales, and extremely high unionization.[16] These factors enabled the UAW to use pattern bargaining to cover the core auto labor markets and take wages out of competition and provided reasons for employers to go along. But, as conditions changed, broad-based bargaining was hard to maintain. Without a supportive policy environment, broad-based bargaining was inherently fragile.

The energy crisis of the 1970s caused gas shortages and high gas prices, which increased consumer demand for more fuel-efficient vehicles than US automakers were producing. Foreign competitors were also becoming increasingly competitive on quality and price as they used innovative production methods, such as just-in-time inventory strategies. As a result, imports rose from 14.6 percent in 1970 to 23.5 percent in 1984.[17] The US economy also suffered a severe recession in the early 1980s, further reducing demand for US autos. Factory overcapacity became a problem. These factors caused US automakers' profits to fall sharply and turn into losses in some years. Though profits recovered, they became less stable than they once had been.[18] Despite employment growth among US auto manufacturers through much of the 1970s, employment in 1981 was lower than it was a decade earlier.[19]

These economic challenges helped lead to the breakdown of pattern-setting in auto assembly and related industries. In order to help save struggling Chrysler and facilitate a federal bailout of the company in 1980, the UAW negotiated a pattern-breaking agreement with lower compensation. In subsequent years, the UAW also engaged in concessionary bargaining, allowing for greater local union flexibility to save jobs at various other assembly plants. Pattern following in auto parts also broke down in the early 1980s, as it did in similar industries such as agricultural equipment manufacturing, as economic pressures and business strategies changed and union density declined.[20] "As auto contracts became less uniform, their influence on settlements in other, related industries, such as agricultural machinery and rubber, declined," one academic review summarized.[21]

While the economic environment contributed to the breakdown of broad-based bargaining, this type of bargaining in the United States is particularly fragile because it depends on very high union density across the relevant labor markets. Very high union density is difficult to maintain in the US system, not only because the process for forming a union is so challenging but also because there are so many ways for employers to escape union coverage and so many financial incentives for them to avoid coverage.[22] While density in auto assembly was virtually 100 percent in the 1970s, any new plant that was built needed to be newly organized in order to be covered by a collective bargaining agreement.[23] This meant that as foreign competitors increasingly set up factories in the United States, they were not automatically covered by existing agreements, and some remained that way permanently as they were unable to be organized, reducing density and coverage rates. Similarly, when US automakers began opening factories in the South, they were also initially nonunion and non-covered: only through years of struggle with massive pressure on the firms were they able to be unionized.[24] (Today the increased use of temporary workers and the ease of moving work to Mexico and elsewhere adds to these de-unionizing pressures.)

Ultimately, erosion in coverage meant that the UAW was only able to negotiate for a smaller portion of the industry and had far less ability to drive toward higher standards across the entire sector, even when economic conditions became more favorable. Instead, the UAW constantly needed to defend what it once had, and it had little ability to spread its standards outward.

The difficulty of maintaining high density and coverage rates in auto assembly was magnified by the fact that a core element of auto production—namely parts manufacturing—had lower density and thus lower coverage. As the Big Three increasingly spun off parts divisions, shrank their workforces, and bought parts from outside suppliers, the UAW represented fewer workers and a smaller share of the auto industry. While parts had generally followed the pattern bargaining set by auto assembly, the pattern was dependent on union power, and, as the UAW weakened even slightly, it did not have the power to maintain high standards. In 1963, auto parts manufacturing was nearly 90 percent organized, and pay was nearly 90 percent of auto assembly rates, but, as density declined, so did standards. In 1974, density in parts was around 80 percent, and pay was 80 percent of auto assembly, and by 1983 density had fallen to 60 percent in parts suppliers, while pay was just two-thirds the level of auto assembly. Parts compensation makes clear how dependent high standards across the entire industry were on extremely high density.[25] In the new system, nonunion parts manufacturing and new factories would automatically be covered through extension mechanisms—and thus these sorts of changes in the industry would not weaken the entire bargaining system.

Some may argue that pattern bargaining deserved to fail because it enabled the UAW to use its strength to irresponsibly drive compensation to uncompetitive levels, causing many of the financial troubles of the American automakers. The UAW was not without blame in the automakers' struggles, especially for not doing more to insist on higher quality, as even the UAW's president acknowledged at the time.[26] Auto assembly wages were also above those in most other US sectors.[27] They were even higher than auto assembly wages in most other countries.

But there were many other influences to consider, and there is significant evidence that the failures of management were much more important. (And US management had successfully fought the UAW in order to retain exclusive authority in production decisions.) For decades in the mid-twentieth century, American auto manufacturers focused on styling and advertising, while their competitors in Germany and Japan worked on technological innovation and improving gas mileage. Thus, by the late 1970s US automakers were no longer producing leading-edge cars with the quality and value that consumers wanted. US managers also earned seven time as much as their Japanese counterparts, vastly outstripping compensation differences between auto assemblers in the two countries. A labor relations textbook by D. Quinn Mills and Janice McCarthy asserts that "decades of poor management" led to many of the troubles faced by US automakers.[28]

There are several other factors to consider that even more directly indicate that broad-based collective bargaining in the United States is workable and likely to succeed under the new system. First, and perhaps most importantly, auto workers in Germany earned slightly more than US auto workers in 1980—and much more today—indicating that broad-based bargaining and high wages are quite compatible with firm success, so long as firms continue to innovate.[29] Indeed, the German industrial relations system—with broad-based bargaining and strong workforce training—is often seen as a critical for the success of the German manufacturing sector.[30] Second, compensation in closely related sectors was only loosely linked to US auto assembly wages, and the connections were heavily dependent on the ability to maintain very high union density. This meant that if union density declined in other sectors, auto wages would inevitably seem quite high—whether they outstripped productivity or not. Indeed, compensation for US auto workers exceeded the compensation for other US manufacturing workers by a much greater degree than was the case in other countries.[31] Competitor countries generally did a better job ensuring that similar work received similar pay, so that most manufacturing workers had high wages, not just auto workers.[32] Third, as troubles in the US auto industry became apparent, the collective bargaining process was used to reduce compensation as well as to innovate numerous cooperative workplace practices that aimed to improve productivity, suggesting that broad-based bargaining can adapt to economic challenges.[33]

The auto industry is not an isolated case. Pattern and other types of broad-based bargaining were relatively common in the United States until the 1980s, existing in industries as varied as steel, telecom, coal, and trucking. Further examination of these examples provides additional evidence of the workability of broad-based bargaining in the United States. These examples also further highlight its fragility under the current system: broad-based bargaining in the United States is dependent on extremely high union density and other economic factors that encourage employers to support it. When these factors started to change, most broad-based bargaining began to break down, and it was largely gone by the end of the 1980s. As professors David Lipsky and Clifford Donn explained in their review of American collective bargaining: "In the 1970s the bargaining structure in many industries, especially in the manufacturing sector, was highly centralized; the key decisions were usually made at the company or industry level by top union and corporate executives. In the 1980s . . . the changing environment had caused bargaining to become more decentralized—more centered on the shop, the plant and the single employer."[34]

In steel, as in the auto industry, broad-based bargaining was achieved through high union density after years of sometimes violent struggle for union representation. Indeed, density was high enough that a 1959 strike was able to shut down 87 percent of the nation's steel production.[35] Also like auto, broad-based bargaining in steel was aided by steel being a very concentrated industry, with a few dominant firms, that made it easier to coordinate bargaining. Broad-based bargaining worked well in steel for several decades, raising standards for closely related industries such as aluminum manufacturing and helping set standards for the larger US economy and enabling firms to profit. Yet in steel, as in auto making, broad-based bargaining weakened due in part to increased foreign competition, plant closings, and a failure of US companies to remain leaders in technological innovation.[36] Unlike in auto, however, broad-based bargaining in the steel industry was achieved through multiple employers coordinating together to negotiate with the union, indicating that more classic sectoral bargaining, not just pattern bargaining, can work in the United States.[37]

Similarly, the telecommunications industry was dominated for decades by a single company, AT&T, and union density was quite high. Yet, even with these favorable conditions, decades of struggle were necessary to achieve national bargaining in 1974. Most communications workers were in a single union, Communications Workers of America (CWA), but a significant percentage were in other unions, indicating that broad-based bargaining can work even when one union does not dominate the industry to the degree as in auto or steel.[38] National telecommunications bargaining lasted for only a decade after it was achieved—it disintegrated relatively quickly as the industry shifted due to technological change facilitating nonunion competition, outsourcing of covered work, and the breakup of AT&T.[39] But it worked fairly well while it lasted, according to an academic review that noted: "AT&T received good and stable profits; workers were well compensated; relatively little output was lost due to strikes; and the telephone system provided a high quality product at a reasonable price."[40]

In railroads—which are not as concentrated as the old telecom industry but still relatively concentrated—broad-based bargaining has existed for a century and continues to this day. Since 1963, an employer organization has conducted bargaining for railroad firms.[41] Workers are represented by twelve different unions—including large unions such as the International Association of Machinists and Aerospace Workers and the International Brotherhood of Electrical Workers and smaller unions such as the American Train Dispatchers Association and Brotherhood of Maintenance of Way Employees.[42] This indicates that a variety of unions can work together under a broad-based bargaining system.

In the coal industry—in contrast, a very decentralized industry with many employers—broad-based multi-employer bargaining was achieved for several decades in the mid-twentieth century, suggesting that concentrated ownership may have made broad-based bargaining easier under the old system but can also work in other environments. Again, extremely high union density was key to forging the multi-employer agreements but could not hold broad-based bargaining together when union density declined in the industry, as nonunion mines in the West accounted for a larger share of production and increased productivity and technological change reduced membership in existing unionized mines.[43] Again, multi-employer bargaining was successful, with one journalist writing that the 1950 broad-based agreement in coal "allowed for a decade of orderly growth and reorganization." During this period, the mineworkers' unions established a market research division to help coal companies plan future investments, providing an important benefit to bargaining for smaller firms that would not have been able to afford such research on their own and thus been at a competitive disadvantage compared to larger firms.[44]

Similarly in trucking, a highly fragmented industry with thousands of firms, the Teamsters used extremely high density to force employers to engage in national, multi-employer bargaining that covered much of the industry for several decades.[45] But as union density declined in the industry and nonunion carriers were increasingly able to undercut the union agreement—in large part because of legal changes in Taft-Hartley that prevented unions from using "secondary" pressures on employers and negotiating "hot cargo" provisions to prevent the transporting of goods from antiunion firms—broad-based bargaining weakened significantly and then deregulation furthered its decline. A number of trucking firms supported multi-employer bargaining as a way to present a unified front and limit union power, and some local unions resisted the national bargaining as a threat to their power, providing additional evidence that some employers benefit from broad-based bargaining, and some unions see threats.[46]

Broad-based bargaining was even successful in the US apparel industry—the prototypical sweatshop industry, with highly mobile factories and layers of contracting between the lead firm and the company doing the actual production.[47] The apparel industry example mirrors many of the themes in the other examples and also shows that broad-based bargaining functioned well in a workforce that was largely composed of female and immigrant workers. Again, high union density—achieved in part because of supportive government policies, including the short-lived National Industrial Recovery Act of 1933—was key to bringing groups of employers together in broad-based bargaining, known in the industry as "jobbers agreements." These jobbers agreements were essential to standardizing compensation and addressing the ability of firms in the industry to move work from factory to factory to avoid unions and high labor standards. They applied to the firms designing and selling apparel as well as to firms doing the sewing and thus covered businesses up and down the supply chain. They also brought many apparel-selling firms together to negotiate as part of industry associations and did the same for numerous manufacturing firms. This broad-based bargaining structure was successful for several decades in the mid-twentieth century at raising wages, enabling companies to profit and stabilizing the industry. Indeed, in the 1950s, apparel workers received the highest hourly rate in the nondurable goods sector. Republican senator Barry Goldwater noted that the jobbers agreements made sweatshops "disappear" and helped "create profits for businesses which were unable to produce profits."[48] But over time, broad-based bargaining in the industry largely fell apart as most apparel work was shipped overseas and union density declined.

While additional examples from the United States could provide further evidence, the point is clear that broad-based bargaining has worked in a range of industries and with many different unions. This indicates that the implementation challenges the new system would face are likely surmountable. This history also highlights that broad-based bargaining would be much easier to achieve and maintain under the new system.

Alternatives

The claim of this book is not just that the new labor system would be workable but also that it would be more effective than alternatives. Before considering the potential alternatives in more detail, readers should understand what the new system would likely achieve. While previous chapters have made clear the benefits of the proposed system, they did not provide estimates of the impact these changes would have. Calculating the impact of bold labor policy changes necessitates a bit of guesswork, so all numbers should be viewed as ballpark estimates, but even rough figures can help illustrate.

Let's start with union density. Estimates from Canada suggest that taking the NLRA closer to how it was before Taft-Hartley and ensuring that workers have strong rights and an easier path to joining a union would roughly double private-sector union density—moving from 6 to 12 percent.[49] Estimates from countries with the Ghent system indicate that it increases union density by around 20 percentage points.[50] This suggests that adapting a robust, American version of the system with unions helping provide public services like workforce training, co-enforcement, and benefits navigation could provide a similar boost. To be conservative, though, assume an increase of a few percentage points less. That would take union density to around 30 percent, which approaches the historical peak in the United States. Though this book has often emphasized the private sector, ensuring that all public-sector workers have union rights and adopting Ghent-like policies in the public sector are also part of the new system.[51] These changes would likely push overall union density above historic highs.

Bargaining coverage would also increase significantly under the new system. Under the old system, union density and bargaining coverage were closely linked and virtually identical. But under the new system, broader-based bargaining would increase coverage well above density levels. A reasonable guess is that around two-thirds of workers of workers would likely be covered by a collective bargaining agreement in the new system.

This coverage estimate is based on a number of rough calculations. First, the new system contains several provisions that would likely increase both density and coverage such as policies that would make it easier for unions to bring multiple employers to the table. One such policy would be master-contract style extension—when a union negotiated a master contract with two different shops in a particular sector, any additional worksites the union organized would automatically be covered by the master contract. Reliable estimates for the impact of these elements are particularly difficult to come by since there is relatively little to compare them to. Still, a reasonable, low-range guesstimate is that these elements would likely boost density and coverage by at least a few percentage points—taking these figures to over one-third in the private sector.

Then prevailing wage-style extension would increase coverage more significantly. The United States has had significant experience with prevailing wages in government contracting as the wage rate paid to 30 percent of workers in a craft and locality.[52] Thus, this is a likely level of density necessary to trigger extension mechanisms in the new system, though the standard could possibly be set at an even lower and more easily attainable level.[53] Density in a number of regions or sectors would be expected to meet the 30 percent threshold, since union density and bargaining coverage from the factors previously described would likely be around one-third of the workforce. Some regions would be way above the threshold, and some would be below. In a sector where density was 70 percent, extension would only increase coverage by 30 percentage points, but in a sector where density was 31 percent, extension would increase coverage by 69 percentage points. So, as a ballpark figure, assume that this kind of extension would lead to coverage that is roughly double the density levels. That would take coverage to around two-thirds of the workforce.

An estimate with coverage being about double the level of density is also reasonable based on comparisons with other countries. Indeed, it is well below the increase in coverage attained in European countries with well-established extension mechanisms. In the Netherlands, for example, coverage is nearly 80 percent, while density is well less than 20 percent, meaning that the Dutch system boosts coverage by more than four times density. Thus, a ballpark estimate with coverage being double density is attainable. It also reasonable to take a conservative approach and assume that extension will increase coverage in the US system less than in Europe based on the theory that US policy tends to intervene less in the labor market than in other countries.

Most of the remaining third of the labor market would be covered by workers' boards. These boards may not count as true collective bargaining coverage because the government is involved in the negotiations, but they still collectively set standards. This collective wage-setting process will provide binding minimum standards in sectors and occupations where job quality has historically been low, such as in domestic work, fast food, and retail—and ensure that no company can escape coverage in the new system.

The impact of these changes would be transformative, though quite hard to estimate with any precision. With union density around one-third of the workforce, collective bargaining coverage about two-thirds, and worker boards covering one-third of the work, compensation would surely increase. A reasonable approximation is that these changes would force compensation for most workers to increase in line with productivity. This is the level of wage increase during the mid-twentieth century, when union density was at similar levels as would be expected under the new system. Wages keeping up with productivity have also been achievable today in several European countries with high coverage levels.[54] Thus, an assumption that the new system would lead to compensation increasing at the level of productivity gains is reasonable. Because collective bargaining and wage board coverage would be much higher than it ever has been in the United States under the new system, it is possible that wages could increase more rapidly than productivity, for at least some period of time. If this continued for a long time, this could be an economic problem, but, as previously discussed, the new system could be adjusted to halt that situation.

The impact these changes would have on economic inequality and gender and racial pay gaps is perhaps even more speculative. As a guesstimate it seems reasonable to expect that overall economic inequality would be reduced by about one-third, possibly by more. US estimates peg the decline of unions from historic highs (roughly the levels that would be achieved under the new system) to their lows today as accounting for about one-third of the rise of wage inequality among men and one-fifth of the rise among women—who started from a lower place and whose labor market opportunities increased during this period.[55] It seems reasonable to assume that increasing union density to historic highs or above would lead to a corresponding decrease in inequality. Because coverage would be much higher than ever, a one-third reduction in inequality is likely a low estimate. Additional evidence that one-third reduction might be a low estimate comes from a number of countries with labor systems similar to those proposed in this book, countries that have seen relatively little increase in economic inequality over recent years.[56] For gender and racial pay gaps, a very rough estimate is that these would shrink by around one third to one half.

Estimates for the impact that the new system would have on democracy are even less precise, since democracy is not easily quantified. Chapter 2 presented evidence highlighting the strong connections between unions and various elements of democracy—including increased participation by citizens, more office-seeking by people with modest incomes, and greater political representation for the views of the non-rich. To attempt to quantify just one part of this impact, consider voting rates. US estimates suggest that each percentage point increase in union density increases voter turnout rates by 0.21 to 0.25 percentage points, with increases highest for those with less education and lower incomes.[57] That suggests the new system would lead to a turnout increase of around 5 or 6 percent—which would translate into the highest turnout in well over a century.[58] And these voters would likely vote in a more progressive manner than the current electorate.[59] Extrapolating out, this suggests that the new system would lead to large swing in the presidential vote share garnered by the Democratic Party, potentially on the order of around 10 percentage points. These kinds of impacts on turnout and vote share would create a very different democratic system from what the United States currently has, even without considering all the other things unions do to represent workers in the political system.

Most of these estimates have been quite rough, but they indicate the transformative potential of the new labor system. They suggest a country with union density at historic highs, collective bargaining coverage nearly double what has ever been achieved in the United States, wages increasing with productivity, inequality one-third lower, and a dramatically different political system. That is the scale of change necessary to address America's underlying problems and a scale that alternatives struggle to achieve.

Other Union-Strengthening Policies

Some supporters of labor unions may hold on to the belief that policies to provide incentives for membership and promote broader-based bargaining are unnecessary. In this view, big policy changes are not needed because unions can rebuild power through better organizing and direct action, such as strikes and boycotts. A related line of thinking holds that achieving the kinds of policy changes labor has long sought, such as getting rid of right-to-work laws, facilitating "card check" sign-up processes, increasing penalties for employer violations of the law, and improving strike rights, would be enough to strengthen the labor movement.

This book recognizes the importance of independent worker action and basic rights. They are absolutely vital and indeed should be seen as part of the new labor system. Organizing and direct action provide the basis for workers to exercise power.

Much of the power that workers have is derived from their ability to disrupt the normal course of business.[60] Not only has this ability been crucial to improving working conditions at times in US history—from great coal strikes to the auto plant sit-down strikes, the teacher strikes in West Virginia and several other states, which led to significant raises and increased school funding, show that disruption still works today. Direct action also helps make political reforms possible. It is hard to imagine broad labor reforms passing without on-the-ground disruptions forcing politicians to deal with worker issues.

Yet there is very little evidence that in the current environment unions can grow in meaningful ways solely through their own efforts. American unions may have been slow to respond to the decline in union density several decades ago and have not always adopted the most effective organizing tactics, but they have now tried almost every strategy possible and have become quite good and inventive at doing so. They have tried direct action and consumer strategies. They have engaged the community and other businesses. They have pursued corporate campaigns as well as digital strategies. As one study put it, "Unions have devoted more energy, resources, and creativity to organizing over the last thirty years than most people (even inside the labor movement) realize."[61] In fact, union organizing in the United States is now seen as the model that unions in other countries seek to emulate.[62]

It is hard to imagine that doing more of the same will produce dramatically different results. In the current environment, even good organizing—whether it is focused on social movement unionism, business unionism, online or mobile organizing, or any other strategy—does not do enough. The National Labor Relations Act structure is a "rat in a wheel" system, according to Larry Mishel, distinguished fellow at the Economic Policy Institute, because it continually forces unions to expend great effort organizing workers just to stay in the same place.[63] In the current system, as new firms and new sectors of the economy are created, they are not covered by union contracts. And unionized firms can contract out, relocate, spin off identical new, nonunion firms, and otherwise slip outside union coverage. This means unions must constantly engage in organizing on a massive scale just to stave off decline. As a study that considered the costs and difficulties of organizing found, "the prospects are dim for a reversal of the downward spiral of labor unions based on increased organizing activity."[64]

It is true that research finds that certain kinds of union organizing strategies are more effective than others.[65] But increased organizing and mobilization does not produce enough growth to reverse labor's decline, as a review of over two hundred studies on union revitalization strategies found.[66] The review concluded, not surprisingly, that organizing can succeed when the policy environment is favorable but makes little headway at other times.

Today only relatively few types of grassroots efforts have any real power to disrupt and force companies and politicians to deal with them. The teacher strikes in West Virginia, for example, were successful because of their massive scale—in all fifty-five counties in the state and affecting over 270,000 students.[67] They were also successful because of the types of workers involved: schools cannot operate without properly trained teachers. The schools probably would have found a way to operate if only food service workers and janitors had gone on strike. Most employers are likely find a way to make do in the face of direct action, especially since most actions workers would engage in are unlikely to achieve the scale of the West Virginia strikes or involve workers as difficult to replace. Direct action and organizing are more promising for those with some market power, but less so for most workers, particularly those who need help the most. Indeed, this is a significant reason why unions increasingly represent workers with higher levels of education than the overall workforce, rather than workers with less education and power.[68]

Further, the teacher strikes in West Virginia and elsewhere also benefited from the supportive decisions of superintendents to cancel school and thus prevent unions and teachers from being fined—indicating that even seemingly independent direct action often benefits from a conducive policy environment.[69] A similar point can also be made about the successful joint labor-management training in the construction trades that produces strong member attachment. The independent efforts that forged the joint training are buttressed by a supportive policy environment. Apprenticeships programs registered by the Department of Labor have high standards and monitoring requirements that many nonunion programs do not meet, and prevailing wage laws allow lower pay for registered apprentices, which provides an incentive for businesses to support registered apprenticeship programs.[70]

Not even the efforts of the US unions most committed to organizing have been able to meaningfully increase density in recent decades. Since 1983, union density has declined in every major private-sector industry, including construction, utilities, manufacturing, transportation, communications, wholesale trade, retail, and finance.[71] Similarly, density has fallen sharply in places as varied as Alabama and Alaska, California and Connecticut, Los Angeles and Las Vegas, and New York City and Atlanta, to name just a few places.[72] There is not a single state or major city in the country where private-sector density has grown significantly in the past several decades.[73] Organizing has not been a particularly successful strategy because the supportive policies are too few and far between.

At a more abstract level, high levels of direct action and organizing are not sustainable over long periods of time. Most workers do not want to be constantly in fight mode and prefer collaborating with their employers.[74] They want their efforts to lead to change and then to go back to their normal routines. But fights with employers would likely need to be ongoing without policy change to help balance power more evenly and lock in the results of organizing efforts.[75]

Unions could also try to pursue greater broader-based bargaining under the current system by changing their organizing tactics, bargaining objectives, and organizational structures.[76] Unions certainly can and should start taking some steps on their own to promote multi-employer bargaining. But, as US history and examples from around the world show, significant increases in broader-based bargaining take much stronger unions or a more supportive policy environment (or both). US unions were able to achieve something approaching sectoral bargaining when density approached 100 percent in the auto and steel industries and well over 50 percent in other industries like telecom. Other countries that have a significant amount of broad-based bargaining but relatively modest density, such as the Netherlands, have supportive extension policies.

These same arguments about the difficulty of organizing workers in the current environment would hold true even if the NLRA were tweaked to be more favorable to workers. While policy changes such as card check and getting rid of right-to-work policies are likely to increase union membership, research finds that these kinds of labor law changes are unlikely to raise unionization rates to anywhere near sufficiency.[77] They would certainly help, but there is little evidence to suggest that they would be enough. Estimates from Larry Mishel indicate that to simply maintain private-sector density requires doubling the scale of current organizing, while an increase of just 4 percentage points would necessitate increasing organizing by seven times, leading him to conclude that "[c]hanging the law to facilitate more organizing is insufficient."[78]

The research on other countries finds a similar story. Unions in Britain have an easier path to majority support than US unions do, but they are still struggling. Parts of Canada have almost everything that US unionists have traditionally wished for—almost a pre–Taft-Hartley version of the National Labor Relations Act, with secondary boycotts, card check, and no right-to-work policies—yet union density is shrinking there too. Unions are in decline even in countries with policies that go well beyond a dream version of the NLRA, such as Germany, with its mandated works councils and board-level representation. In contrast, in countries that have policies designed to encourage union membership, such as through the Ghent system, unions have remained strong. And, of course, countries that encourage broader-based bargaining coverage have been able to maintain much higher coverage than the United States.

Another piece of evidence that suggests that tweaks to the NLRA would not be enough is that the *Janus* Supreme Court decision (that made the public sector effectively right-to-work) has not been as harmful to union density as many union leaders feared.[79] This indicates that right-to-work policies are not as critical as some believed, especially for established unions. Ending right-to-work policies would be helpful but not as helpful as some may have hoped.

As stand-alone solutions, increased organizing and restoring the rights and protections of the original National Labor Relations Act would be insufficient. A better way to think of these actions is as a necessary part of a reform agenda. Organizing workers and disrupting the economy can help to create an impetus for the kinds of policy changes necessary. Organizing will also be important in the new system to pressure employers and the political system to deliver wage and benefit increases. In fact, the US version of a Ghent-like system would be set up to provide incentives to encourage more organizing. Finally, stronger worker rights are also essential to any reform effort because workers cannot engage in any kind of bargaining—let alone broad-based bargaining—if their rights are constantly threatened.

Going well beyond traditional labor law reforms, some people support policies that would require firms to create works councils and put workers on the boards of corporations. These changes would be helpful and should happen. They are compatible with and complimentary to the agenda highlighted in this book, but they are not a replacement or substitute for it.

Works councils can create a collaborative setting for workers to help resolve issues on the job and give workers an additional way to discuss workplace issues among themselves and with managers. This can enhance the internal democracy of corporations and make a firm run better and be more productive.[80] Works councils could even create organizing opportunities and lead to greater unionization. But, on their own, works councils will not do much to raise wages or reduce inequality because they are intended to be a place to discuss almost any issue except compensation. (Similar points can be made about related proposals, such as the creation of independent labor monitors at each workplace.)

Works councils are legally prohibited from discussing wages, which means they are not set up to address America's problems with wage stagnation and inequality. Without broader-based bargaining, works councils would resemble a very weak version of the current enterprise-based bargaining system. If there is no other forum to do so, workers would try to find ways to get around the ban and in effect use works councils as a place to engage in enterprise-style collective bargaining—though with even less power and rights. This is unlikely to be effective in raising compensation, and it can channel conflict back into the worksite, which threatens to undermine the collaborative aspects of works councils. As one study put it, "In establishments covered by collective bargaining agreements works councils are more likely to be engaged in productivity-enhancing activities and less engaged in rent seeking activities than their counterparts in uncovered firms."[81] In other words, without broader-based bargaining raising wages and channeling conflict outside the workplace, works councils are unlikely to function in a collaborative, productivity-enhancing manner.[82] Worse, in places where unions do not exist or do not have sufficient power, works councils would likely be dominated by employers. To function properly, works councils depend on higher-level collective bargaining and strong unions.

Granting worker representation on corporate boards can help ensure that firms are run more democratically and could have a modest impact on wages and economic inequality. Board-level representation policies enable workers to have input on significant decisions that affect the direction of a firm, such as how much to outsource production and the creation of strategies to develop employees' skills. The policy can ensure that the needs and interests of workers—who often have a long-term commitment to a firm and community—are given a voice on par with shareholders, many of whom only have a short-term interest.[83]

Research indicates that board-level representation for workers can constrain CEO pay, reduce economic inequality, and improve job stability—and has the potential to do so in a way that is compatible with strong firm performance.[84]

Still, strong unions are key to making board-level representation work because they help train, educate, and inform worker board members. Without this support, worker board members are unlikely to have the skills and background to read balance sheets, understand corporate finance, or know what is happening in other divisions of the company, among other issues.

It also seems unlikely that that board-level representation on its own would significantly raise wages. Some studies on firms with board-level representation find that they pay only modestly higher wages than otherwise comparable firms or have even lower wages.[85] A particularly revealing study, based on a legal change in Germany that created a quasi-experiment by abolishing worker-elected directors in certain firms and permanently preserved their presence in others, found that board-level representation does not significantly raise wages.[86] More generally, in Germany—the country with perhaps the most robust board-level representation policies in the world, where workers comprise 50 percent of the advisory board members of large firms—wages have stagnated over recent decades, and inequality has risen. Relatively little has changed with Germany's board-level representation laws since 1994. In contrast, the decline of union density and the weakening of industry-wide bargaining in Germany over recent decades are key factors in the country's struggles with slow wage growth and rising inequality.[87]

Even the ability of board-level representation to improve democracy is somewhat limited. The point of board membership is to improve the democratic governance of the firm, and it will certainly help with that. Still, a more democratic firm structure may not be as pro-worker as some may hope. The background of worker board members suggests that they may take into account a greater variety of interests in their decisions than other board members, but worker board members must look out for the best interests of the firm—not the best interests of society—and thus their decisions may not be wildly different from traditional board members. The firm is still capitalistic, and the board members' role is still to maximize profits and the value of their firm.

Importantly, board-level representation does not do much to translate a more democratic firm structure into political power for workers. As a result, it would not do that much to make the country's political democracy responsive to the people. While worker board members would likely be able to limit a firm's anti-worker political activity, they would struggle to drive a positive political agenda for the country's workers. They could not create or fund a pro-worker organization, as the board members representing capital would simply veto them. Still, there is some modest evidence that democracy inside the firm—such as board-level representation provides—can improve the political capabilities of citizens and make them more active.[88] But this is a kind of individual power rather than the kind of organizational power necessary to engage in sustained political fights.

Another kind of bold change to labor law that some have discussed would automatically make all workers members of unions or at least pay dues—a kind of default unionization. These types of proposals would obviously increase union density and boost union finances. There is also a kind of logic to them: all workers benefit from unions, so all workers should join and pay. Still, these kinds of proposals seem outside of the realm of the possible, in that they have not been tried in the United States (and have barely been tried anywhere else). In addition, this kind of reform may not be desirable. It is unclear how workers would react to such a system that compels membership or dues regardless of whether a majority of workers at a worksite want a union. Further, compelling dues payment or membership from all workers could make unions less responsive and accountable to members.[89] Even if these kinds of reforms were possible and desirable, there would still be a need to create an attachment between workers and the union so that workers would be willing and able to take the kinds of powerful actions necessary to make collective bargaining and participatory democracy work properly. It is possible that this attachment could come solely from traditional organizing, but this seems unlikely given all the evidence presented in this book suggesting that additional incentives are necessary to encourage membership and create attachments for many workers. Thus, even with a kind of mandatory unionism, additional recruitment platforms and incentives for joining or participating would still have value in helping pull people in to union activities.

All told, increased organizing is necessary, as are policies to increase workers' rights. They are key parts of the new labor system, but they do not replace the need for strong incentives for membership and broad-based bargaining. There is little evidence that alternative ways to rebuild the labor movement would be as effective at increasing union membership and bargaining coverage, raising wages, and ensuring that government acts in accord with the will of the people.

Nonlabor Policies

Labor modernization is not the only possible way to address America's wage, inequality, and democracy challenges. There are many policies that have little to do with unions that could potentially help. Improving workers' skills, raising the minimum wage, promoting full employment, raising taxes on the wealthy, increasing benefits for poor and middle-class people, campaign finance, and voting reform are all worthy policies. Indeed, they are necessary to help address America's problems. Yet, as discussed at greater length below, these and other alternatives would not do enough on their own. What's more, stronger unions are often necessary to help these alternatives function properly.

Policies to increase education and skills could help many workers earn higher wages and could boost economic productivity. Still, even under a best-case scenario, a skills-only approach would do relatively little to raise wages in the short term. It would take years, perhaps more than a generation, to significantly increase the overall skill and education levels in the United States—which means that under this approach many Americans would likely suffer through wage stagnation for several more decades on top of the decades they have already suffered.

Worse, even over the long term, a skills-based approach is not likely to be particularly effective without a strong labor movement. There is little reason to expect that education would dramatically increase wages without some form of collective bargaining. While most workers would benefit from additional training, there are limits to how much additional training would be helpful. Workers with college degrees or more have fared relatively well compared with their non-college-graduate counterparts, but even college graduates have seen their wages grow slower than productivity over the past two decades.[90] Worse is that training does not always lead to a higher wage—and the returns on training vary widely, particularly by race, gender, and field of study.[91] Even more troubling is that a significant number of jobs simply do not require a college degree or equivalent workforce training. Estimates suggest that roughly one-third of college graduates are working in jobs that do not require a degree.[92]

In short, skills are no guarantee of higher wages or a good job. Not surprisingly, research finds that an education-only strategy won't make much of a dent in overall earnings inequality or do much to raise earnings.[93] Education will make workers more productive, but, without unions, it is employers and not workers who are most likely to seize those productivity gains.

A new labor system could mitigate the weaknesses of a skills-based approach by helping workers gain the power to negotiate for the higher wages their increased education would merit—as well as by ensuring that all work, no matter the level of education, is paid decently. A reformed labor system could also make skills-based strategies work better.[94] Labor unions could help improve the quality of the training, help workers complete the training, and ensure that it leads to a good job.[95] Unions could also ensure that all workers—but especially those with less skills—actually have access to training.[96] A new labor system would also help strengthen the incentives for workers to get additional training by ensuring that investments in human capital lead to higher wages and by setting pay scales that foster a clear connection between greater skills and greater pay. Finally, spending much more money on training likely requires workers to have the power to push companies and governments to make greater investments. The new labor system would give labor that necessary power.

Another potential alternative to the labor movement—increasing taxes on the wealthiest Americans to ensure that they pay their fair share and using the additional revenue to provide additional benefits for lower- and middle-class Americans—is unlikely to deliver as much as a new labor system. The United States clearly needs to raise taxes on the wealthy and boost social spending. Taxes on the wealthy are well below the level they were during the mid-twentieth century, and increasing taxes on rich people can help significantly reduce economic inequality.[97] The United States also provides much skimpier public benefits to its citizens than do most other advanced countries. Virtually all other countries provide universal health care and paid family leave, but the United States does not—and the list of the deficiencies of the US welfare state could go and on.

While higher taxes on the rich and improved government benefits are clearly necessary, they are likely to face significant difficulties in raising middle-class incomes, and they will not build a powerful citizens' organization that can correct the problems with America's democracy. They are part of the solution, but not the whole thing.

Even the most extreme version of this idea—a universal basic income providing a guaranteed level of income to all Americans, no matter their age, whether they are working or not—does not fully address the country's wage and inequality challenges, let alone do much for democracy. Some version of a basic income may very well be a good policy. It may be an important complement to many government antipoverty programs and may help provide a modest improvement in the standard of living for poor people and potentially even the middle class. Indeed, the Alaska Permanent Fund's annual payout (based on oil revenue) of a few hundred to a few thousand dollars to all residents seems to work quite well, though the results from Finland's recent experiment may not be as positive.[98] Still, relying on taxes and transfers to address wage stagnation and extreme inequality suffers from a number of problems.

First, the cost to significantly improve current living standards for most Americans without raising wages is quite large—perhaps impracticably so.[99] Consider, for example, the cost to the government of raising middle-class incomes at the pace of productivity, without wage increases. It would require spending more than twice as much every year as is now spent on Social Security to boost household market incomes for the bottom 80 percent of Americans by income to where they would be had they kept pace with productivity growth over the past twenty-five years.[100] Social Security is by far the largest existing social program; creating a new program roughly double its size may not be practical.

While smaller programs may be more affordable, they would do far less to raise incomes—either maintaining income growth at levels well below productivity growth or only raising incomes for a smaller group, such as the extremely poor.

There are questions about the desirability of creating such a big government program as guaranteed basic income and increasing taxes to the degree necessary to fund it. It would also likely create additional challenges that might not be recognized until the program is up and running. While the experience of Social Security indicates that it is possible for large social programs to work well in the United States, it took decades for Social Security to get to its currents size, and in its early years it provided very few benefits. Social Security did not instantly become the largest government social program but rather evolved over years and years.

Beyond such narrow practical concerns, receiving money or benefits from the government is not actually a wage. Some economists may argue that money is money, and thus a wage and a government benefit are functionally equivalent. At some level it is true that most income is dependent on the governmental structure that enables people to earn a living, and thus there may be less of a distinction than some people claim between a government handout and earned income. But people generally prefer to feel they have earned the money themselves. There is a dignity in earning a living wage that is hard to replace. Doing a job that is valued by society is not just a source of money but can also be a source of pride and placement in the community. A job with a decent wage is a tried and true way for people to feel they are included in society.

Further, the power for workers to earn a living wage creates a different kind of society than one where most people are dependent on government redistribution. It is hard to imagine that a society where some people are extremely wealthy and everyone else depends on a basic income from the government would be as democratic as America currently is, let alone have a true democracy. In this vein, some of the biggest proponents of universal basic income are the superrich of Silicon Valley, who presumably see giving people money less of a challenge to their power and wealth than actually ensuring that workers have adequate power to get paid fairly. Taken to the extreme, a universal basic income that replaces most wage income is akin to a modern version of a feudal society where the peasants depend on the whims of the rich and powerful lords who control government.

Still, for the sake of argument, let's assume a large basic income program could be the product of a real democratic society and create a high standard of living for most people. In this case, basic income might help foster a more harmonious society and the development of worthwhile values. But it also might not. Mass affluence without work would be a big social experiment. Small-scale experiments with modest sums of money suggest that things might work out fine, but there are many reasons to worry that a large and robust basic income program might not work out—from the deep-rooted work ethic to the failures of many other grand social experiments. At a minimum, a massive basic income program would be a big social risk. In contrast, building worker power is reliable and has proven successful at scale.

In total, these concerns suggest that a basic income would be best suited to reducing poverty and modestly improving the living standards of the middle class but less suited to reversing the hollowing out of the middle class or reviving democracy.

To some basic income proponents, these theoretical and practical concerns can be dismissed because, they argue, jobs are disappearing. In the future, there may not be enough work for people, and thus a universal basic income is required, so the story goes. Technology and artificial intelligence will create huge disruptions in the labor market. Indeed, some estimates for the number of jobs that could be lost to technology are huge. Still, a fair amount of research indicates that the disruptions are likely to be significant but more modest—with, for example, the OECD predicting that 10 percent of US jobs are at risk of automation over the next several decades.[101]

The most pessimistic visions of the future are based on the idea that new kinds of jobs will not be created or will be created very slowly, which is at best a kind of guesswork. So far, the experience every time a disruptive technology comes along suggests that it is likely that new jobs will be created. So too does the potential for humans to create new jobs. As long as there are human wants and needs, it is likely there will be work. Humans can invent work at a staggering rate. Decades ago, few could have predicted that there would be industries based around personal trainers, dog walkers, tech support, bloggers, and data storage salespeople. Of course it is possible that this time will be different and that computers will be better able to do everything humans can do, but most likely there will be new kinds of jobs invented as others are destroyed. Even though technology places a number of current jobs at risk, it does not mean there won't be any work in the future.[102]

Still, the basic income proponents are right that something is needed to minimize the human costs of rapid automation. Some relatively small version of a basic income may be an important part of this transition. But the need for additional policies to deal with disruptive technology is also clear. Workers will need protection from invasive technologies, and governments may need to make greater efforts to directly create jobs as well as to ensure that workers financially benefit from new technologies.

Though technological change creates opportunities to make work better, more productive, and higher-paying, technology also provides employers with significant new powers to monitor and control workers, deskill certain jobs, reduce pay, and generally make work worse. This dystopian situation may already exist for some workers. To take the example of just one company, a large retail firm patented in 2016 a cage to put warehouse employees in so they remain out of the way of robots, and the company patented augmented reality glasses in 2017 that can provide workers with real-time instructions on the lenses, as well as allow the company to "detect where a person is at all times and when they have stopped moving."[103] The firm's warehouse workers reportedly have peed in bottles to save time and avoid the company noticing them taking long breaks.[104] There are, of course, many other examples of companies using new technology to closely monitor their workers—for example, by using video cameras to surveil workers, software to monitor workers' facial expressions and tone of voice, and even injecting microchips inside workers' bodies.[105] A basic income does nothing to address the potential for technology to dehumanize workers and make jobs worse. In contrast, a modernized labor system would enable workers to negotiate with employers and governments about the use and control of technology. Workers need some power to ensure that they actually realize the potential benefits of technology, not just a basic income.

Technological change likely also increases the need for policies to create additional jobs. In the midst of the COVID-19 recession, the need for more jobs was clear, with unemployment in 2020 reaching levels higher than at any point since the Great Depression. Still, lack of jobs has been a long-standing problem. Over much of the past several decades the US economy has had a hard time creating enough jobs for most people who want them and has only rarely been at full employment.[106] Labor markets may have been quite tight in 2018 and 2019, but for much of recent decades they have not been. Additional disruption from automation is likely to make this employment problem worse.

Policies to create jobs and promote full employment, such as greater public investments in roads, bridges, child care, and education, or even a "green New Deal" or a jobs guarantee, where the federal government is the employer of last resort, would help to increase employment as well as raise wages and reduce inequality. Promoting full employment provides a great deal of help for those who would otherwise have been unemployed and also benefits those who are already employed. When labor markets are tight and employers have to compete for workers, pay generally increases for most workers. During the late 1990s, for example, when labor markets were very tight, the incomes of high-, middle- and low-income workers increased relatively rapidly and at similar rates. Tight labor markets also make it easier for workers to assert their rights, as the fear of getting fired is lessened when other jobs are available.

Still, full employment policies have clear limitations. While full employment policies are not expected to do much to help promote the democratic responsiveness of government, they can even struggle to raise wages. Tight labor markets provide the most benefits for workers who are willing and able to shop for a new employer. But not every worker wants to threaten to quit in order to receive a pay raise, and not every employer preemptively raises wages to avoid losing employees. Further, some employers dominate local labor markets with monopsony power and limit labor market competition and thus suppress wage levels.

Another problem for full employment policies is that there are signs that a tight labor market may no longer put as much pressure on wages as it used to— likely because the power of workers has been so diminished over recent decades. During 2017, the unemployment rate in the United States was about as low as it had been in over 50 years, yet wages remained stagnant, barely increasing much faster than inflation. It is true that the unemployment rate is not the ideal indicator of labor market tightness, because there are many people who have given up looking for work and are not counted in this measure. It is also possible that wages could increase if labor markets reach an extremely tight level. Indeed, in 2018 and 2019 the unemployment rate continued to fall, and growth for median wages did pick up—but to well below the levels of the late 1990s.[107]

The fact that wages did not rise rapidly during periods of record low unemployment suggests that full employment policies are not enough. So does the fact that wages for men without college educations have actually decreased since the early 1970s—in spite of several periods of very tight labor markets.[108] In addition, evidence from other countries also suggests that tight labor markets may do less for wages than they used to. Over recent years, Canada, Britain, and Australia have all had slow wage growth during periods of relatively low unemployment rates.[109]

Importantly, not only can policies to support full employment faces challenges during good economic times, they will also have an especially hard time raising wages when the underlying private-sector economy remains below full employment. During a period of weak economic growth, the wage for government-supported employment will become the floor that private employers need only match. This is particularly true for the most robust full employment policy—a jobs guarantee, where the number of government-created jobs will increase dramatically during economic downturns.[110] Thus, when the underlying economy is not running at full blast, full employment policies will largely serve to raise wages to the governmental minimum.

A new labor system could compensate for some of the weaknesses of full employment policies and make the policy work better. Unions and collective bargaining can help give power to workers in the democratic process as well as raise wages when the private-sector economy is not extremely tight. Collective bargaining also ensures that when private-sector labor markets are tight, this tightness translates more evenly and directly to real workplace improvements. (Elements of the new labor system, such as prevailing wage-style extension, could be part of any jobs program and provide a kickstart toward full implementation.)

The list of potential alternatives goes on, but they are incomplete solutions and would work better with stronger unions. Reforming trade policy to benefit workers at least as much as multinational companies would help, especially over the long term. But it would have less short-term impact on wages because decisions to make new investments in factories take years to have an effect on labor markets. In addition, the majority of the workforce works in services that are untraded, which means that the wages of most workers are not directly affected by trade.[111]

While raising the minimum wage would help millions of low-income workers, a single minimum wage delivers far more for those at the bottom of the wage distribution than it does for those toward the middle. Even a minimum wage of $15 per hour would put relatively little pressure on the wages of workers with average or slightly above average earnings.[112] The minimum wage needs to be increased, but the new labor system would do more for more workers and complement a higher minimum wage. Workers' boards would be especially useful for workers that would not be impacted much by even a $15 standard. As the economist Arindrajit Dube argues, "wage boards are much better positioned to deliver gains to middle-wage jobs than a single minimum pay standard." His rough modeling of wage boards that produce binding standards for about 30 percent of the workforce suggests that such a policy would increase wages for workers whose wages are at the twentieth percentile by 19 percent, by 15 percent for workers at the fortieth percentile, and by 12 percent for workers at the sixtieth percentile.[113] And, of course, the dramatic increase in collective bargaining under the new system would also raise wages for middle- and upper-middle-income earners.

Further, a high minimum wage is unlikely to work very well without stronger unions, nor would workers' boards. Without strong labor unions, there may not be sufficient political pressure to keep raising standards, and thus the floor might stagnate over time. And, critically, without strong labor unions to enforce minimum standards, it is likely that many, if not most, low-wage employers would violate the law, and thus many workers would not actually receive a legally required high minimum wage.

Wage theft is already rampant in America. It is estimated that workers currently lose over $15 billion per year from minimum wage violations.[114] These violations are not just from small, fly-by-night operations but also from many of the largest companies in the country, indicating just how pervasive wage theft is.[115] Increasing minimum wage levels would only increase the incentive to cheat. Not only does the current American experience suggest that a higher minimum wage would face significant enforcement challenges, so too does the evidence from Canada, Britain, and especially Australia—which has one of highest minimum wages in the world but weak unions and significant problems with wage theft, as discussed in the preceding chapter. Government enforcement agencies are woefully understaffed, and even a significant increase in funding would not be adequate.[116] No amount of government inspectors will ever be able to ensure compliance in every workplace or make workers understand the law and feel comfortable seeking its enforcement. In contrast, strong workplace-based organizations can effectively monitor and police minimum standards and ensure that workers are able to come forward and assert their rights.[117] Which means that in order for a high minimum wage to be most effective at raising wages, unions need to be strengthened.

Policies to promote worker ownership and broad-based profit sharing tend to increase company productivity and are associated with higher total compensation for workers.[118] But significantly expanding these policies—by requiring companies to provide profit sharing to all workers or giving large tax subsidies to companies that do—is not likely to work very well. These kinds of policies would likely cause employers to substitute profit sharing for wages. Under this scenario, total compensation would remain the same—with wages going down and profit sharing or ownership going up. Companies would also likely increasingly contract out work to avoid increasing total compensation. (Similarly, proposals to require or incentivize companies to increase employee wages or pay a set share of profits in compensation would likely encourage companies to shift expenditures around—reclassifying profits as something else and calling employees independent contractors of another company.)

If workers do not have the power to bargain over their total compensation package, forcing companies to provide workers with profit sharing or ownership (or a set percentage of profits) would not necessarily significantly increase compensation for most workers. Instead, it would largely change how workers are paid. Moreover, profit sharing and worker ownership produce the best results for workers and managers when supplemented by high wages and empowerment of workers.[119] That is why profit sharing and ownership should be a subject for collective bargaining rather than a stand-alone solution to the wage challenge. Indeed, bargaining for profit sharing and ownership is likely to be especially important to ensure that workers— not just executives and shareholders— benefit from new job-displacing technologies.

A related set of policies would give workers greater power over the capital they already own—such as in their pensions and 401(k)s—so that it can be managed and invested in a way that promotes good jobs. There is significant potential in this approach. The scale of worker assets is relatively large—public- and private-sector pensions in the United States have over $22 trillion in assets—and smaller-scale experiments by a few pension funds to invest in projects that benefit workers have proven successful at making a good return while creating good union jobs.[120]

Still, there are limits to this strategy, and it will not work very well without strong unions. The primary purpose of this money currently is to provide a secure retirement, rather than to promote good jobs. Even under proposals that would loosen the obligation for retirement funds to put retiree welfare first, this money would still need to provide for workers' retirement, suggesting that the rate of return of potential investments is likely to limit the fund's pro-worker commitment. Further, new money will need to flow into these funds—because much of it will need to be paid out to support current retirees. This additional money will need to come from somewhere. The only real way for workers to gain additional capital is to bargain for it—a government mandate would reduce workers' wages because capital contributions would substitute for wage increases. Further, managing the capital for the benefit of workers would take an organization with a mission to promote workers' interests and expertise in overseeing large pools of money—basically a union. Which is why capital-focused strategies to create good jobs complement strong unions. In a new system, capital strategies could even help fund unions—in a Ghent-like policy—where unions could charge a small fee for overseeing pools of capital in the interests of workers and use their fund management to access and recruit members.

Strengthening the rights of immigrant workers and providing a pathway to citizenship would likely have a modest but meaningful impact on the wages of low-income workers. Although Donald Trump and others blame immigrants for stagnant wages, most research suggests that, in general, immigrants complement US-born workers rather than replace them and thus do not impact wage levels significantly.[121] Even negative estimates suggest that immigration is at most a small part of the wage and employment problem, particularly for middle-income workers. Much of the negative impact immigrants can have on wages is largely due to their lack of legal rights, which weakens the floor, particularly for low-wage workers.[122]

Stronger antitrust enforcement to limit the ability of a few employers to dominate a labor market would help raise workers' wages, since workers would have greater ability to move between employers and force employers to compete for their skills. Antitrust enforcement can also limit the political power of the largest corporations by breaking them into smaller pieces. Improved antitrust enforcement would be an absolutely vital change.[123] Indeed, some research suggests that the growing domination of a few large employers in individual labor markets could be a significant reason why wages are stagnant.[124] Yet breaking up large companies and increased antitrust enforcement may have only a relatively modest impact on wages and a limited effect on democracy. This is not just because increased firm concentration explains only a very small percentage of the gap between pay and productivity since 1979, as some research suggests, but also because labor unions are key in translating the potential for higher wages into reality.[125] Indeed, research finds that firms in uncompetitive labor markets have a much easier time restraining wages when unions are weak.[126]

Wages are unlikely to rapidly increase in a world where workers are dealing with slightly smaller companies facing slightly more competition. And politicians will not suddenly listen to workers instead of companies if firms get a bit smaller. Antitrust legislation and similar policies still leave corporations with far more power than workers in the economy and in democracy.[127] Workers need to be able to bargain for higher wages, and they need to be organized so that politicians are responsive. Corporations may need to be cut down to size, but workers also need to be built up.

A combination of all of these nonlabor policies would certainly make a big difference in the US economy and would raise incomes and reduce economic inequality. But the limits of each of the policies suggests that they would not be sufficient, even in combination. Though a quantification of this claim is perhaps not possible, the evidence from abroad also supports the claim that even a combination of nonlabor policies would not be adequate. While neither Canada nor Australia nor Britain has completely implemented all of the types of policies described previously, each has a much more robust safety net than the United States and has adopted critical elements of these policies. Economic inequality, particularly in Canada and Australia, is much lower than in the United States. But in all of these countries wages are still stagnant for many workers and economic inequality rising rapidly, as discussed in chapter 4.

Put bluntly, alternative policies to raise wages for workers do not really obviate the need for labor unions. Rather, unions minimize the weaknesses of these alternatives and help them work better. Moreover, workers engaged in the collective bargaining process gain agency and organization that can provide the support necessary for these policies to be enacted. Indeed, strong labor unions providing political muscle and organizing public support are almost certainly necessary to sustain (over any length of time) policies promoting full employment, a higher minimum wage, robust training, and a more generous safety net. A sudden surge of political activity could compel politicians to enact some of these policies, but power of strong worker organizations is needed to ensure that a broad set of pro-worker policies are enacted, properly implemented, funded, and enforced.

Similarly, strengthening America's democracy so that government takes more direction from the interests of regular citizens will also require a stronger labor movement. Labor is by no means the only pro-democracy policy necessary. Improvements in campaign finance and voting policies are clearly needed too. But these kinds of democratic reforms would be more likely to achieve their goals if they were complemented by stronger unions and a new labor system.

Healthy democracies generally do not give the wealthy so many ways to spend their money to influence politics, nor do they make voting as difficult or as biased against certain groups of people as the current US political system does. Clearly, reforms will need to reduce the influence of the wealthy—including increased disclosure of contributions, amplification of small contributions, and limits or outright bans on some contributions. Democratic reforms will also need to make it easier and fairer for citizens to participate in the political process by getting rid of restrictive voter identification laws that systematically discriminate against people of color and the young, by making voter registration easier or automatic, and by limiting gerrymandering. Other more dramatic changes may even be necessary, such as ending the Senate filibuster, fixing the unrepresentative electoral college, and even checking an increasingly partisan Supreme Court.

Changing the formal rules of the game would make US elections fairer and thus make it more likely that the government would respond in line with the views and wishes of its citizens. But these kinds of changes have clear limitations, since a fairer system does not automatically translate into the will of the people being carried out.

Campaign finance and voting reforms only address a small part of the process of converting the public's will into policy. There are many elements of the election and governing process that would not be particularly affected by these kinds of changes. Among the many factors before an election even happens include who chooses to run for office, what issues they campaign on, what issues the media choose to focus on, and what issues people hear about and understand. Then there is the question of whether people are able to and chose to vote. The period after the election is just as important or even more so. There are many question to be answered during governing. What policies will elected officials choose to prioritize? Will they follow through on their promises? What vested interests will support or oppose their efforts? What issues will the media discuss? What issues will resonate with the public? Will the public take action to support or oppose a governmental policy? Will the policy be implemented, funded, and enforced?

In order to have a fair shot at influencing each of these stages, the public needs to be organized, engaged, and have an advocate on the inside working for their interests. The wealthy and the powerful certainly do.

At some level, democracy is a contest between people and money. And if the people are not organized, money will always win. This is true even if policies are enacted to limit the influence of money. If the rich cannot give directly to candidates, they will just do more indirect giving. They will increasingly coerce their workers' political activities, spend even more on issue ads and lobbyists, buy more newspapers, TV stations and internet companies, buy additional centers at universities and think tanks, offer more jobs to their former regulators, pay for increasingly extravagant vacations for judges, and hire additional lawyers to contest every policy they do not like. They will use the political structures that are open to them, and they will try even more to frame and limit debates, not just engage in the day-to-day political battles.[128]

The wealthy can have some degree of influence on their own because they can pay legions to do their bidding. But the public needs to be organized to have an impact on who runs for office, what issues candidates focus on during the election and in office, and how the laws are actually implemented and enforced. Most people cannot become super-citizens tracking every governmental action, and they do not want to.[129] Even if they did, they would not have much influence doing so on their own. Most people want and need an organization to help mobilize them at key times and to represent their interests in behind-the-scenes negotiations.

Put differently, democracy has an organization and representation problem. Democracy needs all interests to be effectively organized and represented, but without a strong labor movement, workers are likely to be severely underorganized and underrepresented. While it is theoretically possible that many kinds of groups could organize the public around a broad set of economic and democratic issues, experience has shown that labor is the only organization with the scale and the mission to do so. Labor cannot be the only group organizing and involving citizens in the democratic process and fighting for their interests behind the scenes—other organizations like the PTA, Shriners, Sierra Club, and American Legion matter too. But labor is by far the most important. A healthy civil society is necessary for democracy to work properly, and labor unions are a critical part of civil society. Not surprisingly, research shows that strong unions make government more transparent, effective, and responsive to citizens.[130]

There is also an even deeper problem limiting the effectiveness of democratic reforms: they do little to strengthen the middle class and reduce extreme economic inequality. To be truly effective, democratic reforms need to reduce extreme economic inequality. The more economically unequal a society is, the more the rich will have the ability and incentives to rig the system. Campaign finance and voting reforms can make the rules of the game fairer, but they have a hard time making the power of the players more equal.

At a more abstract level, labor is an essential part of the checks and balances that allow capitalistic democratic governments to function properly. Labor unions can limit the extremes of capitalism from pushing democratic capitalistic systems toward authoritarian rule. And they can limit governments from intruding so much in private business that the system becomes communistic or otherwise destroys the freedoms offered by capitalism. Labor has different interests and spheres of influence than does government or business and can prevent either one from gaining too much power.

A Practical Solution

The new labor system is practical and its implementation challenges manageable, as both US history and international experiences suggest. It is possible to make reasonable determinations for the boundaries of various sectors and occupations. Unions can adapt their structures to the new system, and the new system will work even if unions do so imperfectly. There is little need to worry about significant economic harm in the short run from unions gaining too much power under the new system, and in the long run there is time and opportunity to tweak the system to address this possibility.

Many other changes are needed to address America's wage, inequality, and democracy problems. To rebuild the middle class, ensure stable, long-term wage increases for the vast majority of the population, and make democracy responsive to the will of the people will require that workers increasingly take direct action, as well as a number of policy reforms—including improved skills training, a higher minimum wage, more progressive taxation, and fairer campaign finance and voter registration. But addressing America's challenges also requires a new labor system.

The new labor system would do more than any one of the alternatives. It would increase union density and coverage far more than would relying solely on increased organizing and conventional reforms, such as more robust penalties on employers. The new labor system would also likely do far more to raise wages, reduce economic inequality, and improve the quality of American democracy than nonunion alternatives. Reforms like a higher minimum wage and progressive taxation are necessary but on their own would be very unlikely to achieve anywhere near the impact a new labor system would. Even a combination of alternatives would struggle to ensure, for example, that compensation grows in line with productivity and that voter turnout reaches and stays at historic levels, as would be likely with the new labor system.

The new labor system would also complement other policies and help address their weaknesses. Stronger unions operating under a new labor system would help ensure that workforce training is of high quality and leads to a good job, increase compliance with the minimum wage and other laws, enable workers to more effectively operate on the boards of corporations, and ensure that democratic procedural reforms actually translate into the policy preferences of the public being enacted. Simply put, the new labor system plays a critical role in addressing America's challenges, and cannot be substituted

Moving beyond the kinds of social democratic reforms discussed in this chapter would not solve America's problems. Capitalism's flaws are the source of America's wage stagnation, extreme inequality, and corrupted democracy, but doing away with capitalism would lead to even worse problems. It would inevitably lead to severe restrictions on economic and political freedoms that are incompatible with democracy, as every example that has been tried from the Soviet Union to Cuba shows. Communism is also not very economically efficient, as it has a hard time spurring long-run productivity increases because it lacks the necessary individual incentives and freedoms. Doing away with democracy but keeping capitalism, as is the current model in places like China and Russia, is not appealing either. Capitalism promotes some kinds of individual freedoms that seemingly are in conflict with repressive regimes, though capitalism and political authoritarianism may prove to be compatible over the long run as they share elements of top-down control.[131] But even if capitalism and authoritarianism are compatible, that is a model that few Americans would aspire to.

The answer to America's challenges is to more democratically manage capitalism, and that requires a new labor system.

CREATING THE NEW SYSTEM

A new labor system would help address America's economic and political challenges, is feasible to implement, and would likely work better than alternative policies. Still, there is the matter of enacting the new labor system into law. This is a daunting task.

Passing any kind of labor law reform, let alone a significant overhaul, is quite difficult. The new labor system poses a direct challenge to rich and powerful individuals and corporations, people and institutions that in most circumstances have proven able to block legislation they do not like. Which is why a rare confluence of events is required to make such bold change possible. The task is massive and could take many years, if it ever happens, but there is a path forward.

A close look at the politics of the National Labor Relations Act in 1935 and recent state and local labor modernization efforts as well as insights from political science research indicate that several factors will help determine whether a new labor policy could become law. First and most obviously, there will need to be a strong push from below. Workers and the public will need to push through grassroots activities, and they will also need to elect a majority of politicians willing to vote for pro-union policy. Second, a few elected officials and organizations will need to lead and coordinate the effort. The new labor system will need political champions to drive the legislation and navigate challenges that the new labor system would face on the path to enactment. Third, and most importantly, the intellectual climate will need to shift so that a significant percentage of policy elites come to think of a new labor system as a necessary policy whose time has come. Enough elected officials and other political insiders will need to believe that a new labor system is critical to raising wages, reducing inequality, and making democracy more responsive to the people and would help reduce pay and wealth gaps across race and gender and could even increase societal trust. They will also need to think the policy is workable. In short, they will need to absorb the message of this book.

Grassroots pressure and large electoral majorities combined with organizational muscle and political champions might be enough for many types of issues to succeed, but labor modernization requires far more. Bold changes that overturn old ways of doing things and challenge powerful vested interests require that enough policy makers support the ideas behind the change.[1] The policy needs to be viewed as right for the times—a credible solution to the problem as well as ready to be acted on. Which means that it needs to become something like conventional wisdom among a critical mass of policy elites that a new labor system is necessary to solve America's economic and political challenges.

The path to gaining an electoral majority, institutional support, and a ripe intellectual climate is rough. But signs indicate that the way is not totally blocked. A pro-union electoral majority could exist in the near future, as the public is as supportive of unions as they have been in quite some time, and grassroots energy is growing. Policy champions could emerge as some key union and nonunion worker organizations have begun working on reform policies. Critically, the framing of debate is becoming more favorable to a new labor policy as the intellectual environment is shifting away from a rigid free-market orthodoxy and has become more open to structural economic changes. A small but growing group of academics, advocates, and politicians has begun to make the case for bold labor law changes, and their efforts appear to be gaining traction. Indeed, support for broad-based bargaining has become almost commonplace among prominent Democratic politicians.

The rest of this chapter discusses in greater depth the politics of enacting a new labor system. It begins by exploring whether there might be other ways that the new labor policy could be enacted—such as by drawing support from some businesses. The chapter then teases out the importance of grassroots energy, political majorities, legislative champions, and the intellectual climate by examining state and local labor reform efforts and the passage of the NLRA. The discussion highlights the political difficulties a new labor system faces as well as the potential that favorable factors could align and enable the new labor system to become law. While passage may be a longshot, success rests heavily on enough people coming to accept the premise of this book—that a new labor system could help successfully address critical challenges in America.

.

Other Possible Paths

Before considering the alignment of electoral supermajorities, political champions, and a favorable climate, it is worth exploring other possible ways forward.

Support from business would certainly be helpful. Indeed, very little US legislation has passed in the face of unified business opposition. Big policy changes,
from Social Security to the Affordable Care Act, usually have had some level
of public or private support from a few key business leaders, however, support
from major employers for a new labor system is very unlikely because it would
fundamentally shift power relations between workers and business. But on occasion unified business opposition can be overcome. The NLRA became law despite
virtually unanimous business opposition, and recent state and local labor efforts
passed despite little if any support from business.[2]

Still, the possibility of business support is worth discussing, given its out-
sized political importance. The most likely possibility for some level of support
is that a handful of progressive business leaders offer support, as happened in
some state and local efforts. For example, Seattle billionaire entrepreneur Nick
Hanauer has been a strong supporter of the creation of portable benefits funds,
such as those created by the city's domestic worker bill.[3] In this scenario, support
would most likely come from business leaders whose business would not be particularly affected by the new labor policy. It is even possible that directly affected
businesses could support industry-wide wage setting because it would limit the
ability of competitors to undercut them. Indeed, on a few occasions in US history
businesses have supported industry-wide standards in their sector.[4] And in other
countries employers are often important supporters of multi-employer bargaining systems.[5]

Another possibility is that some business leaders feel that change is inevitable
and seek to shape labor reform to their liking as much as possible, calculating that
other possible changes are worse. A version of this was suggested as a possibility in New York during the wage board process. Though the fast food industry
strongly opposed the wage board and rejected all calls for a $15 minimum hourly
wage, some people in the industry conceded that a smaller wage increase would
be acceptable and showed some willingness to compromise, though ultimately
no comprise was found.[6]

More generally, the fear of radical and disruptive change could prompt some
in the business community to think that limited labor reform would be acceptable. With a new labor system, business would still have profits, their productivity
would likely increase, and CEOs could still get quite rich, in a way that might not
be possible if, for example, policy makers were to ban high CEO pay or tax the rich
at near 100 percent levels.[7] Similarly, communism in the mid-twentieth century

is thought to have encouraged US business and political leaders to smooth out capitalism's rough edges.

Business acceptance of labor reform because of fears of the alternatives is not very likely. Business did not support the National Labor Relations Act, even in the face of political events that could have made them fearful enough to do so: the US economy was in shambles, Senator Huey Long was pushing a plan to "Share Our Wealth" that would have capped incomes and wealth and redistributed to the poor, popular radio host Charles Coughlin encouraged nationalization of major industries, and fascism was rising in Europe.[8] In recent years, major US businesses have supported several antidemocratic efforts in states in order to maintain favorable policies.[9] And, at the extreme, when other countries, such as Germany and Italy, went through particularly disruptive and turbulent economic and political periods, many businesses chose to side with fascists to avoid having to deal with labor.[10]

A related but also unlikely possibility is that Republican Party leadership changes its attitude about labor unions and realizes that a new labor system is actually a conservative way to address wage stagnation, extreme inequality, and the failings of US democracy. Unions are in large part a private solution to market and political regulation. They are not big government. And sectoral bargaining fosters the kind of high-road innovation conservatives claim to revere. Even though elected Republican Party leaders over recent decades have almost uniformly sought to weaken unions, not so long ago a number of Republican leaders supported and worked closely with labor unions.[11] Republican voters are not nearly as hostile to unions as the party is, and some are quite supportive. Still, such an outcome is probably a fantasy in the near term given the grip that free-market ideology has on Republican Party leadership, the leadership's emphasis on maintaining political control, the influence of major campaign contributors, and the party's choice to seek racial division rather than financial improvements for workers.

Favorable Factors

While significant support from the Republican Party or business for a new labor system seems unlikely, there are indications that these political hurdles can be overcome by grassroots efforts, large electoral majorities, political champions, and a favorable intellectual environment—all of which are trending in the right direction.

In the years prior to the passage of the NLRA, there was a sharp increase in worker protests and strike activity that helped put labor issues on the agenda.[12] Similarly, the Fight for $15 strikes that began in the fast food industry helped lead to New York State's decision to empanel a wage board and ultimately raise the minimum. Disruptions to the normal course of business and politics get attention. These brave acts carried real risks for workers, but they were essential in forcing politicians to address labor concerns.

It is hard to know whether the country currently has had enough worker disruptions to put labor at the top of the agenda, though it probably has not. Still, there has been a sharp increase in worker protests in recent years. Indeed, in 2018, more workers went on strike than had in three decades and 2019 saw nearly as many strikes.[13] If this momentum continues to build, labor policy could move up the agenda.

In addition, when the NLRA became law, there were massive pro-labor majorities in Congress, made up mostly of Democrats but a few Republicans as well, and a supportive president.[14] Similarly, most state reforms have come from the likes of New York, California, and Washington, where pro-labor legislators have strong majorities. This indicates what most people with even passing knowledge of US politics already know: a strong majority of pro-labor elected officials is a necessary precondition for passing policies to reform the labor system. (There is currently far more interest in considering these ideas in the Democratic Party than in the Republican Party.) This is especially true if filibuster remains an option in the Senate. But even if it is eliminated, something like a supermajority of pro-union elected officials is still likely required for pro-worker labor legislation to pass both houses of Congress. Any legislator seen as a decisive vote for labor would become a major target for business, and with all their resources they may be able to pick off a few legislators—which is why a large majority of supporters is required.

In order for such an electoral wave to happen, citizens in most of the country—not just those in liberal areas—would need to vote for pro-union policy makers. There is at least some evidence that this is possible, as support for labor is relatively broad and likely increasing.

Nationwide polls show that over 60 percent of the public supports labor unions, which is about as high as public support has been in many decades.[15] Support is likely to continue growing since young adults are the most supportive of unions.[16] Indeed, Millennials—most of today's young adults—are very progressive in their economic views and frequently take action to advance their views.[17]

In addition, the very limited publicly available polling on bold labor policy reform indicates strong public support. A survey designed to test whether workers would join and financially support various types of unions and workers organizations found that roughly 70 percent of workers would join a union that provides benefits and broad-based bargaining. This support was higher than for any other type of worker organization tested.[18] These results should be taken with some skepticism because the proposals were not explained in detail, nor were proposals critiqued, but the fact that the types of proposals described in this book were the most popular is noteworthy. Two separate polls with questions on wage boards found that nearly three-quarters of likely voters support the policy, including the majority of Republicans.[19] The wage board questions may overstate support because of the favorable way they frame the policy and do not discuss opposing arguments. Still, the results are worth noting because they also suggest the potential for strong public support, especially because they likely reflect a type of gut-level response to bold labor reforms, as there had been little public discussion of wage boards or other significant bargaining reforms at the times of the surveys, and the polls gave limited information about the reform.

More importantly, recent labor actions and policy debates indicate widespread support for reform, even in conservative areas. The 2018 teacher strikes in Republican-leaning states like West Virginia, Oklahoma, and Arizona drew broad public support.[20] Further, when citizens have had a chance to directly vote on union policy, the public has backed labor, even though most votes took place in relatively conservative states. To be sure, not every labor-related issue before the general public has resulted in victory for unions, but the losses usually involved a complicating factor that made the public's choice not solely about the labor policy. In 2012, the attempt to recall Wisconsin governor Scott Walker for his antiunion policies failed, but a recall is quite different from a direct vote on his labor program. Similarly, the 2012 Michigan ballot initiative to end right to work failed in part because it required changing a state constitution, something voters are reluctant to do for a general policy matter.[21] But when voters have been able to make a clear and direct choice about labor union policy, they have favored labor. For example, Ohio voters passed a 2011 initiative with over 60 percent in support of overturning Republican legislation to restrict collective bargaining for public-sector workers.[22] In 2018, voters in Missouri overturned the state's right-to-work law by a margin of almost two to one, with more people voting on that ballot initiative than on the state's US senate race, indicating that many people cared strongly about labor issues.[23] Because public-sector bargaining and right to work are two of the least popular labor union issues to debate, these victories may even understate the degree of support for unions in these more conservative states.

While a massive electoral shift is vital to the success of any reform effort, a big wave is necessary but insufficient. Policies need champions and enough organizational muscle behind them to succeed. Senator Robert Wagner's leadership and passion were critical for passage of the NLRA in 1935. Support from the American Federation of Labor was also helpful for the NLRA's passage, even if it was not an overwhelming level of support. Though the AFL worried that unions would need to give up some traditional organizing tactics in exchange for government protections, and some unions within the federation were engaged in significant jurisdictional fights, the AFL provided support for the NLRA and kept pressure on elected officials who feared electoral consequences if they did not support the bill.[24]

Similarly, in recent years labor innovations have not happened in every left-leaning city and state but rather have occurred in places where friendly legislators and unions and other worker organizations have pushed to make them happen. A handful of local unions in Washington, California, and New York have been particularly keen on driving forward new models of organizing and bargaining, far more so than most other unions.[25] And a few nonunion worker organizations have also been strong supporters of moving beyond the current model—particularly those representing domestic workers.

This suggests that legislative champions and a sufficient level of support from unions and worker organizations are necessary to drive a new labor policy forward. While not every union and worker organization needs to make the policy their top priority, enough need to do so. Meanwhile, the other unions need to be generally supportive or at least not strongly opposed.

As this book is being written, not enough national union leaders have championed large-scale labor reform to help drive the policy. Even though the current system is failing, unions still have millions of members and a vested interest in the status quo. Further, some labor leaders still think their unions can be resurrected through increased organizing or only modest changes in labor law. Other unions remain ideologically committed to the idea that they should only engage in "independent" bargaining based solely on their economic power and are resistant to working more closely with government. One of the strengths—and weaknesses—of American unions is that it takes a significant push for them to change. The benefit of this is that they make a stable partner for workers, business, and governments to collaborate with over the long haul and are not easily swayed to take destructive, radical, short-sighted positions. The downside is that unions are not always very nimble and can struggle to break from old ways of doing things. Change is not easy, but unions certainly can change, as their record on race and gender attests.

While not many unions have actively supported creating a new labor system, there are signs of possible change. Service Employees International Union (SEIU) president Mary Kay Henry has been a vocal leader for major labor law reforms to promote broader-based bargaining, and Communications Workers of America (CWA) president Chris Shelton has spoken out in favor of sectoral bargaining.[26] The AFL-CIO has not publicly supported the kinds of reforms in this book, but Richard Trumka, the organization's president, gave a speech in 2017 indicating the need for "bold" reforms that enable all workers, "whether union or not yet union," to collectively bargain, which at least hints that support is possible.[27] Former union presidents have more freedom to express their true feelings, and some, including the UAW's Bob King, have expressed support for sectoral bargaining. Larry Cohen, former president of the CWA, is a vocal champion.[28]

Outside of traditional unions, the National Domestic Workers Alliance—an alliance of sixty affiliate worker organizations—has been a leading voice for new kinds of labor policy. In December 2018, the alliance announced that it was pushing federal legislation to ensure that domestic workers have all the rights other workers do, as well as to create a way to collectively bargain and recruit members—which would occur through a wage board, portable benefits fund, and enforcement, akin to the Seattle domestic worker model.[29] In short, while currently the level of organizational support for a new labor system is relatively modest, it could evolve so that there are more legislative and organizational champions.

The most important factor for determining the success or failure of labor system modernization is likely the idea environment. While measuring the level of intellectual support for an idea is virtually impossible, it is clear that the idea environment was critical in the success of the National Labor Relations Act. In the years prior to the passage of the NLRA in 1935, free-market ideas had been significantly discredited and were losing support because they were unable to do anything about the persistently high unemployment rates in the wake of the Great Depression. This helped make it possible for unions to increasingly be seen as part of the solution to the country's problems. Unions were seen as vital to the economic recovery because they helped increase consumers' purchasing power and were essential to promoting "industrial democracy." Critically, there was also significant labor unrest at the time, with many strikes, which helped create a climate where unions could become viewed as a safe and sensible way to deal with worker grievances.[30]

In contrast, even very modest labor law reforms failed when free-market ideas dominated. At points in the 1970s, 1990s, and 2000s, for example, efforts to ban employers from permanently replacing striking workers or enable "card check" sign-up failed, even though unions had been able to push legislation onto the agenda and though Democrats had a filibuster-proof majority in the Senate and control of all branches of government. Failure in these cases can be blamed on many factors—from the personalities of individual senators to political tactics. But, during the period of these failures, support for "free-market" ideas was rising or well-established, and labor was viewed as just another interest group that was not particularly important to solving national problems.

That prevailing ideas matter—not just power or fear of disruption—can also been seen in a closer look at labor unrest during the passage of the NLRA. Labor unrest was critical to helping put labor issues higher on the political agenda. Still, this probably was not enough on its own to ensure passage.[31] At the peak of strike activity in 1934, Congress passed a very tame resolution rather than the more substantive NLRA. In the months before the NLRA passed in July 1935, strikes dropped significantly, with the number of worker days lost to strikes falling by roughly a third from the prior year.[32]

There are also signs that the intellectual environment was supportive in some of the more recent state and local campaigns. The idea of unions and worker organizations playing a key role in enforcement, for example, has been receiving a growing number of citations in academic and policy publications. The work of professors Janice Fine and Jennifer Gordon has helped push the credibility of the idea.[33] In Seattle, where there has been the most labor reform activity, David Rolf, the former president of SEIU local 775, worked to foster a favorable intellectual climate, doing things like hosting discussions about the need for union innovation, bringing in outside experts to discuss the issues, and writing a book and several policy papers on the subject.[34] Jenny Durkan, the mayor of Seattle, viewed the groundbreaking domestic worker bill as part of the larger project of rebuilding the labor system and thus of fixing the country. As Durkan stated when she was campaigning for office:

> I have made clear that protecting the right of workers to form unions and collectively-bargain is only the baseline. In this changing economy, particularly in the growing "gig" economy, we must find new ways to protect workers and their futures. We must not just be thinking about how we provide wages and benefits today in a fluid marketplace, we must be thinking about what those workers and their families will have decades from now. Working with labor, business, community leaders and experts, I will propose policies that make Seattle a leading laboratory of democracy where new forms of worker organization are explored and prototyped.[35]

The current intellectual environment across the country is not as favorable for labor reform as it is in the progressive cities and states that are leading the way, and nowhere near as favorable as it was during the 1930s when the NLRA passed. But there are indications that the idea of creating a new labor system could ripen. Free-market ideology is losing support, politicians have become more willing to speak positively about labor unions, and labor reform is increasingly building a track record and being discussed in policy circles.

Academic debate about creating a new type of labor system is picking up steam. Law scholars such as Matt Dimick, Kate Andrias, and Brishen Rogers have been writing about bold legal changes that could create sectoral bargaining as well as stronger incentives for membership.[36] In contrast, the vast majority of prior research on labor law reform focused on tweaking extant law. Important progressive think tanks such as the Center for American Progress and the Roosevelt Institute have been promoting bold ideas for labor reform for several years.[37] In 2018, Harvard University's Labor and Worklife Program began a nearly two-year "Clean Slate" process to consider bold changes to labor law involving multiple stakeholders.[38] The final report echoed many of the themes of this book and included dozens of recommendations, most notably proposals for broad-based bargaining.[39] In 2019, the Albert Shanker Institute, a union-affiliated think tank, held a large public conference on sectoral bargaining.[40]

Support for extreme free-market ideas among the public and especially policy elites seems to be in decline. The financial crisis and recession in 2007 and 2008 highlighted many of the weaknesses of extreme free market ideology and the COVID-19 pandemic and subsequent recession have underscored similar lessons. To cite but one poll showing growing public skepticism regarding free-market ideology, in 2018 fewer than half of Americans under age thirty had a positive view of capitalism, as did less than half of supporters of the Democratic Party.[41] Policy elites in the Democratic Party are also clearly moving left on economic issues. The economic policies in the 2016 Democratic Party platform were significantly more progressive than those in the 2012 platform, and the 2020 platform was far more progressive still. The 2020 candidates for the Democratic nomination for president were almost falling over each other to announce bold, left policy ideas, from universal health care and subsidized child care to breaking up large companies and taxing the rich at a greater rate. On the Republican side, Donald Trump has claimed that he is remaking his party into a "workers' party"—and though many of his policies did exactly the opposite, the fact that the leader of the Republican Party talks in these terms about economic issues is significant.[42]

Unions have become increasingly vocal in talking about why they are important, and many politicians seem willing to publicly embrace unions. Indeed, in the aftermath of the *Janus v. AFSCME* Supreme Court decision making the public sector right-to-work, a number of mayors and governors publicly and forcefully declared their support for unions. Dozens of mayors signed a letter stating that "a strong labor movement is necessary for the future of our cities and our country." The governor of New York stated, "We will do everything in our power to protect union members and ensure the labor movement continues to deliver on the promise of the American Dream." And the governor of New Jersey proclaimed, "As a strong advocate for organized labor, I recognize the myriad benefits of employee unionization, as well as the continued challenges unions face in maintaining and growing their membership."[43] These and other policy makers also signed executive orders and legislation designed to build union membership, and some of the policies were championed with the sole purpose of benefiting public-sector unions.[44]

The labor bills that have been introduced in recent years in Congress also suggest that politicians are not only increasingly willing to talk about labor but also open to bold reforms. In contrast to prior years, when legislation tended to focus on one or two more modest changes, several bills introduced would have essentially overturned most of the antiunion provisions of the 1947 Taft-Hartley Act.[45] One of these bills—the Protecting the Right to Organize Act—was passed by the House of Representatives in 2019. The bill did not advance in the Republican-controlled Senate, but in the House, five Republicans voted for the bill along with most Democrats. Having any Republican support for a Democratic bill is remarkably bipartisan these days. Similarly, new federal bills would require that all states allow public-sector workers to collectively bargain, rather than leaving that as a state decision as has been long-standing practice.[46] In 2019, legislation was introduced to create broad-based bargaining and strong incentives for organizational membership for domestic workers.[47] Co-enforcement bills (which provide a role for unions and other worker organizations in the enforcement of workplace laws and have elements that could be considered Ghent-like) have also been introduced in several recent sessions of Congress.[48] While these bills have not come particularly close to becoming law, nor would any one of them constitute a full labor reform, they suggest a greater interest in labor issues and an increased willingness to consider bold ideas.

State and local reform efforts have continued to build. Indeed, in 2019 perhaps the boldest legislation yet was introduced. The Washington State bill would have provided a pathway for broad-based bargaining for independent contractors and created most of the Ghent-like incentives for union membership discussed in this book, including having worker organizations deliver benefits like training and enforcing workplace standards.[49] Also in 2019, the City of Philadelphia enacted an ordinance to create portable benefits for domestic workers that would be operated in ways analogous to the Ghent system.[50]

The continued growth of state and city labor reform (and possibly some federal experimentation with particular industries) is particularly important. This not only helps prove that the reforms can work but also helps make elected officials and the public more comfortable with the idea of a new system. Even the National Labor Relations Act—one of the most fundamental shifts in policy in US history—was built on a number of previous policies, including the World War I labor boards, the Railway Labor Act of 1926, the experiences of the National Industrial Recovery Act of 1933, and the 1934 labor boards. These prior and often smaller-scale efforts helped make legislators comfortable with the ideas of labor policy. State and local efforts can do the same today.

Labor system reform began to trickle into the national debate in recent years and is increasingly being discussed. Sectoral bargaining was mentioned at the 2016 Democratic Party platform hearings, and in 2018 a few progressive members of Congress put out a report discussing sectoral bargaining and other bold labor reforms.[51] During 2017 and 2018, major media including the *New York Times*, *Bloomberg*, and *Vox* started discussing bold labor reforms in some stories.[52]

Most directly relevant to creating a new labor system, in 2019 most of the major candidates in the Democratic presidential primary publicly endorsed sectoral bargaining during their campaigns. Bernie Sanders, Elizabeth Warren, Jay Inslee, Beto O'Rourke, Pete Buttigieg, Cory Booker, Mike Bloomberg, and Julian Castro all released plans for promoting broad-based bargaining, and Joe Biden proposed creating a cabinet-level working group to consider the idea.[53] Though not every plan provided great detail on the new labor system, nor did every candidate regularly champion a plan, the fact that virtually all Democratic presidential candidates were open to or supportive of bold labor reforms similar to those proposed in this book is a massive shift and indicates that the idea climate is becoming quite favorable. It is hard to overstate how important this change is.

What's more is that the 2020 Democratic Party Platform calls for changing labor law "so that it is easier for unions and employers to enter into multi-employer agreements."[54] The platform doesn't provide details on how to do so, but the presence of a goal to increase broad-based bargaining is a significant change. Another sign of the times is a public letter released by a handful of Republican leaders on Labor Day 2020 calling for conservatives to ensure workers have a "seat at the table," and alluding to ideas such as sectoral bargaining, the Ghent system, and workers on corporate boards.[55] While the letter stops short of endorsing any policy changes and was signed by only one elected official, it signals that at least some conservative leaders are starting to change their thinking about unions.

In short, big shifts in economic policy thinking are in the air. These are times when bold ideas that challenge old ways of doing things are needed, and the public and politicians seem increasingly open and interested in such ideas. Whether the intellectual climate shifts so much that it becomes conventional wisdom that the United States needs a new labor system to make the economy and democracy work is impossible to predict. Still, such as shift seems more likely now than at any point in many, many decades.

The Hope

All told, the path to passing major labor reform is quite narrow. A number of factors must continue to evolve favorably. On-the-ground worker activity will need to increase in intensity. The public will have to elect a supermajority of pro-union policy makers to Congress. The labor movement will need to more fully embrace bold reforms. State and local experimentation will need to provide additional policy successes to build on. Most importantly, the intellectual environment must continue evolving toward recognizing the importance of a new labor system in solving the country's economic and political problems.

The window of success may be wider for an incremental approach that seeks labor reform first in occupations or sectors where the National Labor Relations Act does not apply, such as for domestic workers or independent contractors, or in industries where the government is already heavily involved, such as health care or education. That is, the path to a new labor system may come through experimentation in quasi-public industries or in sectors that have been excluded from traditional labor and employment law. Even passing a single experiment at the federal level would be quite difficult, but it might not require quite as large political majorities to be enacted. The incremental approach may even help create a track record that helps foster a more supportive intellectual environment. Still, the more incremental approach could mean giving up an opportunity to get more at one time, and it would not avoid the need to eventually reach critical levels of support on the ground, in Congress, with the labor movement, and in the idea environment.

While enacting the new labor system faces numerous challenges, there is a path to increasing grassroots activism, electing a supportive supermajority, developing political champions, and even fostering a favorable policy window.

Importantly, these factors do not need to stay aligned for very long in order for reform policy to have a lasting impact. If the new labor system is ever able to become law, it is likely that powerful opponents would seek to weaken or undermine its implementation through a variety of strategies, just as they did when the NLRA was passed in 1935. Administrative budgets and regulations would be heavily contested, political supporters targeted, lawsuits filed, studies and news reports on the policy's supposed harms produced, and new "reform" legislation introduced. These efforts would likely have significant financial backing and after some time would probably succeed in at least watering down the original law. The current pro-business makeup of the courts makes it seem very likely that at least some elements of the new labor system would be undermined.[56]

Though the Supreme Court famously upheld the constitutionality of the National Labor Relations Act, the law did not even survive a few years without court decisions weakening it. And the law barely existed for a decade before the Taft-Hartley Act significantly altered it. Still, the NLRA shaped America's economy and democracy for a significant part of the twentieth century. The NLRA led to a sharp increase in union density and coverage and created new rights and a platform for workers to build on for decades even as the law was weakened. Similarly, a new labor system would be able to transform America's economy and democracy in the twenty-first century even if it only lasted a few years in its purest form. Institutions can have powerful and lasting legacies.

The new labor system could also be more robust than the NLRA in the face of attacks and thus survive longer in a useful form. Once the new system was up and running, some employers might be more willing to defend it because it would help solve problems for them—such as the lack of workforce training and getting undercut by low-road firms. Reform would also more fully integrate unions into public institutions—like workers boards and workforce training—meaning that gutting the law would be more complicated because weakening unions would also weaken programs that deliver broad public benefits.

Thus, the new labor system would lead to transformative changes in America's economy and democracy if it became law and could succeed at its goals even if opponents were able to weaken it after passage.

While significant obstacles stand in the way of enacting a new labor system, there are a number of favorable trends that suggest it is possible—including growing public support for unions, workers' increased willingness to engage in direct action, the emergence of some political champions, and a changing intellectual environment that has created an opportunity for debate about labor policy. Indeed, the most important factor favoring the eventual passage of a new labor system is that it would work. As more people realize that labor reform is likely to succeed in addressing some of the country's biggest challenges, support for it should only continue to grow. More of the public may demand a new labor system, champions may more vocally push for it, and elites may increasingly come to believe in its value.

The United States faces deep and enduring challenges—decades of stagnant wages, near record levels of economic inequality, low levels of social trust, racism, large economic divides across race and gender, and a captured political system that too often does the bidding of wealthy elites while ignoring the public's interest. As bad as these problems are, they can foster even more significant social breakdown.

Broad-based bargaining and incentives for union membership would increase density and coverage, which would raise wages, reduce inequality, and make government more responsive to the will of the people. These changes would also help limit racial and gender discrimination and foster social trust, as well as create a level playing field for businesses to compete based on innovation. Not only do political science and economic theory indicate that a new labor system would achieve these results, these outcomes have also been demonstrated in the real world in a variety of settings—in countries around the globe, including those most similar to the United States, as well as in US history and in a few pockets of the country today.

The hope of this book is that it can play a role in making bold labor reform more likely by making the case for a new American labor system.

Notes

INTRODUCTION

1. Steve Fraser, "The Good War and the Workers," *American Prospect*, September 20, 2009, http://prospect.org/article/good-war-and-workers-0.

2. Angus Maddison, "Historical Statistics of the World Historical Economy, GDP and Per Capita GDP, 1-2008 AD," University of Groningen, 2010, https://www.rug.nl/ggdc/historicaldevelopment/maddison/releases/maddison-database-2010.

3. Robert D. Putnam, *Bowling Alone: The Collapse and Revival of American Community* (New York: Simon & Schuster, 2000); David Madland, *Hollowed Out: Why the Economy Doesn't Work without a Strong Middle Class* (Oakland: University of California Press, 2015).

4. David Weil, "Enforcing Labour Standards in Fissured Workplaces: The US Experience," *Economic and Labour Relations Review* 22, no. 2 (2011): 33–54; David Weil, *The Fissured Workplace: Why Work Became So Bad for So Many and What Can Be Done to Improve It* (Cambridge, MA: Harvard University Press, 2014).

5. Thomas A. Kochan et al., "Worker Voice in America: Is There a Gap between What Workers Expect and What They Experience?" *ILR Review* 72 no. 1 (2018): 3–38; Art Swift, "Labor Union Approval Best Since 2003, at 61%," Gallup, August 30, 2017, http://news.gallup.com/poll/217331/labor-union-approval-best-2003.aspx.

6. US Bureau of Labor Statistics, "Work Stoppages Summary," news release, February 8, 2019, https://web.archive.org/web/20200122184028/https://www.bls.gov/news.release/wkstp.nr0.htm; US Bureau of Labor Statistics, "Work Stoppages Summary," news release, February 11, 2020 https://www.bls.gov/news.release/wkstp.nr0.htm.

CHAPTER 1. THE PLAN

1. See Protecting the Right to Organize Act of 2019, H.R. 2474, 116th Cong., 1st sess. (May 2, 2019), https://www.congress.gov/bill/116th-congress/house-bill/2474; Public Service Freedom to Negotiate Act of 2018, H. R. 6238, 115th Cong., 2nd sess. (June 27, 2018), https://www.congress.gov/bill/115th-congress/house-bill/6238. See also Workplace Democracy Act, S 2810, 115th Cong., 2nd sess. (May 9, 2018), https://www.congress.gov/bill/115th-congress/senate-bill/2810.

2. "Collective Bargaining Coverage," OECD.Stat, https://stats.oecd.org/Index.aspx?DataSetCode=CBC; Bernhard Ebbinghaus and Jelle Visser, "When Institutions Matter: Union Growth and Decline in Western Europe, 1950–1995," *European Sociological Review* 15, no. 2 (1999): 135–58; Magnus Rasmussen, "Institutions (Still) Rule: Labor Market Centralization and Trade Union Organization," working paper, October 2017, https://www.researchgate.net/publication/320273351_Institutions_still_Rule_Labor_Market_Centralization_and_Trade_Union_Organization; Lyle Scruggs, "Ghent System and Union Membership in Europe, 1970–1996," *Political Research Quarterly* 55, no. 2 (2002): 275–97; Bo Rothstein, "Labor-Market Institutions and Working-Class Strength," in *Structuring Politics: Historical Institutional in Comparative Analysis*, ed. Sven Steinmo, Kathleen Thelen, and Frank Longstreth (Cambridge, UK: Cambridge University Press, 1992), 33–56; Tim Van Rie, Ive Marx, and Jeoen Horemans, "Ghent Revisited: Unemployment Insurance and

Union Membership in Belgium and the Nordic Countries," *European Journal of Industrial Relations* 17, no. 2 (2011): 125–39; Matthew Dimick, "Labor Law, New Governance, and the Ghent System," *North Carolina Law Review* 90, no. 2 (2012): 319–78.

3. As Joel Rogers argues, "American labor law tends systematically to constrain and fragment worker organization." Joel Rogers, "Divide and Conquer: The Legal Foundations of Postwar US Labor Policy," in *Critical Legal Thought: An American German Debate*, ed. Christian Joerges and David M. Trubek (Baden-Baden, Germany: Nomos Verlagsgesellschaft, 1989), 210–30. See also Joseph B. Rose and Gary N. Chaison, "Unionism in Canada and the United States in the 21st Century: The Prospects for Revival," *Industrial Relations* 56, no. 1 (2001): 34–65, https://www.erudit.org/revue/ri/2001/v56/n1/000140ar.html.

4. Lynn Rhinehart and Celine McNicholas, "Collective Bargaining beyond the Worksite: How Workers and Their Unions Build Power and Set Standards for Their Industries," Economic Policy Institute, May 4, 2020, https://www.epi.org/publication/collective-bargaining-beyond-the-worksite-how-workers-and-their-unions-build-power-and-set-standards-for-their-industries/.

5. Vickie Choitz, Matt Helmer, and Maureen Conway, *Improving Jobs to Improve Care* (Washington, DC: Aspen Institute, 2015), http://www.aspenwsi.org/wordpress/wp-content/uploads/SEIU-CaseStudy.pdf.

6. Note that home care aides providing care to their own family members have lower training requirements. See "Individual Providers," Washington State Department of Social and Health Services, https://www.dshs.wa.gov/altsa/home-and-community-services/individual-providers.

7. Choitz, Helmer, and Conway, *Improving Jobs to Improve Care*. For an additional example of a labor-management training program for health care workers, see "Alaska Health Care Apprenticeship Consortium," Alaska Apprenticeship Training Coordinators Association, accessed April 12, 2019, http://aatca.org/ahcac.

8. Susan C. Reinhard et al., *Raising Expectations: A State Scorecard on Long-Term Services and Supports for Older Adults, People with Physical Disabilities, and Family Caregivers*, 2nd ed. (AARP, Commonwealth Fund, and SCAN Foundation, 2014), http://www.longtermscorecard.org/~/media/Microsite/Files/2014/Reinhard_LTSS_Scorecard_web_619v2_rev_04152016.pdf.

9. David Madland and Malkie Wall, "American Ghent: Designing Programs to Strengthen Unions and Improve Government Services," Center for American Progress, September 18, 2019, https://www.americanprogress.org/issues/economy/reports/2019/09/18/474690/american-ghent.

10. "Schedule of Minimums, 2017 Theatrical and Television Basic Agreement," Writers Guild of America, http://www.wga.org/uploadedFiles/contracts/min2017.pdf. See page 6 for wages, page 28 for residuals, and page 44 for benefits.

11. For additional information and history on collective bargaining by writers, see Catherine Fisk, "Hollywood Writers and the Gig Economy," *University of Chicago Legal Forum* 2017, article 8 (2018): 177–203, https://chicagounbound.uchicago.edu/uclf/vol2017/iss1/8.

12. Wendy Lee, "Netflix Could Play a Key Role in Upcoming Hollywood Labor Drama," *Los Angeles Times*, November 20, 2019; "Reality and Game Show Writers," Writers Guild of America West, https://www.wga.org/the-guild/going-guild/get-involved/reality-game-show.

13. For more on this argument, see Margaret Levi, "Organizing Power: The Prospects for an American Labor Movement," *Perspectives on Politics* 1 no. 1 (2003): 45–68. See also Tito Boeri et al., "Perverse Effects of Centralized Bargaining," Vox CEPR Policy Portal, April 13, 2019, https://voxeu.org/article/perverse-effects-centralised-bargaining.

14. John Budd and Brian McCall, "The Effect of Unions on the Receipt of Unemployment Insurance," *Industrial and Labor Relations Review* 50, no. 3 (1997): 478–92; Barry Hirsch, David MacPherson, and Michael Dumond, "Workers Compensation Recipiency in Union and Nonunion Workplaces," *Industrial and Labor Relations Review* 50, no. 2 (1997): 213–36.

15. See, among many others, Thomas A. Kochan, Harry C. Katz, and Robert B. McKersie, *The Transformation of American Industrial Relations* (New York: Basic Books, 1986); Robert Marshall and Antonio Merlo, "Pattern Bargaining," *International Economic Review* 45 (February 2004): 239–55; Harry Katz, "The Decentralization of Collective Bargaining: A Literature Review and Comparative Analysis," *ILR Review* 47, no. 1 (1993): 3–22; Thomas Anton Kochan and Christine A. Riordan, "Employment Relations and Growing Income Inequality: Causes and Potential Options for Its Reversal," *Journal of Industrial Relations*, 58, no. 3 (2016): 419–40, http://iwer.mit.edu/wp-content/uploads/2016/11/Kochan.Riordan_JIR.Inequality.pdf; Kim Moody, "A Pattern of Retreat: The Decline of Pattern Bargaining," *Labor Notes*, February 16, 2010, https://labornotes.org/.

16. The ICTWSS database finds that in 1980, 10 percent of workers were covered by multi-employer bargaining. Jelle Visser, "ICTWSS: Database on Institutional Characteristics of Trade Unions, Wage Setting, State Intervention and Social Pacts in 51 Countries between 1960 and 2014," version 5.1, September 2016, http://uva-aias.net/en/ictwss. Note that some of this multi-employer bargaining was not necessarily sectoral in nature but rather may have simply combined a few employers.

17. Susan Hayter and Jelle Visser, eds., *Collective Agreements: Extending Labour Protection* (Geneva, Switzerland: International Labour Organization, 2018).

18. Hamid Azari-Rad, Peter Philips, and Mark J. Prus, "State Prevailing Wage Laws and School Construction Costs," *Industrial Relations: A Journal of Economy and Society* 42, no. 3 (2003): 445–57; Michael P. Kelsay, "The Adverse Economic Impact from Repeal of the Prevailing Wage Law in West Virginia," National Alliance for Fair Contracting, January 2015, http://www.faircontracting.org/wp-content/uploads/2015/01/The-Adverse-Economic-Impact-from-Repeal-of-the-PW-Law-in-WV-Dr.-Michael-Kelsay-Full-Report.pdf; Kevin Duncan and Frank Manzo IV, *The Economic, Fiscal, and Social Effects of Kentucky's Prevailing Wage Law* (La Grange: Illinois Economic Policy Institute, 2016), https://illinoisepi.files.wordpress.com/2016/12/kentucky-report-duncan-and-manzo-2016-final.pdf; Kevin Duncan, "The Wage Differential Method: Promising Construction Costs Savings with the Repeal or Weakening of Prevailing Wage Laws that Cannot Be Delivered," National Alliance for Fair Contracting, September 19, 2016, http://www.faircontracting.org/wp-content/uploads/2012/08/Wage-differential-method-critique-Duncan-2016-1.pdf.

19. Bergen County, Ordinance No. 14-07, §5.10.

20. Ohio Revised Code Chapter 4115—Wages and Hours on Public Works (2016), http://law.justia.com/codes/ohio/2016/title-41/chapter-4115/; New Jersey Department of Labor and Workforce Development, "Prevailing Wage Rate Determinations," http://lwd.state.nj.us/labor/wagehour/wagerate/prevailing_wage_determinations.html; Massachusetts General Law 149 § 26, http://www.malegislature.gov/Laws/GeneralLaws/PartI/TitleXXI/Chapter149/Section26.

21. New York Labor Law § 220" (2016); Code of Maryland Regulations 21.11.11.03 (2017), http://www.dsd.state.md.us/comar/comarhtml/21/21.11.11.03.htm.

22. See, for example, the Washington, DC, security guard law §32-1003 (a)(6)(A), which states, "Beginning on July 1, 2019, and no later than July 1 of each successive year, an employer shall pay a security officer working in an office building in the District of Columbia wages, or any combination of wages and benefits, that are not less than the

combined amount of the minimum wage and fringe benefit rate in effect on September 1 of the immediately preceding year for the guard 1 classification established by the United States Secretary of Labor pursuant to Chapter 67 of Title 41 of the United States Code (41 USC. § 6701 et seq.), as amended." DC Code, §32-1003(h), https://code.dccouncil.us/dc/council/code/titles/32/chapters/10.

23. John Baigent, Vince Ready, and Tom Roper, *Recommendations for Labour Law Reform: A Report to the Honourable Moe Sihota, Minister of Labour, Submitted by the Sub-Committee of Special Advisers* (Victoria: British Columbia Ministry of Labour and Consumer Services, 1992); Sara Slinn, "Broader-Based and Sectoral Bargaining Proposals in Collective Bargaining Law Reform: A Historical Review," Osgoode Digital Commons, 2020, https://digitalcommons.osgoode.yorku.ca/all_papers/324; Diane MacDonald, "Sectoral Certification: A Case Study of British Columbia," *Canadian Labor and Employment Law Journal* 5 (1997): 279–83.

24. For information on multi-employer bargaining and its decline in the United States, see, among others, Kochan, Katz, and McKersie, *Transformation of American Industrial Relations*; Marshall and Merlo, "Pattern Bargaining"; Katz, "Decentralization of Collective Bargaining"; Kochan and Riordan, "Employment Relations and Growing Income Inequality"; Moody, "Pattern of Retreat."

25. John-Paul Ferguson, "The Eyes of the Needles: A Sequential Model of Union Organizing Drives, 1999–2004," *Industrial and Labor Relations Review* 62, no. 1 (2008): 3–21.

26. Ferguson, "Eyes of the Needles."

27. See, for example, California State Legislature, "AB-5 Worker Status: Employees and Independent Contractors," September 18, 2019, https://leginfo.legislature.ca.gov/faces/billTextClient.xhtml?bill_id=201920200AB5.

28. Seattle Office of Labor Standards, "Domestic Workers," https://www.seattle.gov/laborstandards/ordinances/domestic-workers-ordinance; Washington State, Senate Bill 5690, 66th Legislature (2019), https://lawfilesext.leg.wa.gov/biennium/2019-20/Pdf/Bills/Senate%20Bills/5690.pdf. Note that the Washington State legislation includes a strong test for employment status.

29. For more details on the selection of multiple unions for a workers' boards as well as other implementation details, see Kate Andrias, David Madland, and Malkie Wall, "A How-To Guide for State and Local Workers' Boards," Center for American Progress, December 11, 2019, https://www.americanprogress.org/issues/economy/reports/2019/12/11/478539/guide-state-local-workers-boards.

30. For more information and an example of how wage boards create a forum for bargaining, see the European Court of Human Rights decision in *Unite the Union v. the United Kingdom*, paragraph 58, in possession of author. See also John Hendy and Keith Ewing, "Article 11(3) of the European Convention on Human Rights: IER Briefing" (Liverpool, United Kingdom: The Institute of Employment Rights, 2017), https://www.ier.org.uk/publications/resources-article-113-european-convention-human-rights.

31. Kate Andrias, "The New Labor Law," *Yale Law Journal* 126, no. 1 (October 2016), https://www.yalelawjournal.org/article/the-new-labor-law. See also Sara Slinn, "Wage Boards for the 21st Century: Revisiting Sectoral Standard-Setting Mechanisms for the Workplace," Osgoode Legal Studies Research Paper, November 1, 2019, https://ssrn.com/abstract=3488079; Rosado Marzán and F. César, "Can Wage Boards Revive U.S. Labor?: Marshaling Evidence from Puerto Rico," *Chicago-Kent Law Review* 95, no. 1, May 3, 2020, https://ssrn.com/abstract=3591984.

32. Andrias, "New Labor Law." Note that local governments must have sufficient home-rule authority to pursue this strategy.

33. "Fast Food Wage Board," New York State Department of Labor, http://labor.ny.gov/workerprotection/laborstandards/wageboard2015.shtm.

34. "Minimum Wage for Fast Food Workers," New York State Department of Labor, factsheet, https://www.labor.ny.gov/formsdocs/factsheets/pdfs/p716.pdf.

35. Seattle City Council, CB No. 119286 (2018), http://seattle.legistar.com/Legislation Detail.aspx?ID=3532201&GUID=232AE887-44C6-4450-A040-84225AD4F11D&Options= Advanced&Search=.

36. Ai-jen Poo, "Out from the Shadows: Domestic Workers Speak in the United States," OpenDemocracy, June 16, 2017, https://www.opendemocracy.net/en/beyond-trafficking-and-slavery/out-from-shadows-domestic-workers-speak-in-united-states/.

37. Kurt Vandaele, "A Report from the Homeland of the Ghent System: The Relationship between Unemployment and Trade Union Membership in Belgium," *Transfer: European Review of Labour and Research* 12, no. 4 (2006): 647–57; David Madland, *The Future of Worker Voice and Power* (Washington, DC: Center for American Progress, 2016), https://cdn.americanprogress.org/wp-content/uploads/2016/10/06051753/WorkerVoice2.pdf.

38. See, for example, Dimick, "Labor Law, New Governance, and the Ghent System."

39. See table 2 in Jochen Clasen and Elke Viebrock, "Voluntary Unemployment Insurance and Trade Union Membership: Investigating the Connections in Denmark and Sweden," *Journal of Social Policy* 37, no. 3 (2008), 438, https://www.research.ed.ac.uk/portal/files/8085688/2008_Voluntary_unemployment_insurance_and_trade_union_membership.pdf.

40. Clasen and Viebrock, "Voluntary Unemployment Insurance and Trade Union Membership."

41. Niels Finn Christiansen, *The Nordic Model of Welfare: A Historical Reappraisal* (Copenhagen: Museum Tusculanum Press, 2005), 109.

42. "Application and Recipiency CY 1988–2018," United State Department of Labor, https://oui.doleta.gov/unemploy/large_carousel.asp?slide=0.

43. For workers' compensation, see Hirsch, MacPherson, and Dumond, "Workers' Compensation Recipiency in Union and Nonunion Workplaces." For unemployment insurance, see Marc Chan, Marios Michaelides, and Sisi Zhang, "Who Receives Unemployment Insurance?" *Research in Applied Economics* 6, no. 3 (2014): 98–128, https://opus.lib.uts.edu.au/bitstream/10453/33633/1/5954-22426-1-PB.pdf.

44. Budd and McCall, "Effect of Unions on the Receipt of Unemployment Insurance Benefits." For last point, see page 481.

45. "History," Black Car Fund, http://www.nybcf.org/history.

46. "F.A.Q.'s," Black Car Fund, http://www.nybcf.org/faqs; *The Indicator*, "Black Car Fund," broadcast January 29, 2018, on *NPR*, https://www.npr.org/templates/transcript/transcript.php?storyId=581626325.

47. "About the IDG," Independent Drivers Guild, https://drivingguild.org/about/; IDG Benefits Fund, https://www.idgbenefits.org/.

48. Karla Walter, "Public Sector Training Partnerships Build Power," Center for American Progress, October 3, 2019, https://www.americanprogress.org/issues/economy/reports/2019/10/03/475355/public-sector-training-partnerships-build-power.

49. Celine McNicholas, Zane Mokhiber, and Adam Chaikof, "Two Billion Dollars in Stolen Wages Were Recovered for Workers in 2015 and 2016—and That's Just a Drop in the Bucket," Economic Policy Institute, December 13, 2017, https://www.epi.org/publication/two-billion-dollars-in-stolen-wages-were-recovered-for-workers-in-2015-and-2016-and-thats-just-a-drop-in-the-bucket.

50. Seema N. Patel and Catherine L. Fisk, "California Co-Enforcement Initiatives That Facilitate Workers Organizing," *Harvard Law and Policy Review* 12 (2017), https://harvardlpr.com/wp-content/uploads/sites/20/2017/11/Patel-Fisk-CoEnforcement.pdf. Note also that case studies suggest that partnerships with unions have noticeably improved enforcement outcomes. For instance, Patel and Fisk describe a UCLA study that found that, between 2008 and 2011, the vast majority of workers (83 percent) who

got judgements for unpaid wages never actually received any money. After the California Division of Labor Standards Enforcement contracted with the Wage Justice Center (WJC) to enforce unpaid judgements, the WJC dramatically improved judgement enforcement, obtaining over $8.25 million on behalf of 5,500 workers.

51. Budd and McCall, "Effect of Unions on the Receipt of Unemployment Insurance Benefits," 478. See also Stephen J. Trejo, "The Effects of Overtime Pay Regulation on Worker Compensation," *American Economic Review* 81, no. 4 (1991): 719–40.

52. For more on this concept, see David Madland and Alex Rowell, "How State and Local Governments Can Strengthen Worker Power and Raise Wages," Center for American Progress, May 2, 2017, https://www.americanprogressaction.org/issues/economy/reports/2017/05/02/166640/state-local-governments-can-strengthen-worker-power-raise-wages/.

53. "Joint Compliance Monitoring Program: Los Angeles Unified School District and All Work Preservation Groups, Rules of Engagement (Fiscal Year 2019–20)," Los Angeles Unified School District, http://www.laschools.org/contractor/lc/documents/download/work-preservation/Rules_of_Engagement.pdf; City of Los Angeles, *Labor Compliance Manual* (City of Los Angeles, 2014), https://bca.lacity.org/Uploads/labor/LABOR%20COMPLIANCE%20MANUAL.pdf.

54. Tia Koonse, Miranda Dietz, and Annette Bernhardt, *Enforcing City Minimum Wage Laws in California: Best Practices and City-State Partnerships* (Los Angeles: UCLA Center for Labor Research and Education; Berkeley: UC Berkeley Center for Labor Research and Education, 2015), http://laborcenter.berkeley.edu/pdf/2015/minimum-wage-enforcement.pdf.

55. Janice Fine and Jennifer Gordon, "Strengthening Labor Standards Enforcement through Partnerships with Workers' Organizations," *Politics and Society* 38, no. 4 (2010): 552–85.

56. For general info on co-enforcement, see Fine and Gordon, "Strengthening Labor Standards Enforcement through Partnerships with Workers' Organizations." For specifics on city policy, see Janice Fine, *Co-Production: Bringing Together the Unique Capabilities of Government and Society for Stronger Labor Standards Enforcement* (Labor Innovations for the 21st Century, 2015), http://theliftfund.org/wp-content/uploads/2015/09/LIFT ReportCoproductionOct_ExecSumm-rf_4.pdf; Koonse, Dietz, and Bernhardt, *Enforcing City Minimum Wage Laws in California*; "2015 Guidelines," Seattle Office of Labor Standards, Community Outreach and Education Fund, http://www.seattle.gov/Documents/Departments/CivilRights/ols-fund_guidelines-2015.pdf; Libby Schaaf and Sabrina Landreth, "Proposed Amended Midcycle Policy Budget for Fiscal Year 2016–17," May 26, 2016, http://www2.oaklandnet.com/oakca1/groups/cityadministrator/documents/policy/oak059136.pdf.

57. Angela Hanks and David Madland, "Opinion: Young Workers Deserve Better Training," *MarketWatch*, April 5, 2018, https://www.marketwatch.com/story/young-workers-deserve-better-training-2018-04-04.

58. Anthony P. Carnevale, Stephen J. Rose, and Andrew R, Hanson, *Certificates: Gateway to Gainful Employment and College Degrees* (Washington, DC: Georgetown University Center on Education and the Workforce, 2012), https://cew.georgetown.edu/wp-content/uploads/2014/11/Certificates.FullReport.061812.pdf; Clive Belfield and Thomas Bailey, "The Labor Market Returns to Sub-Baccalaureate College: A Review," working paper, Center for Analysis of Postsecondary Education and Employment, March 2017, https://capseecenter.org/wp-content/uploads/2017/04/labor-market-returns-sub-baccalaureate-college-review.pdf.

59. Hanks and Madland, "Young Workers Deserve Better Training."

60. "Labor Market Training Expenditures as a Percent of GDP in OECD Countries, 2011," Hamilton Project, June 19, 2014, https://www.hamiltonproject.org/charts/

labor_market_training_expenditures_as_a_percent_of_gdp_in_oecd_countries_20. Note that recent, comprehensive data on training is limited; and there are mixed opinions about the state of training in the United States. See, for instance, Peter Cappelli, "Skill Gaps, Skill Shortages, and Skill Mismatches: Evidence for the US," NBER Working Paper 20382, National Bureau of Economic Research, 2014, https://www.nber.org/papers/w20382.pdf; and Robert Lerman, "Are Employers Providing Enough Training? Theory, Evidence, and Policy Implications," paper prepared for National Academy of Sciences Symposium on the Supply Chain for Middle-Skill Jobs: Education, Training, and Certification Pathways, n.d., https://sites.nationalacademies.org/cs/groups/pgasite/documents/webpage/pga_168146.pdf.

61. Angela Hanks and David Madland, "Better Training and Better Jobs," Center for American Progress, February 22, 2018, https://www.americanprogress.org/issues/economy/reports/2018/02/22/447115/better-training-better-jobs/.

62. For further discussion of the system, see Hanks and Madland, "Better Training and Better Jobs."

63. Alison Booth, Marco Francesconi, and Gylfi Zoega, "Unions, Work-Related Training, and Wages: Evidence for British Men," *ILR Review* 57, no. 1 (2003): 68–91; Christian Dustmann and Uta Schönberg, "Training and Union Wages," *Review of Economics and Statistics* 91, no. 2 (2009): 363–76; Jason Heyes and Mark Stuart, "Bargaining for Skills: Trade Unions and Training at the Workplace," *British Journal of Industrial Relations* 36, no. 3 (1998): 459–67.

64. Cihan Bilginsoy, "The Hazards of Training: Attrition and Retention in Construction Industry Apprenticeship Programs," *ILR Review* 57, no. 1 (2003): 54–67; Cihan Bilginsoy, "Unemployment, the Great Recession, and Apprenticeship Attrition in the US," *Journal of Vocational Education and Training* 70, no. 2 (2017): 171–92.

65. Lameck Onsarigo et al., *The Economic, Fiscal, and Social Effects of Ohio's Prevailing Wage Law* (Midwest Economic Policy Institute, 2017), https://midwestepi.files.wordpress.com/2016/05/bowling-green-su-kent-state-ohio-pw-study-4-10-17.pdf; Duncan and Manzo, "Economic, Fiscal, and Social Effects of Kentucky's Prevailing Wage Law."

66. Robert W. Glover and Cihan Bilginsoy, "Registered Apprenticeship Training in the US Construction Industry," *Education and Training* 47, no. 4/5 (2005): 337–49.

67. See, for example, Alexander Hertel-Fernandez and Ethan Porter, "Bread and Butter or Bread and Roses? Experimental Evidence on Why Public Sector Employees Support Unions," unpublished paper, SSRN, 2018, https://papers.ssrn.com/sol3/papers.cfm?abstract_id=3214662.

68. For a summary of this research, see Hanks and Madland, "Better Training and Better Jobs."

69. CSEA/VOICE, http://voicecsea.org/.

70. Counting U.S. Postsecondary and Secondary Credentials (Washington, DC: Credential Engine, 2019), https://credentialengine.org/wp-content/uploads/2019/09/Counting-US-Postsecondary-and-Secondary-Credentials_190925_FINAL.pdf; Stephanie Cronen, Meghan McQuiggan, and Emily Isenberg, "Adult Training and Education: Results from the National Household Education Surveys Program of 2016: First Look," Institute of Education Sciences, National Center for Education Statistics, September 2017, https://www.insidehighered.com/sites/default/server_files/files/2017103_2016%20ATES%20First%20Look%20Report_for508c_090617.pdf.

71. "Class Information," Culinary Academy of Las Vegas, http://www.theculinaryacademy.org/class-info.

72. Jeffrey Waddoups, "Union-Management Training Partnerships in the Hotel Industry: The Cases of Las Vegas and San Francisco," unpublished paper, January 2002, https://www.researchgate.net/publication/228819216_Union-Management_Training_Partnerships_in_the_Hotel_Industry_The_Cases_of_Las_Vegas_and_San_Francisco; "Our History," Culinary Academy of Las Vegas, http://www.theculinaryacademy.org/our-history.

73. "FAQ," Culinary Academy of Las Vegas, http://www.theculinaryacademy.org/fre quently-asked-questions; "About Us," Culinary Academy of Las Vegas, http://www.the culinaryacademy.org/about.

74. "FAQ," Culinary Academy of Las Vegas.

75. Mia Gray and James DeFillippis, "Learning from Las Vegas: Unions and Post-industrial Urbanization," *Urban Studies* 52, no. 9 (2014): 1683–701.

76. Gray and DeFillippis, "Learning from Las Vegas."

77. *Mark Janus v. American Federation of State, County, and Municipal Employees Council 31*, brief of amici curiae, Governor Tom Wolf and others.

78. *Mark Janus v. American Federation of State, County, and Municipal Employees Council 31*, brief of amici curiae, fifteen unions and umbrella organizations that provide services to affiliated unions and associations representing nearly half a million public safety employees.

79. Hanks and Madland, "Better Training and Better Jobs."

80. For more details on how to build power in workers' boards see Andrias, Madland, and Wall, "How-To Guide for State and Local Workers' Boards."

81. "Samuel Gompers," AFL-CIO, https://aflcio.org/about/history/labor-history-people/samuel-gompers.

82. Joseph A. McCartin, *Labor's Great War: The Struggle for Industrial Democracy and the Origins of Modern American Labor Relations, 1912–1921* (Chapel Hill: University of North Carolina Press, 1997), 56. See also "Samuel Gompers."

83. Samuel Gompers, "Labor's Participation in Government," *American Federationist* 23, no. 2 (1916): 105–10.

84. For a broad perspective on the roles unions play, see, among others, Hoyt Wheeler, *The Future of the American Labor Movement* (Cambridge, UK: Cambridge University Press, 2002); K. D. Ewing, "The Function of Trade Unions," *Industrial Law Journal* 34, no. 1 (2005): 1–22; Sidney Webb and Beatrice Webb, *The History of Trade Unionism* (New York: Longmans, Green, 1894).

85. Roger Waldinger et al., "Helots No More: A Case Study of the Justice for Janitors Campaign in Los Angeles," in *Organizing to Win: New Research on Union Strategies*, ed. Kate Bronfrenbrenner et al. (Ithaca, NY: Cornell University Press, 1997), 102–19; Harold D. Hunt and Isilay Civan, "Sweeping Changes? Unionization and the Bottom Line," *Tierra Grande 1784* (July 2006), https://assets.recenter.tamu.edu/documents/articles/1784.pdf; and Christian Erickson et al., "Justice for Janitors in Los Angeles: Lessons from Three Rounds of Negotiations," *British Journal of Industrial Relations*, 40, no. 3 (2002): 543–67.

86. See, for example, Chris W. Street, "UAW: California Legislature Requires Tesla Pay Fair and Responsible Wages," *Breitbart*, December 22, 2017, https://www.breitbart.com/local/2017/12/22/uaw-cal-legislature-requires-tesla-pay-fair-responsible-wages.

87. Assembly Bill No. 1387: An Act to Amend Section 2055 of, and to Repeal Section 2067 of the Labor Code, Relating to Car Washes," California State Assembly, 2013–2014 sess., http://www.leginfo.ca.gov/pub/13-14/bill/asm/ab_1351-1400/ab_1387_bill_20130418_amended_asm_v98.pdf. For other examples of unions using nonunion policy to support bargaining, see Ben Sachs, "Despite Preemption: Making Labor Law in Cities and States," *Harvard Law Review* 124, no. 5 (2011): 1154–224, https://harvardlawreview.org/wp-content/uploads/pdfs/vol124_sachs.pdf.

88. Arthur M. Schlesinger Jr., *The Coming of the New Deal, 1933–1935* (New York: Houghton Mifflin, 2003), esp. 90–92.

CHAPTER 2. UNIONS AS THE SOLUTION

1. For more on how wages are a product of both social and economic forces, see Dustin Avent-Holt and Donald Tomaskovic-Devey, "A Relational Theory of Earnings Inequality," *American Behavioral Scientist* 58, no. 3 (January 2013): 379–99.

2. John Schmitt and Janelle Jones, *Where Have All the Good Jobs Gone?* (Washington, DC: Center for Economic and Policy Research, 2012), http://cepr.net/documents/publica tions/good-jobs-2012-07.pdf.

3. Brendan Duke, "When I Was Your Age," Center for American Progress, March 3, 2016, https://www.americanprogress.org/issues/economy/reports/2016/03/03/131627/ when-i-was-your-age. See also David Leonhardt, "The Fleecing of Millennials," *New York Times*, January 27, 2019.

4. Annette Bernhardt et al., *Broken Laws, Unprotected Workers: Violations of Employ-ment and Labor Laws in America's Cities* (Chicago: Center for Urban Economic Devel-opment; New York: National Employment Law Project; Los Angeles, UCLA Institute for Research on Labor and Employment, 2009), https://www.nelp.org/wpcontent/ uploads/2015/03/BrokenLawsReport2009.pdf. For wage theft in large companies, see Philip Mattera, *Grand Theft Paycheck: The Large Corporations Shortchanging Their Work-ers' Wages* (Washington, DC: Good Jobs First and Jobs with Justice Education Fund, 2018), https://www.goodjobsfirst.org/sites/default/files/docs/pdfs/wagetheft_report.pdf.

5. Alexander J. S. Colvin, *The Growing Use of Mandatory Arbitration* (Washington, DC: Economic Policy Institute, 2018), https://www.epi.org/publication/the-growing-use-of-mandatory-arbitration-access-to-the-courts-is-now-barred-for-more-than-60-million-american-workers.

6. Evan Starr, J. J. Prescott, and Norman Bishara, "Noncompetes in the U.S. Labor Force," University of Michigan Law & Econ Research Paper 18-013 (2019), https://ssrn.com/ abstract=2625714. See also Karla Walter, "States Must Act to Protect Workers from Exploit-ative Noncompete and No-Poach Agreements," Center for American Progress, April 2, 2019, https://www.americanprogress.org/issues/economy/news/2019/04/02/467955/ states-must-act-protect-workers-exploitative-noncompete-no-poach-agreements.

7. Alexander Hertel-Fernandez, *Politics at Work: How Companies Turn Their Workers into Lobbyists*, Studies in Postwar American Political Development (Oxford, UK: Oxford University Press, 2018).

8. "Median/Average Hourly Wages," State of Working America Data Library, Eco-nomic Policy Institute, https://www.epi.org/data/#/?subject=wage-avg&g=. Emmanuel Saez finds that there has been "total stagnation in the real incomes of the bottom 50%" since the late 1960s. Emmanuel Saez, "Income and Wealth Inequality: Evidence and Policy Implications," *Contemporary Economic Policy* 35, no. 1 (2017): 7–25, https://eml.berkeley. edu/~saez/SaezCEP2017.pdf.

9. Mary C. Daly, Bart Hobijn, and Joseph H. Pedtke, "Disappointing Facts about the Black-White Wage Gap," *FRBSF Economic Letter* (Federal Reserve Bank of San Francisco), September 5, 2017, https://www.frbsf.org/economic-research/files/el2017-26.pdf.

10. Lisa J. Dettling et al., "Recent Trends in Wealth-Holding by Race and Ethnicity: Evidence from the Survey of Consumer Finances," *FEDS Notes* (Board of Governors of the Federal Reserve System), September 27, 2017, https://www.federalreserve.gov/econres/ notes/feds-notes/recent-trends-in-wealth-holding-by-race-and-ethnicity-evidence-from-the-survey-of-consumer-finances-20170927.htm. See also Darrick Hamilton, and William Darity, Jr., "The Political Economy of Education, Financial Literacy, and the Racial Wealth Gap," *Federal Reserve Bank of St. Louis Review* 99, no. 1 (2017): 59–76, https://files. stlouisfed.org/files/htdocs/publications/review/2017-02-15/the-political-economy-of-education-financial-literacy-and-the-racial-wealth-gap.pdf.

11. "The Productivity-Pay Gap," Economic Policy Institute, July 2019, https://www.epi. org/productivity-pay-gap.

12. David Leonhardt, "Our Broken Economy, in One Simple Chart," *New York Times*, August 7, 2017.

13. Moritz Kuhn, Moritz Schularick, and Ulrike I. Steins, "Income and Wealth Inequal-ity in America, 1949–2016," Opportunity & Inclusive Growth Institute Working Paper 9,

Federal Reserve Bank of Minneapolis, June 2018, https://www.minneapolisfed.org/insti
tute/working-papers-institute/iwp9.pdf.

14. Lawrence Mishel and Jessica Schieder, "CEO Compensation Surged in 2017," Economic Policy Institute, August 16, 2018, https://www.epi.org/publication/ceo-compen
sation-surged-in-2017.

15. "Top 1% National Income Share," World Inequality Database, https://wid.
world/world/#sptinc_p99p100_z/GB;US;DE;FR/2017/eu/k/p/yearly/s/false/5.7349999
99999999/30/curve/false/region.

16. "Distribution of Family Income: Gini Index," *The World Factbook*, Central Intelligence Agency, https://www.cia.gov/library/publications/the-world-factbook/rankorder/
2172rank.html.

17. Eric Levitz, "America's Version of Capitalism Is Incompatible with Democracy,"
Intelligencer—New York Magazine, May 23, 2018, http://nymag.com/intelligencer/2018/05/
americas-brand-of-capitalism-is-incompatible-with-democracy.html; Jedidiah Britton-
Purdy, "Normcore," *Dissent*, Summer 2018, https://www.dissentmagazine.org/article/
normcore-trump-resistance-books-crisis-of-democracy.

18. Quoted in Jack Beatty, *Age of Betrayal: The Triumph of Money in America, 1865–
1900* (New York City: Vintage Books, 2008), xv.

19. David Madland, *Hollowed Out: Why the Economy Doesn't Work without a Strong
Middle Class* (Oakland: University of California Press, 2015), 67.

20. Robin Einhorn, *American Taxation, American Slavery* (Chicago: University of Chicago Press, 2006); Eric Zolt "Inequality, Collective Action, and Taxing and Spending Patterns of State and Local Governments," *Tax Law Review* 62, no. 4 (2009): 445–504; Sun
Go and Peter Lindert, "The Curious Dawn of American Public Schools," NBER Working
Paper 13335, National Bureau of Economic Research, August 2007, https://www.nber.org/
papers/w13335.pdf.

21. Einhorn, *American Taxation, American Slavery*; Larry M. Bartels, *Unequal Democracy: The Political Economy of the New Gilded Age* (Princeton, NJ: Princeton University
Press, 2008); Martin Gilens, "Inequality and Democratic Responsiveness," *Public Opinion
Quarterly* 69, no. 5 (2005): 778–96; Martin Gilens and Benjamin I. Page, "Testing Theories
of American Politics: Elites, Interest Groups, and Average Citizens," *Perspectives on Politics*
12, no. 3 (2014): 564–81.

22. Larry M. Bartels, *Unequal Democracy: The Political Economy of the New Gilded Age*
(Princeton, NJ: Princeton University Press, 2008); Martin Gilens, "Inequality and Democratic Responsiveness," *Public Opinion Quarterly* 69, no. 5 (2005): 778–96; Martin Gilens
and Benjamin I. Page, "Testing Theories of American Politics: Elites, Interest Groups, and
Average Citizens," *Perspectives on Politics* 12, no. 3 (2014): 564–81.

23. "Are Government Officials Crooked 1958–2014," American National Election
Studies, https://electionstudies.org/resources/anes-guide/top-tables/?id=61.

24. "Public Trust in Government: 1958–2019," Pew Research Center, April 11, 2019,
https://www.people-press.org/2019/04/11/public-trust-in-government-1958-2019.

25. Madland, *Hollowed Out*, 105–7, 90–92.

26. For a good overview of the material basis of oligarchy, see Jeffrey Winters, *Oligarchy*
(Cambridge University Press, 2012); for an example of a specific agenda in recent years,
see Gordon Lafer, *The One Percent Solution* (Ithaca, NY: Cornell University Press, 2017).

27. Madland, *Hollowed Out*, 76–78; lobbying based on "Ranked Sectors," Center
for Responsive Politics, https://www.opensecrets.org/lobby/top.php?indexType=c&show
Year=2018, for the year 2018. Ratios were calculated by comparing spending by the Labor
sector to the sum of spending by all other sectors, excluding Labor, Other, and Ideology/
Single-Issue.

28. Madland, *Hollowed Out*, 82–85.

29. Eric Uslaner, "Trust and the Economic Crisis of 2008," *Corporate Reputation Review* 13, no. 2 (2010): 110–23, https://www.researchgate.net/publication/45349108_Trust_and_the_Economic_Crisis_of_2008.

30. For a summary of this research, see David Madland, "Trust," chapter 2 in *Hollowed Out*.

31. Madland, *Hollowed Out*, 39. See also Eric M. Uslaner, *Divided Citizens: How Inequality Undermines Trust in America* (New York City: Demos, 2002).

32. Christian Albrekt Larsen, *The Rise and Fall of Social Cohesion: The Construction and De-construction of Social trust in the US, UK, Sweden, and Denmark* (Oxford University Press, 2013), 91.

33. Eric Uslaner, *The Decline of Comity in Congress* (Ann Arbor: University of Michigan Press, 1997); Howard Rosenthal, Keith Poole, and Nolan McCarthy, "Political Polarization and Income Inequality," unpublished paper, SSRN, 2003, https://ssrn.com/abstract=1154098; John Voorheis, Nolan McCarty, and Boris Shor, "Unequal Incomes, Ideology, and Gridlock: How Rising Inequality Increases Political Polarization," unpublished paper, SSRN, 2015, https://papers.ssrn.com/sol3/papers.cfm?abstract_id=2649215.

34. Eric Uslaner, *The Moral Foundations of Trust* (Cambridge, UK: Cambridge University Press, 2010).

35. Madland, *Hollowed Out*.

36. See, for example, Madland, *Hollowed Out*.

37. Aristotle, *The Politics; and The Constitution of Athens*, edited by Stephen Everson (Cambridge, UK: Cambridge University Press, 1996); Clement Fatovic, *America's Founding and the Struggle over Economic Inequality* (Lawrence: University of Kansas Press, 2015); Francis Fukuyama, "The Future of History: Can Liberal Democracy Survive the Decline of the Middle Class," *Foreign Affairs*, January/February 2012, 53–61.

38. Aristotle, *Politics; and The Constitution of Athens*.

39. James Madison, "Federalist No. 10," in *The Federalist Papers* (1787).

40. Ganesh Sitaraman, *The Crisis of the Middle Class Constitution* (New York: Alfred A. Knopf, 2017), 3.

41. Steven Levitsky and Daniel Ziblatt, *How Democracies Die* (New York: Crown, 2018).

42. See, for example, Danny Hakim and Michael Wines, "'They Don't Really Want Us to Vote': How Republicans Made It Harder," *New York Times*, November 3, 2018.

43. See, for example, German Lopez, "The Past Year of Research Has Made It Very Clear: Trump Won Because of Racial Resentment," *Vox*, December 15, 2017, https://www.vox.com/identities/2017/12/15/16781222/trump-racism-economic-anxiety-study; Lynn Vavreck, John Sides, and Michael Tesler, *Identity Crisis: The 2016 Presidential Campaign and the Battle for the Meaning of America* (Princeton, NJ: Princeton University Press, 2018); Brian F. Schaffner, Matthew MacWilliams, Tatishe Nteta, "Explaining White Polarization in the 2016 Vote for President: The Sobering Role of Racism and Sexism," paper prepared for presentation at the Conference on the US Elections of 2016: Domestic and International Aspects, January 8–9, 2019, https://www.idc.ac.il/en/schools/government/uselections/Documents/Schaffner-Brian%20.pdf. See also Kate Ratliff et al., "Engendering Support: Hostile Sexism Predicts Voting for Donald Trump over Hillary Clinton in the 2016 Presidential Election," *Group Processes and Intergroup Relations* 22, no. 4 (2017): 578–93.

44. David Madland et al., "President Trump's Policies Are Hurting American Workers," Center for American Progress Action Fund, 2018, https://www.americanprogressaction.org/issues/economy/reports/2018/01/26/168366/president-trumps-policies-hurting-american-workers.

45. Vavreck, Sides, and Tesler, *Identity Crisis*, 75, 80; Thomas Ferguson et al., "The Economic and Social Roots of Populist Rebellion: Support for Donald Trump in 2016," Working Paper 83, Institute for New Economic Thinking, October 2018, https://www.ineteconomics.org/uploads/papers/WP_83-Ferguson-et-al.pdf.

46. For information on negative partisanship, see Thomas Edsall, "What Motivates Voters More Than Loyalty? Loathing," *New York Times*, March 1, 2018; Shanto Iyengar and Masha Krupenkin, "The Strengthening of Partisan Affect," *Political Psychology* 39, no. 4 (February 2018): 201–18.

47. "Exit Polls: National President," CNN, last modified November 23, 2016, https://www.cnn.com/election/2016/results/exit-polls.

48. Robert P. Jones et al., *Anxiety, Nostalgia, and Mistrust: Findings from the 2015 American Values Survey* (Washington, DC: Public Religion Research Institute, 2015), https://www.prri.org/wp-content/uploads/2015/11/PRRI-AVS-2015-1.pdf.

49. See Uslaner, *Moral Foundations of Trust*; and Madland, *Hollowed Out*.

50. Lynn Vavreck, John Sides, and Michael Tesler, political scientists from George Washington University, the University of California, Irvine, and the University of California, Los Angeles, respectively, argue that an important part of Trump's election was "how people explained economic outcomes . . . and especially whether they believed hardworking white Americans were losing ground to less deserving minorities." Vavreck, Sides, and Tesler, *Identity Crisis*, 177. See also Judith Goldstein and Margaret Peters, "Nativism or Economic Threat: Attitudes toward Immigrants during the Great Recession," *International Interactions* 40, no. 3 (2014): 376–401, for a discussion of how economic threats and policy views on immigrants interact.

51. For further discussion of these themes, see Angela Hanks and David Madland, "Better Training and Better Jobs: A New Partnership for Sectoral Training," Center for American Progress, February 22, 2018, https://www.americanprogress.org/issues/economy/reports/2018/02/22/447115/better-training-better-jobs.

52. For a review of this research, see David Madland and Alex Rowell, "Unions Help the Middle Class, No Matter the Measure," Center for American Progress Action Fund, June 9, 2016, https://cdn.americanprogress.org/wp-content/uploads/2016/06/08122007/BenefitsOfUnions-brief.pdf.

53. Christian E. Weller, David Madland, and Alex Rowell, "Building Middle-Class Wealth through Unions," *Challenge: The Magazine of Economic Affairs* 60, no. 1 (2017): 40–50.

54. Richard Freeman et al., "Bargaining for the American Dream: What Unions Do for Mobility," Center for American Progress, September 9, 2015, https://www.americanprogress.org/issues/economy/reports/2015/09/09/120558/bargaining-for-the-american-dream.

55. Josh Bivens et al., "How Today's Unions Help Working People: Giving Workers the Power to Improve Their Jobs and Unrig the Economy," Economic Policy Institute, August 24, 2017, https://www.epi.org/publication/how-todays-unions-help-working-people-giving-workers-the-power-to-improve-their-jobs-and-unrig-the-economy.

56. Marion G. Crain and Ken Matheny, "Beyond Unions, Notwithstanding Labor Law," *UC Irvine Law Review* 4, no. 2 (2014), 561–608, https://papers.ssrn.com/sol3/papers.cfm?abstract_id=2549099; J. Hagedorn et al., "The Role of Labor Unions in Creating Working Conditions that Promote Public Health," *American Journal of Public Health* 106 (2016): 989–95; Judith A. Scott, "Why a Union Voice Makes a Real Difference for Women Workers: Then and Now," *Yale Journal of Law and Feminism* 21, no. 1 (2009): 233, 235, https://digitalcommons.law.yale.edu/yjlf/vol21/iss1/9/; and Taylor E. Dark, *The Unions and the Democrats* (Ithaca, NY: Cornell University Press, 2001).

57. Fuller context: "Before the politically induced decline in union strength . . . unions probably were the most effective advocate for public policies advantageous to the less affluent." David Jacobs and Lindsey Myers, "Union Strength, Neoliberalism, and Inequality: Contingent Political Analyses of US Income Differences since 1950," *American Sociological Review* 79, no. 4 (2014): 752–74.

58. Janice Fine and Jennifer Gordon, "Strengthening Labor Standards Enforcement through Partnerships with Workers' Organizations," *Politics and Society* 38, no. 4 (2010):

552–58; David Weil, "Individual Rights and Collective Agents: The Role of Old and New Workplace Institutions in the Regulation of Labor Markets," NBER Working Paper 9565, National Bureau of Economic Research, March 2003, https://www.nber.org/papers/w9565.pdf; Brooke E. Liermann, "To Assure Safe and Healthful Working Conditions: Taking Lessons from Labor Unions to Fulfill OSHA's Promises," *Loyola Journal of Public Interest Law* 12 (2010): 1–37, https://www.browngold.com/wbcntntprd1/wp-content/uploads/to_assure_safe_and_healthful_working_conditions1.pdf.

59. Mark Harcout, Geoffrey Wood, and Sondra Harcourt, "Do Unions Affect Employer Compliance with the Law? New Zealand Evidence for Age Discrimination," *British Journal of Employment Relations* 42, no. 3 (2004): 527–41; Benjamin Amick et al., "Protecting Construction Worker Health and Safety in Ontario, Canada: Identifying a Union Safety Effect," *Journal of Occupational and Environment Medicine* 57, no. 2 (December 2015): 1337–42; Wayner Lewchuck, "The Limits of Voice: Are Workers Afraid to Express Their Health and Safety Rights?" *Osgoode Hall Law Journal* 50, no. 4 (2013): 789–812; Deadly Skyline: An Annual Report on Construction Fatalities in New York State" (New York: New York Committee for Occupational Safety and Health, 2017), http://nycosh.org/wp-content/uploads/2017/01/DeadlySkyline2017_NYS-ConstructionFatalitiesReport_final_NYCOSH_May.pdf; Harry Miller et al., "An Analysis of Safety Culture and Safety Training: Comparing the Impact of Union, Non-Union, and Right to Work Construction Venues," *Online Journal for Workforce Education and Development* 9, no. 2 (2013), https://opensiuc.lib.siu.edu/ojwed/vol6/iss2/5/; Alison D. Morantz, "Coal Mine Safety: Do Unions Make a Difference?" *ILR Review* 66, no. 1 (2013): 88–116; Tae-Youn Park, Eun-Suk Lee, and John W. Budd, "What Do Unions Do for Mothers? Paid Maternity Leave Use and the Multifaceted Roles of Labor Unions," *ILR Review* 72, no. 3 (2018); David Cooper and Teresa Kroeger, "Employers Steal Billions from Workers' Paychecks Each Year," Economic Policy Institute, 2017, https://www.epi.org/publication/employers-steal-billions-from-workers-paychecks-each-year-survey-data-show-millions-of-workers-are-paid-less-than-the-minimum-wage-at-significant-cost-to-taxpayers-and-state-economies; Dionne Pohler and Chris Riddell, "Multinationals' Compliance with Employment Law: An Empirical Assessment Using Administrative Data from Ontario, 2004 to 2015," *ILR Review* 72, no. 3 (2018): 606–35.

60. Bruce Western and Jake Rosenfeld, "Unions, Norms, and the Rise in US Wage Inequality," *American Sociological Review* 76, no. 4 (2011): 513–37. See also David Card, Thomas Lemieux, and W. Craig Riddell, "Unions and Wage Inequality," *Journal of Labor Research* 25, no. 4 (2004): 519–59; John DiNardo, Nicole M. Fortin, and Thomas Lemieux, "Labor Market Institutions and the Distribution of Wages, 1973–1992," *Econometrica* 64, no. 5 (1996): 1001–44; Richard B. Freeman, "How Much Has De-Unionisation Contributed to the Rise in Male Earnings Inequality?," NBER Working Paper 3826, National Bureau of Economic Research, August 1991, https://www.nber.org/papers/w3826.

61. For a summary, see Madland and Rowell, "Unions Help the Middle Class"; Jonas Pontusson, David Rueda, and Christopher R. Way, "Comparative Political Economy of Wage Distribution: The Role of Partisanship and Labour Market Institutions," *British Journal of Political Science* 32 (2002): 281–308; Thomas A. Kochan and Christine A Riordan, "Employment Relations and Growing Income Inequality: Causes and Potential Options for Its Reversal," *Journal of Industrial Relations* 58, no. 3 (2016): 419–40; Brantly Callaway and William J. Collins, "Unions, Workers, and Wages at the Peak of the American Labor Movement," *Explorations in Economic History* 68 (2018): 95–118, https://www.nber.org/papers/w23516.pdf; Qinglin Hu and Dean M. Hanink, "Declining Union Contract Coverage and Increasing Income Inequality in US Metropolitan Areas," *Professional Geographer* 70, no. 3 (2018): 453–62; Henry S. Farber et al., "Unions and Inequality over the Twentieth Century: New Evidence from Survey Data," NBER Working Paper 24587, National Bureau

of Economic Research, May 2018, https://www.nber.org/papers/w24587.pdf; Frank Levy and Peter Temin, "Inequality and Institutions in the 20th Century America," NBER Working Paper 13106, National Bureau of Economic Research, May 2007, https://www.nber.org/papers/w13106.pdf; John Ahlquist, "Labor Unions Political Representation, and Economic Inequality," *Annual Review of Political Science* 20 (2017): 409–32.

62. Stephanie Moller, et al., "Determinants of Relative Poverty in Advanced Capitalist Democracies," *American Sociological Association* 68, no. 1 (2003): 22–51; David Brady, Andrew S. Fullerton, and Jennifer Moren Cross, "Putting Poverty in Political Context: A Multi-Level Analysis of Adult Poverty across 18 Affluent Democracies," *Social Forces* 88, no. 1 (2009): 271–300; Dean Baker, "Unions: The Best Fix to Poverty," Center for Economic and Policy Research, September 15, 2013, https://web.archive.org/web/20170224041341/http://cepr.net/blogs/cepr-blog/unions-the-best-fix-to-poverty.

63. David Brady, Regina S. Baker, and Ryan Finnigan, "When Unionization Disappears: State-Level Unionization and Working Poverty in the United States," *American Sociological Review* 78, no. 3 (2013): 872–96.

64. Freeman et al., "Bargaining for the American Dream."

65. Bartels, *Unequal Democracy*; Gilens, "Inequality and Democratic Responsiveness."

66. Gilens and Page, "Testing Theories of American Politics."

67. Steven J. Rosentone and John Hansen, *Mobilization, Participation, and Democracy in America* (London: Macmillan, 1993). For general information on the importance of mobilization, see Kay Lehman Schlozman, Sidney Verba, and Henry E. Brady, *The Unheavenly Chorus: Unequal Political Voice and the Broken Promise of American Democracy* (Princeton, NJ: Princeton University Press, 2013). On the importance of unions for education and mobilization, see, for example, Torben Iversen and David Soskice, "Information, Inequality, and Mass Polarization: Ideology in Advanced Democracies," *Comparative Political Studies* 48, no. 13 (2015): 1781–1813; Veronica Terriquez, "Schools for Democracy: Labor Union Participation and Latino Immigrant Parents' School-Based Civic Engagement," *American Sociological Review* 76, no. 4 (2011): 581–601; Peter Levine, "The Legitimacy of Labor Unions," *Hofstra Labor and Employment Law Journal* 18, no 2 (2001): 529–53, https://scholarlycommons.law.hofstra.edu/hlelj/vol18/iss2/8.

68. Jasmine Kerrissey and Evan Schofer, "Union Membership and Political Participation in the United States," *Social Forces* 91, no. 3 (2013): 895–928.

69. David Madland and Nick Bunker, "Unions Make Democracy Work for the Middle Class," Center for American Progress Action Fund, January 25, 2012, https://www.americanprogressaction.org/issues/economy/reports/2012/01/25/10913/unions-make-democracy-work-for-the-middle-class; Kerrissey and Schofer, "Union Membership and Political Participation in the United States"; Jonathan E. Booth, Daniela Lup, and Mark Williams, "Union Membership and Charitable Giving in the United States," *Industrial and Labor Relations Review* 70, no. 4 (2016): 835–64; Jake Rosenfeld, *What Unions No Longer Do* (Cambridge, MA: Harvard University Press, 2014); James Feigenbaum, Alexander Hertel-Fernandez, and Vanessa Williamson, "From the Bargaining Table to the Ballot Box: Political Effects of Right to Work Laws," NBER Working Paper 24259, National Bureau of Economic Research, February 2019, https://www.nber.org/papers/w24259.pdf; Alex Bryson, Rafael Gomez, and Tobias Kretschmer, "What Accounts for the Union Member Advantage in Voter Turnout? Evidence from the European Union, 2002–2008," *Industrial Relations* 69, no. 4 (2014): 732–65; Roland Zullo, "Union Cities and Voter Turnout," Labor and Employment Relations Association 58th annual meeting, Champaign, Illinois, 2006; Roland Zullo, "Union Membership and Political Inclusion," *ILR Review* 62, no. 1 (2008), 22–38.

70. Benjamin Radcliff and Patricia Davis, "Labor Organization and Electoral Participation in Industrial Democracies," *American Journal of Political Science* 44, no. 1 (2000): 132–41.

71. It is worth noting that major decisions about capital investment or the scope or direction of the enterprise are in the core of entrepreneurial control and need not be discussed at all. An additional virtue of centralized bargaining is that these issues become less of a concern to workers.

72. Carole Pateman, *Participation and Democratic Theory* (Cambridge, UK: University of Cambridge Press, 1970); Robert Dahl, *A Preface to Economic Democracy* (Oakland: University of California Press, 1986).

73. John Hibbing and Elizabeth Theiss-Morse, *Stealth Democracy: Americans' Beliefs about How Government Should Work* (Cambridge, UK: Cambridge University Press, 2002).

74. Ethan Kaplan, Jörg L. Spenkuch, and Haishan Yuan, "Natural Disasters, Moral Hazard, and Special Interests in Congress," unpublished paper, 2019, http://econweb.umd.edu/~kaplan/natural_disasters.pdf.

75. This is especially true since ACORN went out of existence.

76. Martin Gilens, *Affluence and Influence: Economic Inequality and Political Power in America* (Princeton, NJ: Princeton University Press, 2012); Gilens and Page, "Testing Theories of American Politics."

77. Campaign contributions based on "Election Overview: Totals by Sector," Center for Responsive Politics, https://www.opensecrets.org/overview/sectors.php?cycle=2018, for the years 1990 and 2018. Ratios were calculated by comparing spending by the Labor sector to the sum of spending by all other sectors, excluding Labor, Other, and Ideology/Single-Issue.

78. Lobbying based on "Lobbying: Ranked Sectors," Center for Responsive Politics, https://www.opensecrets.org/lobby/top.php?indexType=c&showYear=2018, for the year 2018. Ratios were calculated by comparing spending by the Labor sector to the sum of spending by all other sectors, excluding Labor, Other, and Ideology/Single-Issue.

79. Gilens and Page, "Testing Theories of American Politics"; Gilens, *Affluence and Influence.*

80. Daniel Stegmueller, Michael Becher, and Konstantin Käppner, "Labor Unions and Unequal Representation," draft "for presentation at workshop on *Unions and the Politics of Inequality,*" Université de Genève, April 13–14, 2018, https://pdfs.semanticscholar.org/b6c b/09ba8ea6eeea82da1ddc3ead47a819625c07.pdf. See also Patrick Flavin, "Labor Union Strength and the Equality of Political Representation," *British Journal of Political Science* 48, no. 4 (2018): 1075–91.

81. Susan Orr, "Forming a More Democratic Unions: Organized Labor and American Democracy, Ideals and Institutions," unpublished dissertation, 2010. See also K. Sabeel Rahman, *Democracy Against Domination* (Oxford, UK: Oxford University Press, 2016); Suresh Naidu, "Problems against Symptoms: Economic Democracy and Inequality," *Items: Insights from the Social Sciences* (Social Science Research Council), September 6, 2016, https://items. ssrc.org/problems-against-symptoms-economic-democracy-and-inequality. See also John Halpin and Connor Williams, "The Progressive Intellectual Tradition in America," Center for American Progress, April 14, 2010, https://www.americanprogress.org/issues/democracy/reports/2010/04/14/7677/the-progressive-intellectual-tradition-in-america.

82. In addition to many works cited above, see Felicia Wong, K. Sabeel Rahman, and Dorian Warren, "Democratizing Economic Power to Break the Cycle of American Inequality," *Stanford Social Innovation Review,* Winter 2020, https://ssir.org/articles/entry/democratizing_economic_power_to_break_the_cycle_of_american_inequality.

83. Jacob S. Hacker and Paul Pierson, *Winner-Take-All Politics: How Washington Made the Rich Richer—and turned Its Back on the Middle Class* (New York: Simon & Schuster, 2010), 57.

84. Cheol-Sung Lee, "Labor Unions and Good Governance: A Cross-National, Comparative Analysis," *American Sociological Review,* 72, no. 4 (2007): 585–609.

85. Rankings of democratic quality include "Tables and Ratings," in *Freedom in the World 2018: The Annual Survey of Political Rights and Civil Liberties* (Lanham, MD: Rowman & Littlefield, 2019), 1219–29, https://freedomhouse.org/report/freedom-world-2018-table-country-scores; Economist Intelligence Unit, *Democracy Index 2017: Free Speech under Attack* (Economist Intelligence Unit, 2018), https://spcommreports.ohchr.org/TMResultsBase/DownLoadFile?gId=34079; "Polity data series," Wikipedia, accessed March 9, 2019, https://en.wikipedia.org/wiki/Polity_data_series. While there are many trade union members in China and other less than democratic countries, these organizations are not independent but rather arms of the state. Similarly, in countries that were ruled in authoritarian ways that incorporated unions (e.g., Argentina, Mexico, and Egypt), under this state corporatist model "independent unions are banned and state officials typically vet union leaders for political allegiance." Jasmine Kerrisey and Evan Schofer, "Labor Unions and Political Participation in Comparative Perspective," *Social Forces* 97, no. 1 (2018): 427–64.

86. Phil Fishman, "Democracy, Union Made," *American Interest*, September 1, 2007, https://www.the-american-interest.com/2007/09/01/democracy-union-made. According to Ho Keun Song, writing in 1999 about unions in Korea, "The labour movement played the most influential and decisive role in the struggle against authoritarianism in the past two decades and in triggering the transition to democracy in 1987. Organized labour put formidable pressure on authoritarian leadership in all three major regimes when NSMs [new social movements] were underdeveloped." Ho Keun Song, *Labour Unions in the Republic of Korea: Challenge and Choice* (Geneva: International Institute for Labour Studies, 1999), https://library.fes.de/pdf-files/gurn/00164.pdf, 35. See also Ruth Berins Collier and James Mahoney, "Labor and Democratization: Comparing the First and Third Waves in Europe and Latin America," Working Paper 62-95, Institute for Research on Labor and Employment, May 1995, http://irle.berkeley.edu/files/1995/Labor-and-Democratization.pdf.

87. C. N. Trueman, "Trade Unions and Nazi Germany," The History Learning Site, https://www.historylearningsite.co.uk/nazi-germany/trade-unions-and-nazi-germany; Paul W. Drake, *Labor Movements and Dictatorships* (Baltimore: Johns Hopkins University Press, 1996); "The Tradeoff of Labor and Neoliberal Economics: The Case for Chile in the 1990s," Council on Hemispheric Affairs, August 3, 2011, http://www.coha.org/the-tradeoff-of-labor-and-neoliberal-economics-the-case-of-chile-in-the-1990s; András Tóth, "The New Hungarian Labour Code—Background, Conflicts, Compromises," working paper, Friedrich Ebert Foundation Budapest, June 2012, http://www.fesbp.hu/common/pdf/Nachrichten_aus_Ungarn_june_2012.pdf.

88. For details on unions and Peron, see Laura Tedesco, *Democracy in Argentina: Hope and Disillusion* (London: Taylor and Francis, 1999); for Egypt and more general info, see Kerrisey and Schofer, "Labor Unions and Political Participation in Comparative Perspective."

89. Volker Berghahn and Detlev Karsten, *Industrial Relations in West Germany* (New York: Berg, 1989); Labour Relations Act of 1995, South Africa.

90. Among many others, see, for example, V. Bhasker, Alan Manning, and Ted To, "Oligopsony and Monopsonistic Competition in Labor Markets," *Journal of Economic Perspectives* 16, no. 2 (2002): 155–74, http://discovery.ucl.ac.uk/15468/1/15468.pdf; Alan Manny, *Monopsony in Motion: Imperfect Competition in Labor Markets* (Princeton, NJ: Princeton University Press, 2005).

91. Richard Freeman and James Medoff, *What Do Unions Do?* (New York City: Basic Books, 1984). See also James T. Bennett and Bruce E. Kaufman, eds., *What Do Unions Do? A Twenty-Year Perspective* (Piscataway, NJ: Transaction Publishers, 2007).

92. Freeman and Medoff, *What Do Unions Do?*, 14.

93. As one review of the research put it, "Union density appears to have little or no impact on comparative labor market performance." Toke S. Aidt and Zafaris Tzannatos, "Trade Unions, Collective Bargaining, and Macroeconomic Performance: A Review," *Industrial Relations Journal* 39, no. 4 (2008): 258–25. See also, among many others, David Metcalf, "Unions and Productivity, Financial Performance and Investment: International Evidence," Center for Economic Performance, July 2002, http://eprints.lse.ac.uk/20072; Franz Traxler and Bernd Brandl, "Collective Bargaining, Inter-Sectoral Heterogeneity and Competitiveness: A Cross-National Comparison of Macroeconomic Performance," *British Journal of Industrial Relations* 50, no. 1 (2012): 73–98; Barry T. Hirsch, "What Do Unions Do for Economic Performance?," *Journal of Labor Research* 25, no. 3 (2004): 415–55; Naercio Menez-Filho and John Van Reenen, "Unions and Innovation: A Survey of the Theory and Empirical Evidence," Centre for Economic Policy Research, Discussion Paper 3792, January 2003, http://cep.lse.ac.uk/textonly/people/vanreenen/papers/DP3792.pdf; Dale Belman and Richard N. Block, "The Impact of Collective Bargaining on Competitiveness and Employment," in *Bargaining for Competitiveness: Law, Research, and Case Studies*, ed. Richard N. Block (Kalamazoo, MI: W. E. Upjohn Institute for Employment Research, 2003), 45–74; and Dean Baker et al., "Unemployment and Labor Market Institutions: The Failure of the Empirical Case for Deregulation," September 2004, http://cepr.net/documents/publications/cepa200404.pdf. For a review of the economic effects of unions by a non-economist, see Wolfgang Streeck, "The Sociology of Labor Markets and Trade Unions," in *The Handbook of Economic Sociology*, eds. Neil J. Smelser and Richard Swedberg (New York: Russell Sage Foundation, 2005), 254–83.

94. See, for example, John Schmitt, "Why Does the Minimum Wage Have No Discernable Effect on Employment?," Center for Economy and Policy Research, February 2013, http://cepr.net/documents/publications/min-wage-2013-02.pdf; Sylvia Allegretto et al., "The New Wave of Local Minimum Wage Policies: Evidence from Six Cities," Center on Wage and Employment Dynamics, September 6, 2018, http://irle.berkeley.edu/files/2018/09/The-New-Wave-of-Local-Minimum-Wage-Policies.pdf. For a related line of research on a different workplace policy, see Joan C. Williams et al., Stable Scheduling Increases Productivity and Sales: The Stable Scheduling Study (San Francisco: Worklife Law; Chicago: University of Chicago School of Social Service Administration; Chapel Hill: University of North Carolina, Kenan-Flagler Business School, 2018), https://worklifelaw.org/publications/Stable-Scheduling-Study-Report.pdf.

95. Daron Acemoglu and James Robinson, "Economic versus Politics: Pitfalls of Policy Advice," *Journal of Economic Perspectives* 27, no. 2 (2013): 173–92; Madland, *Hollowed Out*.

96. Acemoglu and Robinson, "Economic versus Politics."

97. David Madland and Alex Rowell, "Combating Pay Gaps with Unions and Expanded Collective Bargaining," Center for American Progress Action Fund, June 28, 2018, https://www.americanprogressaction.org/issues/economy/reports/2018/06/28/170469/combating-pay-gaps-unions-expanded-collective-bargaining; Christian E. Weller and David Madland, "Union Membership Narrows the Racial Wealth Gap for Families of Color," Center for American Progress, September 4, 2018, https://www.americanprogress.org/issues/economy/reports/2018/09/04/454781/union-membership-narrows-racial-wealth-gap-families-color.

98. Bernard D. Meltzer, "The National Labor Relations Act and Racial Discrimination: The More Remedies, the Better?" *University of Chicago Law Review* 42, no. 1 (Fall 1974): 1–44, https://chicagounbound.uchicago.edu/cgi/viewcontent.cgi?article=11907&context=journal_articles.

99. Sean Farhang and Ira Katznelson, "The Southern Imposition: Congress and Labor in the New Deal and Fair Deal," *Studies in American Political Development* 19 (Spring 2005): 1–30, https://gspp.berkeley.edu/assets/uploads/research/pdf/article_4.pdf.

100. John Smith, "AFL-CIO's Richard Trumka on Racism and Obama," *YouTube*, July 20, 2008, https://www.youtube.com/watch?v=7QIGJTHdH50; John Nichols, "AFL-CIO's Trumka Embraces All Workers—Including Immigrants," *Nation*, September 19, 2009, https://www.thenation.com/article/afl-cios-trumka-embraces-all-workers-including-immigrants.

101. Bivens et al., "How Today's Unions Help Working People."

102. Michelle J. Budig, Joya Misra, and Irene Boeckmann, "Work-Family Policy Trade-Offs for Mothers? Unpacking the Cross-National Variation in Motherhood Earnings Penalties," *Work and Occupations* 43, no. 2 (2016): 119–77.

103. Francine D. Blau and Lawrence M. Kahn, "Understanding International Differences in the Gender Pay Gap," *Journal of Labor Economics* 21, no. 1 (2003): 106–44.

104. Elise Gould and Celine McNicholas, "Unions Help Narrow the Gender Wage Gap," Economic Policy Institute, April 3, 2017, https://www.epi.org/blog/unions-help-narrow-the-gender-wage-gap. See also Marta M. Elvira and Ishak Saporta, "How Does Collective Bargaining Affect the Gender Pay Gap?," *Work and Occupations* 28, no. 4 (2001): 469–90, for evidence that women in unionized establishments experience smaller pay gaps than their counterparts in establishments without unions.

105. Bivens et al., "How Today's Unions Help Working People."

106. Jake Rosenfeld and Meredith Kleykamp, "Organized Labor and Racial Wage Inequality in the United States," *American Journal of* Sociology 117, no. 5 (2015): 1460–502. Note that Rosenfeld and Kleykamp found that during their sample's time period, black and white workers received similar union wage premiums.

107. Weller and Madland, "Union Membership Narrows the Racial Wealth Gap for Families of Color."

108. Seema Mody, "Hotels Are Arming Workers with Panic Buttons to Combat Harassment," CNBC, September 6, 2018, https://www.cnbc.com/2018/09/06/major-hotels-arm-workers-with-panic-buttons-to-fight-harassment.html; David Robb, "SAG-AFTRA Bans Auditions in Hotel Rooms and Residences," *Deadline*, April 12, 2018, https://deadline.com/2018/04/hollywood-actors-hotel-rooms-residences-auditions-banned-sag-aftra-1202362990.

109. Brief of the Human Rights Campaign, Lambda Legal Defense and Education Fund, Inc., the National Center for Lesbian Rights, the National LGBTQ Task Force, and PFLAG as Amici Curiae in Support of Respondents, *Janus v. AFSCME*, 585 US (2018), https://www.supremecourt.gov/DocketPDF/16/16-1466/28491/20180119143902718_16-1466%20bsac%20HRC.pdf. See also Gerald Hunt and Monica Bielski Boris, "The Lesbian, Gay, Bisexual, And Transgender Challenge To American Labor," chap. 4 in *The Sex of Class: Women Transforming American Labor*, ed. Dorothy Sue Cobble (Ithaca, NY: Cornell University Press, 2015).

110. Dorothy Sue Cobble, *The Other Women's Movement: Workplace Justice and Social Rights in Modern America* (Princeton, NJ: Princeton University Press, 2004).

111. Paul Frymer and Jacob M. Grumbach, "Labor Unions and White Racial Politics," *American Journal of Political Science*, June 29, 2020, https://doi.org/10.1111/ajps.12537.

112. Blau and Kahn, "Understanding International Differences in the Gender Pay Gap"; Aidt and Tzannatos, "Trade Unions, Collective Bargaining, and Macroeconomic Performance"; Francine D. Blau and Lawrence M. Kahn, "Gender Differences in Pay," NBER Working Paper 7732, National Bureau of Economic Research, June 2000, http://www.nber.org/papers/w7732.pdf.

113. Valerie Wilson and William M. Rodgers III, "Black-White Wage Gaps Expand with Rising Wage Inequality," Economic Policy Institute, September 20, 2016, https://www.epi.org/publication/black-white-wage-gaps-expand-with-rising-wage-inequality. See also Leslie McCall, "Sources of Racial Wage Inequality in Metropolitan Labor Markets: Racial,

Ethnic, and Gender Differences," *American Sociological Review,* 66 (2001): 520–41, for research showing that overall black-white wage gaps are lower in metropolitan areas with higher union membership.

114. On the relationship between inequality and trust, see Uslaner, *Moral Foundations of Trust,* 193–97. For a somewhat related argument about the importance of broad-based economic growth creating conditions that allow for addressing discrimination, see Benjamin M. Friedman, *The Moral Consequences of Economic Growth* (New York City: Vintage Books, 2006).

115. For a summary of this research, see Madland and Rowell, "Combating Pay Gaps with Unions and Expanded Collective Bargaining."

116. See, among others, Dorian T. Warren, "The American Labor Movement in the Age of Obama: The Challenges and Opportunities of a Racialized Political Economy," *Perspectives on Politics* 8, no. 3 (2010): 847–60.

117. Daniel Hautzinger, "How Pullman Porters Laid Groundwork for the Civil Rights Movement," *WTTW,* February 22, 2019, https://interactive.wttw.com/playlist/2019/02/22/pullman-porters; Hugh B. Hammett, "Labor and Race: The Georgia Railroad Strike of 1909," *Labor History* 16 (1975): 470–84; James Gilbert Cassady, "African Americans and the American Labor Movement," *Prologue Magazine* 29, no. 2 (1997), https://www.archives.gov/publications/prologue/1997/summer/american-labor-movement.html; "History of Labor Unions Analysis," *Shmoop,* https://www.shmoop.com/study-guides/history/history-labor-unions/analysis; and Nelson Lichtenstein, *State of the Union: A Century of American Labor* (Princeton, NJ: Princeton University Press, 2002), 92.

118. For evidence of unions late to reform, see, for example, Paul Frymer, *Black and Blue: African Americans, the Labor Movement, and the Decline of the Democratic Party* (Princeton, NJ: Princeton University Press, 2007).

119. Ryan Grim and Aida Chavez, "Minneapolis Police Union President: "I've Been Involved in Three Shootings Myself, and Not a One of Them Has Bothered Me," *Intercept,* June 2, 2020, https://theintercept.com/2020/06/02/minneapolis-police-union-bob-kroll-shootings/; Samantha Michaels, "Minneapolis Police Union President Allegedly Wore a 'White Power Patch' and Made Racist Remarks," Mother Jones, May 30, 2020, https://www.motherjones.com/crime-justice/2020/05/minneapolis-police-union-president-kroll-george-floyd-racism/.

120. "AFL-CIO General Board Recommends Police Reform, Calls for Defense Secretary, Chairman of Joint Chiefs of Staff and President of Minneapolis Police Union to Resign," AFL-CIO, June 9, 2020, https://aflcio.org/press/releases/afl-cio-general-board-recommends-police-reform-calls-defense-secretary-chairman; Hamilton Nolan, "SEIU President: Expelling Police Unions from the Labor Movement 'Has to Be Considered,' *In These Times,* June 19, 2020, https://inthesetimes.com/working/entry/22610/mary-kay-henry-seiu-expel-police-unions-black-lives-matter-labor-movement; Elliott Almond, "Major California Police Unions Call for Reforms, Removal of Racist Officers," *Mercury News,* June 14, 2020, https://www.mercurynews.com/2020/06/14/california-largest-police-unions-unveil-reform-plan-in-joint-statement/; Jacob Bogage, "Thousands of Workers Walk Out in 'Strike for Black Lives,'" *Washington Post,* July 20, 2020, https://www.washingtonpost.com/business/2020/07/20/strike-for-black-lives/.

121. Lawrence Mishel, "Diversity in the New York City Union and Nonunion Construction Sectors," Economic Policy Institute, March 2, 2017, https://www.epi.org/publication/diversity-in-the-nyc-construction-union-and-nonunion-sectors.

122. Robert W. Glover and Cihan Bilginsoy, "Registered Apprenticeship Training in the US Construction Industry," *Education + Training* 47, no. 4/5 (2005): 337–49.

123. For a discussion of this, see Jake Rosenfeld, "The Timing Was Terrible: Deunionization and Racial Inequality," chap. 5 in *What Unions No Longer Do.*

124. For some history of the mineworkers during World War I, for example, see Joseph A. McCartin, *Labor's Great War: The Struggle for Industrial Democracy and the Origins of Modern American Labor Relations, 1912–1921* (Chapel Hill: University of North Carolina Press, 1997), 123–28.

125. AFL-CIO, *A Short History of American Labor* (Washington, DC: AFL-CIO, 1981).

126. McCartin, *Labor's Great War,* 151–53.

127. "Labor Movement Was Critical Ally to Civil Rights Movement," *All Things Considered*, NPR, August 27, 2013, https://www.npr.org/templates/story/story.php?storyId=216191855.

128. Ted Conover, "The Strike That Brought MLK to Memphis," *Smithsonian,* January 2018, https://www.smithsonianmag.com/history/revisiting-sanitation-workers-strike-180967512.

129. John Brueggemann and Terry Boswell, "Realizing Solidarity: Sources of Interracial Unionism during the Great Depression," *Work and Occupations* 25, no. 4 (1998), 436–82; Frymer, *Black and Blue.*

130. "The Origins of American Trade Unionism," Digital History, http://www.digital history.uh.edu/disp_textbook.cfm?smtID=2&psid=3191.

131. "History of the ILGWU: Early Struggles," Cornell University ILR School, http://ilgwu.ilr.cornell.edu/history/earlyStruggles.html; "History of the ILGWU: Social Unionism," Cornell University ILR School, http://ilgwu.ilr.cornell.edu/history/socialUnionism.html.

132. "Women's Rights: Breaking the Gender Barrier: A Woman's Place Is in Her Union," Special Collections and University Archives, University of Maryland Libraries, https://www.lib.umd.edu/unions/social/womens-rights.

133. "San Jose Employee Strike over Equal Pay for Women," *New York Times,* July 6, 1981; Walter Goodman, "Equal Pay for 'Comparable Worth' Growing as Job-Discrimination Issue," *New York Times,* September 4, 1984.

134. For some of the legal changes that led to the "duty of fair representation," see Archibald Cox, "The Duty of Fair Representation," *Villanova Law Review* 2, no. 2 (1957): 151–77, https://digitalcommons.law.villanova.edu/cgi/viewcontent.cgi?referer=http://scholar.google.com/&httpsredir=1&article=3236&context=vlr; "The Duty of Fair Representation," American Bar Association, https://www.americanbar.org/content/dam/aba/events/labor_law/basics_papers/nlra/fair_representation.authcheckdam.pdf.

135. Farber et al., "Unions and Inequality over the Twentieth Century."

136. Bivens et al., "How Today's Unions Help Working People."

137. For additional information, see Lane Windham, *Knocking on Labor's Door* (Chapel Hill: University of North Carolina Press, 2017).

138. Bivens et al., "How Today's Unions Help Working People."

139. U.S. Bureau of Labor Statistics, "News Release: Union Members—2019," January 2, 2020, https://www.bls.gov/news.release/pdf/union2.pdf.

140. Kate Bronfenbrenner and Dorian Warren, "Race, Gender, and the Rebirth of Trade Unionism," Digital Commons@ILR, ILR School, Cornell University, June 2007, http://digitalcommons.ilr.cornell.edu/articles/829.

141. For some background on the diversity of union leadership, see Bronfenbrenner and Warren, "Race, Gender, and the Rebirth of Trade Unionism." For information on corporate board diversity, see Missing Pieces Report: The 2016 Board Diversity Census of Women and Minorities on Fortune 500 Boards (Deloitte/Alliance for Board Diversity, 2016), https://www2.deloitte.com/us/en/pages/center-for-board-effectiveness/articles/board-diversity-census-missing-pieces.html.

142. "Lee Saunders, President," American Federation of State, County, and Municipal Employees, https://www.afscme.org/union/leadership/lee-saunders; *Questions and Answers about AFSCME* (Washington, DC: AFSCME, 2017).

143. "Mary Kay Henry, President," Service Employees International Union, accessed March 14, 2019, https://www.advocate.com/business/2012/09/01/labor-day-tribute-mary-kay-henry.

144. "Randi Weingarten, AFT President," American Federation of Teachers, accessed March 14, 2019, https://jwa.org/teach/livingthelegacy/biographies/weingarten-randi.

145. "Our President," National Education Association, https://www.nea.org/about-nea/leaders/president.

146. "Leadership," AFL-CIO, accessed March 14, 2019, https://aflcio.org/about-us/leadership.

147. "Women in Unions," Status of Women in the States, accessed March 14, 2019, https://statusofwomendata.org/women-in-unions/. For African American leadership at the second level, see also Erin Evans, "The Top Black Labor Union Leaders," *Root*, September 5, 2010, https://www.theroot.com/the-top-black-labor-union-leaders-1790867923.

CHAPTER 3. THE CONTOURS OF A MODERN LABOR SYSTEM

1. Note that unions may not meet the definition to be a "pure" public good. It is theoretically possible for unions to negotiate wage increases for only their members—but an employer usually extends these gains to other workers to reduce the incentive to join and thus to weaken the union. Union contracts could also be rival in consumption because wage increases for certain types of workers could limit wage increases for other types of workers.

2. Mancur Olson, *The Logic of Collective Action: Public Goods and the Theory of Groups* (Cambridge, MA: Harvard University Press, 1971).

3. For examples of employer support for various labor systems, see, among others, Kathleen Thelen, "Varieties of Labor Politics in the Developed Democracies," in *Varieties of Capitalism: The Institutional Foundations of Comparative Advantage*, eds. Peter A. Hall and David Soskice (Oxford University Press, 2001), 71–103; Peter Swenson, *Capitalists against Markets* (Oxford University Press, 2002).

4. Thomas Frank, "It's Time to Give Voters the Liberalism They Want," *Wall Street Journal*, November 19, 2008.

5. For research on the impact of outsourcing on wages and unionization, see Arindrajit Dube and Ethan Kaplan, "Does Outsourcing Reduce Wages in Low-wage Service Occupations? Evidence from Janitors and Guards," *ILR Review* 63, no. 2 (2010): 287–306, http://econweb.umd.edu/~kaplan/empiricaloutsourcing.pdf.

6. Todd E. Vachon, Michael Wallace, and Allen Hyde, "Union Decline in a Neoliberal Age: Globalization, Financialization, European Integration, and Union Density in 18 Affluent Democracies," *Socius: Sociological Research for a Dynamic World* 2 (2016): 1–22, https://doi.org/10.1177%2F2378023116656847.

7. Jacob Hacker, "Policy Drift: The Hidden Politics of US Welfare State Retrenchment," in *Beyond Continuity: Institutional Change in Advanced Political Economies*, eds. W. Streeck and K. Thelen (Oxford University Press, 2005), 40–82.

8. Gordon Lafer, *Neither Free nor Fair* (Washington, DC: Jobs With Justice: 2007), https://www.jwj.org/neither-free-nor-fair.

9. Kate Bronfenbrenner, "No Holds Barred—The Intensification of Employer Opposition to Organizing," Briefing Paper 235, Economic Policy Institute, May 20, 2009, https://digitalcommons.ilr.cornell.edu/cgi/viewcontent.cgi?article=1037&context=reports.

10. Stephen H. Norwood, *Strikebreaking and Intimidation: Mercenaries and Masculinity in Twentieth-Century America* (Chapel Hill: University of North Carolina Press, 2002).

11. Bronfenbrenner, "No Holds Barred."

12. John-Paul Ferguson, "The Eyes of the Needles: A Sequential Model of Union Organizing Drives, 1999–2004," *Industrial Relations Review* 62, no. 1 (2008): 3–21.

13. "Right-to-Work Resources," National Conference of State Legislatures, accessed March 19, 2019, http://www.ncsl.org/research/labor-and-employment/right-to-work-laws-and-bills.aspx.

14. Joseph McCartin, "Bargaining for the Future: Rethinking Labor's Recent Past and Planning Strategically for Its Future" (Kalmanovitz Initiative for Labor and the Working Poor, Georgetown University, Washington, DC, June 18, 2014).

15. See Kate Andrias, "The New Labor Law," *Yale Law Journal* 126, no. 1 (2016), https://www.yalelawjournal.org/article/the-new-labor-law, especially note 126.

16. Josiah Bartlett Lambert, *"If the Workers Took a Notion": The Right to Strike and American Political Development* (Ithaca, NY: Cornell University Press, 2005). For more on the importance of disruption for less powerful groups, see Frances Fox Piven and Richard Cloward, *Poor People's Movements: Why They Succeed, How They Fail* (New York: Vintage, 1977).

17. Stan Karp and Adam Sanchez, "The 2018 Wave of Teacher Strikes: A Turning Point for Our Schools?" *Rethinking Schools* 32, no. 4 (2018), https://www.rethinkingschools.org/articles/the-2018-wave-of-teacher-strikes. Note that teacher strikes are illegal in many states. Milla Sanes and John Schmitt, "Regulation of Public Sector Collective Bargaining in the States," Center for Economic and Policy Research, 2014, https://www.cepr.net/documents/state-public-cb-2014-03.pdf.

18. "The Right to Strike," National Labor Relations Board, https://www.nlrb.gov/strikes.

19. "Secondary Boycotts (Section 8(b)(4))," National Labor Relations Board, https://www.nlrb.gov/rights-we-protect/whats-law/unions/secondary-boycotts-section-8b4.

20. Wiebke Warneck, *Strike Rules in the EU 27 and Beyond: A Comparative Overview* (Brussels: European Trade Union Institute for Research, Education and Health and Safety, 2007), https://www.asi.is/media/7581/Strike_rules_in_the_EU27.pdf.

21. Lance A. Compa, "Human Rights and Workers' Rights in the United States," AFL-CIO, 2006, https://digitalcommons.ilr.cornell.edu/cgi/viewcontent.cgi?article=1129&context=laborunions.

22. Human Rights Watch, *Unfair Advantage: Workers' Freedom of Association in the United States under International Human Rights Standards* (New York: Human Rights Watch, 2000), https://www.hrw.org/reports/2000/uslabor.

23. William Forbath, *Law and the Shaping of the American Labor Movement* (Cambridge, MA: Harvard University Press, 1991); William Domhoff, "The Rise and Fall of Labor Unions in the U.S," Who Rules America?, https://whorulesamerica.ucsc.edu/power/history_of_labor_unions.html; Suresh Naidu and Noam Yuchtman, "Labor Market Institutions in the Gilded Age of American Economic History," NBER Working Paper 22117, National Bureau of Economic Research, 2016, https://www.nber.org/papers/w22117.pdf.

24. Clayton Anti-Trust Act (1914); Norris-LaGuardia Act (1932).

25. Joseph A. McCartin, *Labor's Great War: The Struggle for Industrial Democracy and the Origins of Modern American Labor Relations, 1912–1921* (Chapel Hill: University of North Carolina Press, 1997).

26. National Labor Relations Act, 29 USC § 151 (1935).

27. See James Atleson, *Labor and the Wartime State: Labor Relations and Law during World War II* (Urbana: University of Illinois Press, 1998); "World War II Labor Measures," Encyclopedia.com, https://www.encyclopedia.com/history/encyclopedias-almanacs-transcripts-and-maps/world-war-ii-labor-measures. Even during this period of favorable Congressional and executive policymaking, the courts in cases such as *National Labor Relations Board v. Mackay Radio & Telegraph Co.* (1938) were still not very supportive of labor.

28. Richard Freeman, "Spurts in Union Growth: Defining Moments and Social Processes," chap. 8 in *The Defining Moment: The Great Depression and the American Economy in the Twentieth Century*, ed. Michael D. Bordo, Claudia Goldin, and Eugene N. White (Chicago: University of Chicago Press, 1998).

29. For a review of social movement research see, David Madland, 2015. "A Wink and a Handshake: Why the Collapse of the U.S. Pension System has Provoked Little Protest," PhD dissertation, Georgetown University.

30. Indeed, even the increases in organizing and slight increases in density in the mid-1930s prior to 1937 can at least be partially attributed to the policy climate during the 1933 passage of the National Industrial Recovery Act, which included union rights. As Frances Fox Piven and Richard Cloward argue, the act's labor provisions "were to have an unprecedented impact on the unorganized working people of the country, not so much for what they gave, as for what they promised." Piven and Cloward, *Poor People's Movements*, 110.

31. For the NLRA, see James Gross, *Broken Promise: The Subversion of US Labor Relations* (Philadelphia, PA: Temple University Press, 1995); for the courts, see Julius Getman, "The National Labor Relations Act: What Went Wrong; Can We Fix It?" *Boston College Law Review* 45, no. 1 (2003): 125–46, https://lawdigitalcommons.bc.edu/bclr/vol45/iss1/3.

32. Cynthia Estlund, "The Ossification of American Labor Law," *Columbia Law Review* 102, no. 6 (2002): 1527–612; Jefferson Cowie, "Reframing the New Deal: The Past and Future of American Labor and the Law," *Theoretical Inquiries in Law* 17, no. 1 (2016): 13–38, http://www7.tau.ac.il/ojs/index.php/til/article/view/1371.

33. Bronfenbrenner, "No Holds Barred."

34. A Bill to Protect the Economic Rights of Labor in the Building and Construction Industry by Providing for Equal Treatment of Craft and Industrial Workers, H.R. 5900, 94th Cong., 1st sess. (1975), https://www.congress.gov/bill/94th-congress/house-bill/5900; Striker Replacement Bill, S. 55, 103rd Cong., 1st sess. (1993), https://www.govtrack.us/congress/bills/103/s55/text/is; Employee Free Choice Act, H.R. 5000, 114th Cong., 2nd sess. (2016), https://www.congress.gov/114/bills/hr5000/BILLS-114hr5000ih.pdf; and Wage Act, S.2143, 115th Cong., 1st sess. (2017), https://www.congress.gov/115/bills/s2143/BILLS-115s2143is.pdf.

35. "Right-to-Work Resources."

36. Act 10, Wisconsin A.B. 11 (2011), https://docs.legis.wisconsin.gov/2011/related/acts/10; David Madland and Alex Rowell, "Attacks on Public-Sector Unions Harm States: How Act 10 Has Affected Education on Wisconsin," Center for American Progress Action Fund, 2017, https://www.americanprogressaction.org/issues/economy/reports/2017/11/15/169146/attacks-public-sector-unions-harm-states-act-10-affected-education-wisconsin.

37. See, for example, An Act Relating to Employment Matters Involving Public Employees, Iowa H.F. 291 (2017), https://www.legis.iowa.gov/legislation/BillBook?ba=HF291&ga=87.

38. Nelson Lichtenstein, "Busted: The Decline of Unions: Introduction," in *The Age of Inequality: Corporate America's War on Working People*, ed. Jeremy Gantz (Brooklyn, NY: Verso, 2017), 53–55.

39. Henry S. Farber et al., "Unions and Inequality over the Twentieth Century: New Evidence from Survey Data," NBER Working Paper 24587, National Bureau of Economic Research, 2018, https://www.nber.org/papers/w24587.

40. Daniel Tope and David Jacobs, "The Politics of Union Decline: The Contingent Determinants of Union Recognition Elections and Victories," *American Sociological Review* 74, no. 5 (2009): 842–64.

41. Thomas A. Kochan et al., "Worker Voice in America: Is There a Gap between What Workers Expect and What They Experience?" *ILR Review* 72, no. 1 (2018): 3–38; Richard B. Freeman, "Do Workers still Want Unions? More Than Ever," Economic Policy Institute, February 22, 2007, http://www.sharedprosperity.org/bp182/bp182.pdf.

42. Art Swift, "Labor Union Approval Best since 2003, at 61%," *Gallup News*, August 30, 2017, http://news.gallup.com/poll/217331/labor-union-approval-best-2003.aspx.

43. Joseph E. Slater, *Public Workers: Government Employee Unions, the Law, and the State, 1900–62* (Ithaca, NY: Cornell University Press, 2004), 1, 3.

44. Slater, *Public Workers*, 12.

45. Barry T. Hirsch and David A. MacPherson, "Union Membership and Coverage Database from the CPS," accessed March 21, 2019, http://unionstats.com/. For state policies, see Milla Sanes and John Schmitt, *Regulation of Public Sector Collective Bargaining in the States* (Washington, DC: Center for Economic and Policy Research, 2014), http://cepr.net/documents/state-public-cb-2014-03.pdf.

46. Henry S. Farber, "Union Membership in the United States: The Divergence between the Public and Private Sectors," Working Paper 503, Princeton University, Industrial Relations Section, September 2005, https://core.ac.uk/download/pdf/6894934.pdf.

47. Hirsch and MacPherson, "Union Membership and Coverage Database from the CPS."

48. "Trade Union [Density]," OECD.Stat, accessed March 21, 2019, https://stats.oecd.org/Index.aspx?DataSetCode=TUD.

49. Bernhard Ebbinghaus and Jelle Visser, "When Institutions Matter, Union Growth and Decline in Western Europe, 1950–1995," *European Sociological Review* 15, no. 2 (1999): 135–58. See also Peter Lange and Lyle Scruggs, "Where Have All the Members Gone? Union Density in the Era of Globalization," 1998,https://pdfs.semanticscholar.org/c0d6/c1630387866a4911ed21ea8361ee008208cd.pdf; Jelle Visser, "Why Fewer Workers Join Unions in Europe: A Social Custom Explanation of Membership Trends," *British Journal of Industrial Relations* 40, no. 3 (2002): 403–30. For a country-specific study showing the importance of policy, even in seemingly autonomous industrial relations, see Stephen J. Silva, *Holding the Shop Together: German Industrial Relations in the Postwar Era* (Ithaca, NY: Cornell University Press, 2013).

50. For chambers of commerce, see Katherine House, *Revenue Models: An Examination of Income Trends for Chambers of Commerce* (Alexandria, VA: American Chambers of Commerce Executives, 2013), http://www.theoaklandchambernetwork.com/ACCE_RMWP_Insperity__1_.pdf; for Planned Parenthood, see "How Federal Funding Works at Planned Parenthood," I Stand with Planned Parenthood, https://www.istandwithpp.org/defund-defined/how-federal-funding-works-planned-parenthood.

51. FY 2019 Congressional Justification and FY 2017 Annual Performance Report (US Small Business Administration, 2019), https://www.sba.gov/sites/default/files/aboutsbaarticle/SBA_FY_2019_CBJ_APR_2_12_post.pdf, 20.

52. To give just a small sample, labor policies around the world include requiring workers to join a union in order to get a public benefit, promoting the right to strike, mandating that companies join an employer association to collectively bargain, enabling unions to sign closed shop arrangements with employers, having government arbitrate employment disputes so that employer power does not dictate results, and requiring each worksite to have a democratically elected worker organization.

53. Note also that the fact of policy supporting unions can cause workers to be more likely to think that their employers are susceptible to change. See Benjamin I. Sachs, "Law, Organizing, and the Status Quo Vulnerability," *Texas Law Review* 96, no. 2 (2017): 351–77, https://texaslawreview.org/wp-content/uploads/2017/12/Sachs.pdf.

54. See, among many others, Ebbinghaus and Visser, "When Institutions Matter"; Magnus Rasmussen, "Institutions (Still) Rule: Labor Market Centralization and Trade Union Organization," working paper, 2017, https://www.researchgate.net/publication/320273351_Institutions_still_Rule_Labor_Market_Centralization_and_Trade_Union_Organization; Magnus Bergli Rasmussen and Jonas Pontusson, "Working-Class Strength by Institutional Design? Unionization, Partisan Politics, and Unemployment Insurance Systems, 1870 to 2010," *Comparative Political Studies* 51, no. 6 (2017): 793–828; Bruce Western, *Between Class and Markets: Postwar Unionization in the Capitalist Democracies*

(NJ: Princeton University Press, 1997); Bo Rothstein, "Labor-Market Institutions and Working-Class Strength," chap. 2 in *Structuring Politics: Historical Institutionalism in Comparative Analysis*, eds. Sven Steinmo, Kathleen Thelen, and Frank Longstreth (New York: Cambridge University Press, 1992).

55. Kurt Vandaele, "A Report from the Homeland of the Ghent System: The Relationship between Unemployment and Trade Union Membership in Belgium," *Transfer: European Review of Labour and Research* 12, no. 4 (2006): 647–57; Tim Van Rie, Ive Marx, and Jeoen Horemans, "Ghent Revisited: Unemployment Insurance and Union Membership in Belgium and the Nordic Countries," *European Journal of Industrial Relations* 17, no. 2 (2011): 125–39; Matthew Dimick, "Labor Law, New Governance, and the Ghent System," *North Carolina Law Review* 90, no. 2 (2012): 1–55, https://papers.ssrn.com/sol3/papers.cfm?abstract_id=1680900; Lyle Scruggs, "The Ghent System and Union Membership in Europe, 1970–1996," *Political Research Quarterly* 55, no. 2 (2002): 275–97; Laust Høgedahl, "The Ghent Effect for Whom? Mapping the Variations of the Ghent Effect across Different Trade Unions in Denmark," *Industrial Relations Journal* 45, no. 6 (2014): 469–85; Jochen Clasen and Elke Viebrock, "Voluntary Unemployment Insurance and Trade Union Membership: Investigating the Connections in Denmark and Sweden," *Journal of Social Policy* 37, no. 3 (2008): 433–51.

56. "Collective Bargaining Coverage," OECD.Stat, accessed March 22, 2019, https://stats.oecd.org/Index.aspx?DataSetCode=CBC; Ebbinghaus and Visser, "When Institutions Matter"; Rasmussen, "Institutions (Still) Rule"; Scruggs, "Ghent System and Union Membership in Europe"; Rothstein, "Labor-Market Institutions and Working-Class Strength"; Rie, Marx, and Horemans, "Ghent Revisited."

57. Rothstein, "Labor-Market Institutions and Working-Class Strength"; "Trade Union Density." OECD.stat, accessed March 26, 2019, https://stats.oecd.org/Index.aspx?DataSetCode=TUD.

58. Jens Lind, "The End of the Ghent System as Trade Union Recruitment Machinery?" *Industrial Relations Journal* 40, no. 6 (2009): 510–23; Anders Kjeillberg, "The Decline in Swedish Union Density since 2007," *Nordic Journal of Working Life Studies* 1, no. 1 (2011): 67–93, https://portal.research.lu.se/ws/files/3462138/2064087.pdf; Petri Böckerman and Roope Uusitalo, "Erosion of the Ghent System and Union Membership Decline: Lessons from Finland," *British Journal of Industrial Relations* 44, no. 2 (2006): 283–303, http://citeseerx.ist.psu.edu/viewdoc/download?doi=10.1.1.500.3957&rep=rep1&type=pdf. Research indicates that Ghent systems have grown to promote membership as government subsidies were increased. Rasmussen and Pontusson, "Working-Class Strength by Institutional Design."

59. Christian Lyhne Ibsen, Jonas Toubol, Daniel Sparwath Jensen, "Social Customs and Trade Union Membership: A Multi-Level Analysis of Workplace Union Density Using Micro-Data," *European Sociological Review* 33, no. 4 (2017): 504–17; Jonas Toubol and Carsten Stroby Jensen, "Why Do People Join Trade Unions? The Impact of Workplace Union Density on Union Recruitment," *Transfer: European Review of Labour and Research* 20, no. 1 (2014): 135–54.

60. See "Belgium," Worker-participation.eu, accessed March 26, 2019, https://www.worker-participation.eu/National-Industrial-Relations/Countries/Belgium.

61. See Gerhard Bosch and Claudia Weinkpof, "Reducing Wage Inequality: The Role of the State in Improving Job Quality," *Work and Occupations* 44, no. 1 (2016): 68–88.

62. "Union Access to Workplaces," FindLaw New Zealand, accessed March 26, 2019, https://www.findlaw.co.nz/articles/4280/union-access-to-workplaces.aspx; Ebbinghaus and Visser, "When Institutions Matter."

63. Guy Mundlak, "Organizing Workers in 'Hybrid Systems': Comparing Trade Union Strategies in Four Countries—Austria, Germany, Israel and the Netherlands," *Theoretical*

Inquiries in Law 17, no. 1 (2016): 163–200, http://www7.tau.ac.il/ojs/index.php/til/article/view/1376.

64. Ebbinghaus and Visser, "When Institutions Matter."

65. Ebbinghaus and Visser, "When Institutions Matter"; Rasmussen, "Institutions (Still) Rule."

66. The Right to Strike and the ILO: The Legal Foundations (International Trade Union Confederation, 2014), https://www.ilo.org/wcmsp5/groups/public/---ed_dialogue/---actrav/documents/genericdocument/wcms_245669.pdf.

67. For strike rights, see Weibke Warneck, *Strike Rules in the EU27 and Beyond: A Comparative Overview* (Brussels: European Trade Union Institute for Research, Education and Health and Safety, 2007), https://www.asi.is/media/7581/Strike_rules_in_the_EU27.pdf. For strike frequency, see "Strikes—Map of Europe," European Trade Union Institute, https://www.etui.org/Services/Strikes-Map-of-Europe. For density, see "Trade Union Density." OECD.stat, accessed March 26, 2019, https://stats.oecd.org/Index.aspx?DataSetCode=TUD.

68. See Rae Cooper and Bradon Ellem, "Cold Climate: Australian Unions, Policy, and the State," *Comparative Labor Law and Policy Journal* 38, no. 1 (2017): 418. For density, see Jelle Visser, "ICTWSS: Database on Institutional Characteristics of Trade Unions, Wage Setting, State Intervention and Social Pacts in 51 Countries between 1960 and 2014," University of Amsterdam, http://uva-aias.net/en/ictwss.

69. Martin H. Malin and Catherine Fisk, "After *Janus*," *California Law Review*, 2018, https://ssrn.com/abstract=3245522.

70. Note that David Rolf, president of Service Employees International Union Local 775 in Seattle, among others, argues that in our current system "only a minority of workers is ever likely to benefit from collective bargaining." David Rolf, "Toward a 21st-Century Labor Movement," *American Prospect*, April 18, 2016, http://prospect.org/article/toward-21st-century-labor-movement. For a more complete discussion, see David Rolf, *The Fight for Fifteen: The Right Wage for a Working America* (New York: New Press, 2016).

71. For some work on the importance of high replacement costs of workers for worker power, see Howard Kimeldorf, "Worker Replacement Costs and Unionization: Origins of the US Labor Movement," *American Sociological Review* 78, no. 6 (2013): 1033–62.

72. "Although the average size of establishments rose through the expansionary years of the 1990s, it has fallen during each year of the first decade of the 2000s; a primary explanation is that new establishments are starting and staying smaller." Eleanor J. Choi and James R. Speltzer, "The Declining Average Size of Establishments: Evidence and Explanations," *Monthly Labor Review*, March 2012, 50–65, https://www.bls.gov/opub/mlr/2012/03/art4full.pdf.

73. Organisation for Economic Co-operation and Development (OECD), "Collective Bargaining in a Changing World of Work," chap. 4 in *OECD Employment Outlook 2017* (Paris: OECD Publishing, 2017), https://www.oecd-ilibrary.org/sites/empl_outlook-2017-en/1/2/4/index.html?itemId=/content/publication/empl_outlook-2017-en&_csp_=55459d499ec59fbfddc806ba1252bdeb&itemIGO=oecd&itemContentType=book#chap00004; Minawa Ebisui, "Non-standard Workers: Good Practices of Social Dialogue and Collective Bargaining," Working Paper 36, International Labour Office, April 2012, http://www.ilo.org/wcmsp5/groups/public/---ed_dialogue/---dialogue/documents/publication/wcms_179448.pdf; Rasmussen, "Institutions (Still) Rule."

74. For an interesting discussion of the importance of employer interests in the establishment of sectoral bargaining, see Swenson, *Capitalists against Markets*.

75. For Spain and Portugal, see *ITUC Frontlines Report: April 2013* (Brussels: International Trade Union Confederation, 2013), https://www.ituc-csi.org/IMG/pdf/en_ituc_frontlines_full_report_april_2013_web.pdf; and Reinhard Naumann, "Reregulating the Extension of Collective Agreements in Portugal: A Case Study," chap. 4 in *Collective*

Agreements: Extending Labour Protection, eds. Susan Hayter and Jelle Visser (Geneva: International Labour Organization, 2018), https://www.ilo.org/wcmsp5/groups/public/ ---dgreports/---dcomm/documents/publication/wcms_633672.pdf. For Britain and Australia, see chapter 4 of this book. For Uruguay, see Maria Lorena Cook and Joseph Bazler, "Bringing Unions Back In: Labour and Left Governments in Latin America," Digital Commons@ILR, ILR School, Cornell University, April 2013, https://digitalcommons.ilr. cornell.edu/cgi/viewcontent.cgi?referer=&httpsredir=1&article=1166&context=working papers. For Norway, see Lawrence Kahn, "Against the Wind: Bargaining Recentralisation and Wage Inequality in Norway 1987–91," *Economic Journal* 108 no. 448 (1998): 603–45.

76. See, among others, Torgeir Aarvaag Stokke, "The Anatomy of Two-Tier Bargaining Models," *European Journal of Industrial Relations* 14, no. 1 (2008): 7–24.

77. "Collective Bargaining Coverage"; "Trade Union Density."

78. See, among others, Jelle Visser, *Wage Bargaining Institutions—From Crisis to Crisis* (Brussels: European Commission, 2013), http://ec.europa.eu/economy_finance/publica tions/economic_paper/2013/pdf/ecp488_en.pdf; *ITUC Frontlines Report*.

79. OECD, "Collective Bargaining in a Changing World of Work." See also Jelle Visser, "What Happened to Collective Bargaining during the Great Recession?" *IZA Journal of Labor Policy* 5, article no. 9 (2016), https://doi.org/10.1186/s40173-016-0061-1.

80. Michael Wallerstein, "Wage Setting Institutions and Pay Inequality in Advanced Industrial Societies," *American Journal of Political Science* 43, no. 3 (1999): 649–80.

81. Toke S. Aidt and Zafiris Tzannatos, "Trade Unions, Collective Bargaining, and Macroeconomic Performance: A Review," *Industrial Relations Journal* 39, no. 4 (2008): 259–95. See also Wallerstein, "Wage Setting Institutions and Pay Inequality"; *ITUC Frontlines Report*; Francine Blau and Lawrence Kahn, "Understanding International Differences in the Gender Pay Gap," *Journal of Labor Economics* 21, no. 1 (2003): 106–44. Francine Blau and Lawrence Kahn find that centralization decreases inequality—largely as a matter of middle to bottom, not top to middle. Francine D. Blau and Lawrence M. Kahn, "Wage Structure and Gender Earnings Differentials: An International Comparison," *Economica* 63, no. 250 (1996): S29–S62. See also Jonas Pontusson, David Rueda, and Christopher R. Way, "Comparative Political Economy of Wage Distribution: The Role of Partisanship and Labour Market Institutions," *British Journal of Political Science* 32, no. 2 (2002): 281–308.

82. For evidence on the move away from centralized bargaining, see Eurofund, *Collective Bargaining in Europe in the 21st Century* (Luxembourg: Publications Office of the European Union, 2015), https://digitalcommons.ilr.cornell.edu/cgi/viewcontent.cgi? referer=https://www.google.com/&httpsredir=1&article=1490&context=intl.

83. Kahn, "Against the Wind."

84. Cook and Bazler, "Bringing Unions Back In"; Marcos Supervielle and Mariela Quiñones, "Uruguay's Miracle: Redistribution and the Growth of Unionism," *Global Dialogue* 10, no. 1, http://globaldialogue.isa-sociology.org/uruguays-miracle-redistribution-and-the-growth-of-unionism; Álvaro Padrón and Achim Wachendorfer, "Trade Unions in Transformation: Uruguay: Building Trade Union Power," Friedrich Ebert Stiftung, November 2017, http://library.fes.de/pdf-files/iez/13845.pdf.

85. See, for example, Tali Kristal and Yinon Cohen, "Decentralization of Collective Agreements and Rising Wage Inequality in Israel," *Industrial Relations* 46, no. 3 (2007): 613–35, http://www.columbia.edu/~yc2444/Decentralization%20of%20Collective%20 Wage%20Agreements%20and%20Rising%20Wage%20Inequality%20In%20Israel.pdf; as well as the discussion of Australia, New Zealand, and Britain in chapter 4 of this book.

86. Alice Kügler, Uta Schönberg, and Ragnhild Schreiner, "Productivity Growth, Wage Growth and Unions," European Central Bank Forum on Central Bank, 2018, https://www. ecb.europa.eu/pub/conferences/shared/pdf/20180618_ecb_forum_on_central_banking/ Schoenberg_Uta_Paper.pdf. See also Torsten Müller and Thorsten Schulten, "Germany: Parallel Universes of Collective Bargaining," chap. 12 in *Collective Bargaining in Europe: Towards*

an Endgame, vol. 2, ed. Torsten Müller, Kurt Vandaele, and Jeremy Waddington (Brussels: European Trade Union Institute, 2019), https://www.etui.org/sites/default/files/CB%20 Vol%20II%20Chapter%2012.pdf. Note also the discussion about how to address problems in German collective bargaining in Thorsten Schulten, "German Collective Bargaining— from Erosion to Revitalisation?," in *Industrial Relations in Germany: Dynamics and Perspectives*, ed. Martin Behrens and Heiner Dribbusch (Baden-Baden: Nomos, 2019), 11–30.

87. Kügler, Schönberg, and Schreiner, "Productivity Growth, Wage Growth and Unions."

88. Nathan Wilmers, "Solidarity within and across Workplaces: How Cross-Workplace Coordination Affects Earnings Inequality," *RSF: The Russell Sage Foundation Journal of the Social Science* 5, no. 4 (2019): 190–215, https://www.rsfjournal.org/content/rsfjss/5/4/190. full.pdf.

89. Thomas Anton Kochan and Christine A. Riordan, "Employment Relations and Growing Income Inequality: Causes and Potential Options for Its Reversal," *Journal of Industrial Relations* 58, no. 3 (2016), 419–40.

90. Visser, "Wage Bargaining Institutions"; *ITUC Frontlines Report.*

91. Blau and Kahn, "Understanding International Differences in the Gender Pay Gap."

92. Blau and Kahn, "Understanding International Differences in the Gender Pay Gap"; Francine D. Blau and Lawrence M. Kahn, "Gender Differences in Pay," *Journal of Economic Perspectives* 14, no. 4 (2000): 75–99; Brenda Gannon et al., "Inter-Industry Wage Differentials and the Gender Wage Gap: Evidence from European Countries," *Economic and Social Review* 38, no. 1 (2005): 135–55; Florentino Felgueroso, María José Pérez-Villadóniga, and Juan Prieto, "Collective Bargaining and the Gender Wage Gap: A Quantile Regression Approach," Working Paper 2007-06, FEDEA, March 2007, http://documentos.fedea.net/ pubs/dt/2007/dt-2007-06.pdf; Gillian Whitehouse, "Legislation and Labour Market Gender Inequality: An Analysis of OECD Countries," *Work, Employment, and Society* 6, no. 1 (1992): 65–86. For more on pathways that unionization and increased bargaining centralization might use to reduce racial and gender pay gaps, see Francine D. Blau and Lawrence M. Kahn, "International Differences in Male Wage Inequality: Institutions versus Market Forces," NBER Working Paper 4678, National Bureau of Economic Research, 1994, http:// www.nber.org/papers/w4678; Ronald Schettkat, "Institutions in the Economic Fitness Landscape: What Impact Do Welfare State Institutions Have on Economic Performance?," IZA—Institute of Labor Economics, January 2003, http://ftp.iza.org/dp696.pdf.

93. Jill Manzo, Robert Bruno, and Frank Manzo IV, *State Prevailing Wage Laws Reduce Racial Income Gaps in Construction* (La Grange: Illinois Economic Policy Institute, 2018), https://illinoisepi.files.wordpress.com/2018/02/ilepi-pmcr-prevailing-wage-reduces-racial-income-gaps-final.pdf.

94. For public-sector evidence, see Hadas Mandel and Moshe Semyonov, "Gender Pay Gap and Employment Sector: Sources of Earnings Disparities in the United States, 1970–2010," *Demography* 51 (2014): 1597–1618; and Eric Grodsky and Devah Pager, "The Structure of Disadvantage: Individual and Occupational Determinants of the Black-White Wage Gap," *American Sociological Review* 66 (2001): 542–67, https://scholar. harvard.edu/files/pager/files/asr_grodskypager.pdf. See also David Cooper, Mary Gable, and Algernon Austin, "The Public-Sector Jobs Crisis: Women and African Americans Hit Hardest by Job Losses in State and Local Governments," Economic Policy Institute, May 2, 2012, https://www.epi.org/publication/bp339-public-sector-jobs-crisis. For evidence that the racial pay gap remains constant in the public sector but is higher for higher-income workers in the private sector, see John S. Heywood and Daniel Parent, "Performance Pay and the White-Black Wage Gap," *Journal of Labor Economics* 30, no. 2 (2012): 249–90; Governmentwide Strategy on Advancing Pay Equality in the Federal Government (Washington, DC: United States Office of Personnel Management, 2014), https://www.opm.gov/policy-data-oversight/pay-leave/reference-materials/reports/

Governmentwide-Strategy-on-Advancing-Pay-Equality-in-the-Federal-Government. pdf. For minimum wage evidence, see Francine D. Blau and Lawrence M. Khan, "Swimming Upstream: Trends in the Gender Wage Differential in the 1980s," *Journal of Labor Economics* 15, no. 1 (1997): 1–42.

95. Nadja Bergmann and Claudia Sorger, "Some Facts about the Gender Pay Gap in Austria" Gender Pay Gap, June 2015, http://www.genderpaygap.eu/documents/Fact sheet_Austria.pdf; Jill Rubery and Damian Grimshaw, "Gender and the Minimum Wage," chap. 9 in *Regulating for Decent Work*, eds. Sangheon Lee and Deirdre McCann (London: Palgrave Macmillan, 2011). Note also that Spanish research shows that bargaining above firm level is particularly effective at reducing gender pay gaps among lower-wage workers but less effective than firm-level bargaining at reducing pay gaps among more highly paid workers. Felgueroso, Pérez-Villadóniga, and Prieto, "Collective Bargaining and the Gender Wage Gap."

96. For evidence of the productivity-enhancing benefits of higher wages, see, among others, Justin Wolfers and Jan Zilinsky, "Higher Wages for Low-Income Workers Lead to Higher Productivity," Peterson Institute for International Economics, January 13, 2015, https://www.piie.com/blogs/realtime-economic-issues-watch/higher-wages-low-income-workers-lead-higher-productivity; Nick Bunker, "Abundance and the Direction of Technological Growth," Washington Center for Equitable Growth, February 18, 2016, http://equitablegrowth.org/abundance-and-the-direction-of-technological-growth; Rebecca Riley and Chiara Rosazza Bondibene, "Raising the Standard: Minimum Wages and Firm Productivity," NIESR Discussion Paper 449, National Institute of Economic and Social Research, 2015, http://www.niesr.ac.uk/sites/default/files/publications/Minimum%20 wages%20and%20firm%20productivity%20NIESR%20DP%20449.pdf; Michael Reich, Peter Hall, and Ken Jacobs, "Living Wages and Economic Performance: The San Francisco Airport Model," Institute of Industrial Relations, March 2003, http://laborcenter.berkeley. edu/pdf/2003/sfo_mar03.pdf.

97. Douglas Hibbs and Hakan Locking, "Wage Dispersion and Productive Efficiency: Evidence for Sweden," *Journal of Labor Economics* 18, no. 4 (2000): 755–82; Karl Ove Moene and Michael Wallerstein, "Pay Inequality," *Journal of Labor Economics* 15, no. 3 (1997): 403–30. For examples of pay for similar workers depending on the firm they work for, see Alan B. Krueger and Lawrence H. Summers, "Efficiency Wages and the Inter-Industry Wage Structure," *Econometrica* 56, no. 2 (1988): 259–93; Chad Syverson, "What Determines Productivity?," *Journal of Economic Literature* 49, no. 2 (2011): 326–65, http:// home.uchicago.edu/syverson/productivitysurvey.pdf.

98. While not all research shows positive productivity effects from works councils, most studies do. See Steffen Mueller, "Works Councils and Establishment Productivity," *Industrial and Labor Relations Review* 65, no. 4 (2012): 880–98; Steffen Mueller, "Works Councils and Labour Productivity: Looking beyond the Mean," *British Journal of Industrial Relations* 53, no. 2 (2015): 308–25; John T. Addison, Claus Schnabel, and Joachim Wagner, "Works Councils in Germany: Their Effects on Establishment Performance," *Oxford Economic Papers* 53, no. 4 (2001): 659–94; Olaf Hübler and Uwe Jirjahn, "Works Councils and Collective Bargaining in Germany: The Impact on Productivity and Wages," *Scottish Journal of Political Economy* 50, no. 4 (2003): 471–91. See also "Co-determination: Works Council Pays Off," Hans-Böckler-Stiftung, June 2010, https://web.archive.org/web/20190719185852/http://www.boeckler.de/35927_35964. htm. For US-focused studies on general labor-management partnership, see Jody Hoffer Gittell, Andrew Von Nordenflycht, and Thomas A. Kochan, "Mutual Gains or Zero Sum? Labor Relations and Firm Performance in the Airline Industry," *Industrial and Labor Relations Review* 57, no. 2 (2004), 163–80; Eileen Appelbaum, Jody Hoffer Gittell, and Carrie Leana, "High-Performance Work Practices and Sustainable Economic

Growth," Center for Economic and Policy Research, April 2011, http://cepr.net/report/
high-performance-work-practices-and-sustainable-economic-growth.

99. Teresa Ghilarducci, "Freeman and Medoff, What Do Unions Do?" *Journal of Legislation* 12, no. 1 (1985): 119–21, https://scholarship.law.nd.edu/cgi/viewcontent.cgi?
article=1358&context=jleg. On cooperation, see also Thelen, "Varieties of Labor Politics
in the Developed Democracies," 71. Thelen writes, "Collective bargaining above the level
of the firm supports plant-level cooperation by 'bracketing' divisive distributional issues
and 'depersonalizing' industrial conflict." See also Hübler and Jirjahn, "Works Councils
and Collective Bargaining in Germany"; Stefan Zagelmeyer, "The Employer's Perspective
on Collective Bargaining Centralization: An Analytical Framework," *International Journal
of Human Resource Management* 16, no. 9 (2005): 1623–39; Matthew Dimick, "Productive
Unionism," *UC Irvine Law Review* 4 (2014): 679–724; Scruggs, "Ghent System and Union
Membership in Europe"; Stephen Deery and Roderick Iverson, "Labor-Management
Cooperation: Antecedents and Impact on Organizational Performance," *Industrial and
Labor Relations Review* 58, no. 4 (2005): 588–609; and Robert Buchele and Jens Christiansen, "Labor Relations and Productivity Growth in Advanced Capitalist Economies,"
Radical Political Economics 31, no. 1 (1999): 87–110.

100. Anke Hassel, "What Does Business Want? Labour Market Reforms in CMEs
and Its Problems," chap. 9 in *Beyond Varieties of Capitalism: Conflict, Contradictions,
and Complementarities in the European Economy*, eds. Bob Hancké, Martin Rhodes, and
Mark Thatcher (Oxford, UK: Oxford University Press, 2007); Christian Dustmann and
Uta Schönberg, "Training and Union Wages," *Review of Economics and Statistics* 91, no. 2
(2009): 363–76; Organisation for Economic Co-operation and Development, "Collective Bargaining: Levels and Coverage," chap. 5 in *OECD Employment Outlook: July 1994*
(Paris: OECD, 1994), 167–208, http://www.oecd.org/els/emp/2409993.pdf; Stefan Zagelmeyer, *Governance Structures and the Employment Relationship: Determinants of Employer
Demand for Collective Bargaining in Britain* (Oxford, UK: Peter Lang AG, 2004), 166;
Marius R. Busemeyer and Torben Iversen, "Collective Skill Systems, Wage Bargaining,
and Labor Market Stratification," chap. 8 in *The Political Economy of Collective Skill Formation*, eds. Marius R. Busemeyer and Christine Trampusch (Oxford: Oxford University
Press, 2011).

101. See, among others, Richard Freeman and James Medoff, *What Do Unions Do* (New
York: Basic Books, 1984); Gittell, Von Nordenflycht, and Kochan, *"Mutual Gains or Zero
Sum?"; Eileen Appelbaum, Jody Hoffer Gittell, and Carrie Leana, "High-Performance
Work Practices and Sustainable Economic Growth," Center for Economic and Policy
Research, 2011, https://www.researchgate.net/publication/228470237_High-Performance_
Work_Practices_and_Sustainable_Economic_Growth. On cooperation, see also Deery
and Iverson, "Labor-Management Cooperation"; Buchele and Christiansen, "Labor Relations and Productivity Growth in Advanced Capitalist Economies."

102. Bronfenbrenner, "No Holds Barred."

103. Note that there are many instances when unions negotiate improvements that
benefit nonunion workers, including safety standards and wage increases. Note also that
unions commonly advocate for public policies that support workers broadly, and in fact
sometimes these policies provide little specific benefit for their members—for example,
their advocacy for increased minimum wages and increased access to health care.

104. Thomas A. Kochan, *Shaping the Future of Work: What Future Worker, Business,
Government, and Education Leaders Need to Do for All to Prosper* (New York: Business
Expert Press, 2016).

105. *Economic Report of the President, Together with the Annual Report of the Council of
Economic Advisors* (Washington, DC: US Government Printing Office, 2015), http://www.
nber.org/links/cea_2015_erp.pdf; C. Jeffrey Waddoups, "Did Employers in the United

States Back Away from Skills Training during the Early 2000s?," *ILR Review* 69, no. 2 (2015): 405–34; Chris Benner, Laura Leete, and Manuel Pastor, *Staircases or Treadmills? Labor Market Intermediaries and Economic Opportunity in a Changing Economy* (New York City: Russell Sage Foundation, 2007).

106. "America's Workforce: We Can't Compete if We Cut," flyer, National Skills Coalition, 2017, http://www.nationalskillscoalition.org/resources/publications/file/Americas-workforce-We-cant-compete-if-we-cut.pdf.

107. "Labor Market Training Expenditures as a Percent of GDP in OECD Countries, 2011," chart, Hamilton Project, http://www.hamiltonproject.org/charts/labor_market_training_expenditures_as_a_percent_of_gdp_in_oecd_countries_20.

108. David J. Deming et al., "The Value of Postsecondary Credentials in the Labor Market: An Experimental Study," *American Economic Review* 106, no. 3 (2016): 778–806, https://www.aeaweb.org/articles?id=10.1257/aer.20141757. For evidence of the mixed quality of US training coupled with high costs, see Clive Belfield and Thomas Bailey, "The Labor Market Returns to Sub-Baccalaureate College: A Review," CAPSEE Working Paper, Center for Analysis of Postsecondary Education and Employment, March 2017, https://capseecenter.org/wp-content/uploads/2017/04/labor-market-returns-sub-baccalaureate-college-review.pdf.

109. Organisation for Economic Co-operation and Development, *Skills Matter: Further Results from the Survey of Adult Skills* (Paris: OECD Publishing, 2016), 24, https://read.oecd-ilibrary.org/education/skills-matter_9789264258051-en#page24.

110. For a good study of the differences in training structures and policy in countries with enterprise bargaining compared to higher-level bargaining, see Kathleen Thelen, *How Institutions Evolve* (Cambridge, UK: Cambridge University Press, 2004).

111. Sheila Maguire et al., Tuning into Local Labor Markets: Findings from the Sectoral Employment Impact Study (Philadelphia: Public/Private Ventures, 2010), http://ppv.issuelab.org/resources/5101/5101.pdf; Richard Hendra et al., Encouraging Evidence on a Sector-Focused Advancement Strategy: Two-Year Impacts from the Work Advance Demonstration" (Washington, DC: MDRC, 2016), http://www.mdrc.org/sites/default/files/2016_Workadvance_Final_Web.pdf.

112. Guy Vernon and Mark Rogers, "Where Do Unions Add Value? Predominant Organizing Principle, Union Strength and Manufacturing Productivity Growth in the OECD," *British Journal of Industrial Relations* 51, no. 1 (2013): 1–27.

113. Aidt and Tzannatos, "Trade Unions, Collective Bargaining, and Macroeconomic Performance."

114. See, among others, Susan Hayter, ed., "Executive Summary—The role of collective bargaining the global economy: Negotiating for social justice," International Labor Organization, 2011, https://www.ilo.org/wcmsp5/groups/public/---dgreports/---dcomm/---publ/documents/publication/wcms_159204.pdf, which concludes, "Collective bargaining compresses wage structures and reduces wage inequality, including the gender pay gap. The volume does not find any evidence that this is at the cost of economic efficiency. At a macroeconomic level, highly coordinated and centralized collective bargaining has a positive effect on earnings equality without any negative employment effect." Reassessing the role of policies and institution for labor market performance, Andrea Bassani and Romain Duval find that "highly centralised and/or coordinated wage bargaining systems are estimated to reduce unemployment." Andrea Bassani and Romain Duval, *Employment Patterns in OECD Countries: Reassessing the Role of Policies and Institutions* (Paris: Organisation for Economic Co-operation and Development, 2006), https://www.oecd.org/employment/emp/36888714.pdf. See also Servaas Storm and C. W. M. Naastepad, "Labor Market Regulation and Productivity Growth: Evidence for Twenty OECD Countries (1984–2004)," *Industrial Relations* 48, no. 4 (2009): 629–54.

115. Author's analysis using "Trade in Goods and Services, Imports, Exports, % of GDP, 2017," OECD Data, accessed March 28, 2019, https://data.oecd.org/trade/trade-in-goods-and-services.htm. See also *ITUC Frontlines Report*, which notes, "In the last decade it would appear that countries with high synchronisation had an export sector roughly double the size of other advanced economies."

CHAPTER 4. LESSONS FROM CANADA, BRITAIN, AND AUSTRALIA

1. Seymour Martin Lipset, "Trade Unions and Social Structure: I," *Industrial Relations* 1, no. 1 (1961): 75–89; Wolfgang Streeck, The Sociology of Labor Markets and Trade Unions," in *The Handbook of Economic Sociology*, ed. N. J. Smelser and R. Swedberg (NJ: Princeton University Press, 2005), 254–83, https://www.ssoar.info/ssoar/bitstream/handle/document/19500/ssoar-2005-streeck-the_sociology_of_labor_markets.pdf?sequence=1.

2. Note that there are a few ways that Canadian labor law is inferior to that of the United States, as, for example, US workers have broader rights to engage with their coworkers in "concerted activity" without fear of employer retaliation.

3. Craig Riddell, "Unionization in Canada and the United States: A Tale of Two Countries," in *Small Differences That Matter: Labor Markets and Income Maintenance in Canada and the United State*, eds. David Card and Richard B. Freeman (University of Chicago Press, 1993), 109–46, https://economics.ubc.ca/files/2013/05/pdf_paper_craig-riddell-unionization-canada-unitedstates-tale.pdf.

4. Légis Québec, "Chapter D-2: Act Respecting Collective Agreement Decrees," http://legisquebec.gouv.qc.ca/en/ShowDoc/cs/D-2. Note also that Canada has a few other policies that help encourage sectoral bargaining that apply in limited circumstances, such as the Federal Status of the Artist Act.

5. Riddell, "Unionization in Canada and the United States"; John Godard, "Do Labor Laws Matter? The Density Decline and Convergence Thesis Revisited," *Industrial Relations* 42, no. 3 (2003): 458–92.

6. See, for example, Riddell, "Unionization in Canada and the United States."

7. Ishak Saporta and Bryan Lincoln, "Managers' and Workers' Attitudes toward Unions in the US and Canada," *Relations Industrielles/Industrial Relations* 50, no. 3 (1995): 550–66; Terry Thomason and Silvana Pozzebon, "Managerial Opposition to Union Certification in Quebec and Ontario," *Relations Industrielles/Industrial Relations* 53, no. 4 (1998): 750–71; Karen Bentham, "Employer Resistance to Union Certification: A Study of Eight Canadian Jurisdictions," *Relations Industrielles/Industrial Relations* 57, no. 1 (2002), https://papers.ssrn.com/sol3/papers.cfm?abstract_id=1669335.

8. Michele Campolieti, Rafael Gomez, and Morley Gunderson, "Managerial Hostility and Attitudes towards Unions: A Canada-US Comparison," *Journal of Labor Research* 34 (2012): 99–119. Note that because of the more favorable legal structure in Canada, employer hostility may not be expressed to the degree it is in the United States.

9. See, for example, Michele Campolieti, Rafael Gomez, and Morley Gunderson, "What Accounts for the Representation Gap? Decomposing Canada—US Differences in the Desire for Collective Voice," *Journal of Industrial Relations* 53, no. 4 (2011): 425–49; Riddell, "Unionization in Canada and the United States."

10. Scott Legree, Tammy Schirle, and Mikal Skuterud, "The Effect of Labour Relations Laws on Union Density Rates: Evidence from Canadian Provinces," Vancouver School of Economics, CLSSRN Working Papers, 2014, https://ideas.repec.org/p/ubc/clssrn/clsrn_admin-2014-42.html.

11. Riddell, "Unionization in Canada and the United States." For 2018, see "Union Status by Industry," Statistics Canada, accessed April 1, 2019, https://www150.statcan.gc.ca/t1/tbl1/en/tv.action?pid=1410013201&pickMembers%5B0%5D=2.5&pickMembers

%5B1%5D=4.1. For coverage estimates, see Andrew Jackson, "Solidarity Forever? Trends in Canadian Union Density," *Studies in Political Economy* 74 (2004): 125–46.

12. "Union Status by Industry."

13. Diane Galarneau and Thao Sohn, "Insights on Canadian Society: Long-term Trends in Unionization," Statistics Canada, November 2013, 4, table 2, https://www150. statcan.gc.ca/n1/en/pub/75-006-x/2013001/article/11878-eng.pdf?st=0HYrVzCH; Jackson, "Solidarity Forever?"; "Union Status by Industry."

14. Galarneau and Sohn, "Insights on Canadian Society," 34, chart 2. Note that even looking at a shorter time period, such as since 1997, private-sector density has declined in virtually all provinces, though it has been steady in a two small provinces, Prince Edward Island and Newfoundland and Labrador. See "Union Status by Geography," Statistics Canada, accessed April 1, 2019, https://www150.statcan.gc.ca/t1/tbl1/en/tv.action?pid= 1410012901&pickMembers%5B0%5D=2.5&pickMembers%5B1%5D=3.1&pickMembers %5B2%5D=4.1.

15. For unionization and coverage rates, see "Union Status by Geography."

16. Jim Stanford, "Looking Back on the Moment of Truth: An International Perspective," in *A New Kind of Union, Unifor and the Birth of the Modern Canadian Union*, Fred Wilson (Toronto: James Lorimer, 2019), 218, figure 2.

17. For productivity-wage decoupling, see James Uguccioni and Andrew Sharpe, *Decomposing the Productivity-Wage Nexus in Selected OECD Countries, 1986–2013* (Ottawa: Centre for the Study of Living Standards, 2016), http://www.csls.ca/reports/ csls2016-16.pdf. For slow median wage growth, especially for young men, see René Morissette, Carnet Picot, and Yuqian Lu, "The Evolution of Canadian Wages over the Last Three Decades," Statistics Canada, March 2013, 23, chart 6, https://www150.statcan.gc.ca/n1/en/ pub/11f0019m/11f0019m2013347-eng.pdf?st=O3oSDDmG.

18. Matthew Brzozowski et al., "Consumption, Income, and Wealth Inequality in Canada," *Review of Economic Dynamics* 13, no. 1 (2010): 52–75; David A. Green, W. Craig Riddell, and France St-Hilaire, "Income Inequality in Canada: Driving Forces, Outcomes and Policy," Institute for Research on Public Policy, February 23, 2017, http://irpp.org/ research-studies/income-inequality-in-canada/.

19. Green, Riddell, and St-Hilaire, "Income Inequality in Canada," figure 2.

20. Green, Riddell, and St-Hilaire, "Income Inequality in Canada," figure 3.

21. Green, Riddell, and St-Hilaire, "Income Inequality in Canada," figure 5.

22. Leah F. Vosko and Mark Thomas, "Confronting the Employment Standards Enforcement Gap: Exploring the Potential for Union Engagement with Employment Law in Ontario, Canada," *Journal of Industrial Relations* 56, no. 5 (2014): 631–52; *Unpaid Wages, Unprotected Workers: A Survey of Employment Standards Violations* (Toronto: Workers' Action Centre, 2011), http://workersactioncentre.org/wp-content/uploads/2016/07/ unpaidwagesunprotectedworkers_eng.pdf; It's More than Poverty: Employment Precarity and Household Well-being (Poverty and Employment Precarity in Southern Ontario, 2013), https://www.unitedwaygt.org/document.doc?id=91; "Workers' Stories of Exploitation and Abuse: Why BC Employment Standards Need to Change: Summary Report," BC Employment Standards Coalition, 2017, http://bcemploymentstandardscoalition.com/ wp-content/uploads/2017/05/Summary-Report-Workers-Stories-of-Exploitation-and- Abuse.pdf.

23. David Card, Thomas Lemieux, and W. Craig Riddell, "Unions and Wage Inequality," *Journal of Labor Research* 25, no. 4 (2004): 519–59.

24. Brzozowski et al., "Consumption, Income, and Wealth Inequality in Canada"; Green, Riddell, and St-Hilaire, "Income Inequality in Canada"; Donald J. Boudreaux et al., The Myth of Middle-Class Stagnation in Canada (Fraser Institute, 2016), https://www.fraser institute.org/sites/default/files/the-myth-of-middle-class-stagnation-in-canada-post.pdf.

25. See, for example, Eric Tucker, "Shall Wagnerism Have No Dominion?" *Just Labour* 21 (Spring 2014), https://ssrn.com/abstract=2433551; Godard, "Do Labor Laws Matter"; Joseph B. Rose, "The Prospects for Union Renewal in Canada," in *Proceedings of the 60th Annual Meeting of the Labor and Employment Relations Association: LERA* (Labor and Employment Relations Association, 2008), 101–7, http://www.lerachapters.org/OJS/ojs-2.4.4-1/index.php/LERAMR/article/view/1341; Christopher Schenk, "Fifty Years after PC 1003: The Need for New Directions," in *Labour Gains, Labour Pains: 50 Years of PC 1003*, ed. Cy Gonick, Paul Phillips, and Jesse Vorst (Halifax: Fernwood, 1995), 195–214; Paul C. Weiler, *Governing the Workplace: The Future of Labor and Employment Law* (Cambridge, MA: Harvard University Press, 1990); and Ethan Phillips, "The Unfinished Business of Labour Law Reform in Ontario: A Strategy for Implementing Sectoral Bargaining," *Canada Fact Check,* January 12, 2018, https://canadafactcheck.ca/bill148ontariolabourlawsectoralbargaining.

26. David Doorey, "The Model of Sectoral Bargaining Everyone Is Whispering About," Canadian Law of Work Forum, May 6, 2016, http://lawofwork.ca/?p=8574.

27. Joseph Rose and Gary Chaison, "Unionism in Canada and the United States in the 21st Century: The Prospects for Revival," *Relations Industrielles* 56, no. 1 (2001): 34–65.

28. Unifor, *Building Balance, Fairness and Opportunity in Ontario's Labor Market* (Unifor, 2015), https://www.unifor.org/sites/default/files/attachments/unifor_final_submission_ontario_changing_workplaces.pdf. See also Unifor, "Make It Fair: Restoring Balance, Fairness and Opportunity in B.C.'s Labour Market" ("Submission Response by Unifor on the Recommendations for Amendments to the Labour Relations Code, B.C. Labour Relations Code Review"), Unifor, November 30, 2018, https://engage.gov.bc.ca/app/uploads/sites/332/2019/01/Unifor.pdf.

29. Marty Warren, "Tim Hortons Workers Need a Union," *Star* (Toronto), January 11, 2018. For other unions that have supported sectoral bargaining, see, for example, David Sparrow and Sue Milling, "Submission to the Changing Workplaces Review: Respect the Artist," ACTRA Toronto, June 16, 2015, https://cirhr.library.utoronto.ca/sites/cirhr.library.utoronto.ca/files/ontario_workplace_review/ACTRA.pdf; CWA Canada Associate Members, "Submission to the Changing Workplaces Review," September 18, 2015, https://cirhr.library.utoronto.ca/sites/cirhr.library.utoronto.ca/files/ontario_workplace_review/CWA%20Canada%20Associate%20Members.pdf; Fred Hahn, "Changing Workplaces Review: Response to Interim Report," CUPE/SCFP Ontario, October 7, 2016, https://cirhr.library.utoronto.ca/sites/cirhr-edit.library.utoronto.ca/files/ontario_workplace_review_phase2/CUPE%20Ontario%20%281%29.pdf.

30. For a good summary, see Sara Slinn, "Broader-Based and Sectoral Bargaining Proposals in Collective Bargaining Law Reform: A Historical Review," working paper, "forthcoming in (2020) Labour / Le Travail, Vol. 85," https://digitalcommons.osgoode.yorku.ca/all_papers/324.

31. For legislation that was passed, see "Archived—A Plan for Fair Workplaces and Better Jobs (Bill 148)," Government of Ontario, https://www.ontario.ca/page/plan-fair-workplaces-and-better-jobs-bill-148.

32. "The Ontario Federation of Labour's Submission in Response to the 2016 Changing Workplaces Review: Special Advisors' Interim Report," Ontario Federation of Labour, 2016, https://cirhr.library.utoronto.ca/sites/cirhr-edit.library.utoronto.ca/files/ontario_workplace_review_phase2/Ontario%20Federation%20of%20Labour%20%281%29.pdf; *A New Code for New Times: Meeting the Challenge of Precarious Work*, "AFL Submission to the 2017 Workplace Legislation Review," (Alberta Federation of Labor, 2017), https://www.una.ab.ca/files/uploads/2017/3/Appendix_A_A_New_Code_for_New_Times.pdf.

33. "Recommendations for Labour Law Reform: A Report to the Honourable Moe Sihota, Minister of Labour, Submitted by the Sub-Committee of Special Advisers, John

Baigent, Vince Ready, Tom Roper," British Columbia, Ministry of Labour and Consumer Services, 1992; Slinn, "Broader-based and Sectoral Bargaining Proposals in Collective Bargaining Law Reform"; Diane MacDonald, "Sectoral Certification: A Case Study of British Columbia," *Canadian Labor and Employment Law Journal* 5 (1997): 279–83; David Doorey, "The Model of Sectoral Collective Bargaining Everyone Is Whispering About," Canadian Law of Work Forum, May 6, 2016, http://lawofwork.ca/?p=8574.

34. Chris Howell, *Trade Unions and the State: The Construction of Industrial Relations Institutions in Britain, 1890–2000* (Princeton, NJ: Princeton University Press, 2005), 130. See also Jelle Visser, "ICTWSS: Database on Institutional Characteristics of Trade Unions, Wage Setting, State Intervention and Social Pacts in 51 Countries between 1960 and 2014," University of Amsterdam, http://www.uva-aias.net/en/ictwss.

35. For coverage around 1980, see Howell, *Trade Unions and the State*, 130; Keith Ewing and John Hendy, "New Perspectives on Collective Labour Law: Trade Union Recognition and Collective Bargaining," *Industrial Law Journal* 46, no. 1 (2017): 23–51.

36. Visser, "ICTWSS: Database on Institutional Characteristics of Trade Unions, Wage Setting, State Intervention and Social Pacts." For more on the decline of multi-employer bargaining, see Willy Brown, Alex Bryson, and John Forth, "Competition and the Retreat from Collective Bargaining," NIESR Discussion Paper 318, National Association of Economic and Social Research, August 2008, http://www.niesr.ac.uk/sites/default/files/publi cations/210808_110817.pdf.

37. "Trade Union Statistics 2017," National Statistics (UK), https://www.gov.uk/gov ernment/statistics/trade-union-statistics-2017; Department for Business, Energy, & Industrial Strategy, "Trade Union Membership 2017: Statistical Bulletin," National Statistics (UK), Department for Business, Energy and Industrial Strategy, May 2018, https:// assets.publishing.service.gov.uk/government/uploads/system/uploads/attachment_data/ file/712543/TU_membership_bulletin.pdf.

38. "Collective Bargaining Coverage," Organisation for Economic Co-operation and Development, accessed April 5, 2019, https://stats.oecd.org/Index.aspx?DataSetCode=CBC.

39. This paragraph is largely based on Howell, *Trade Unions and the State*.

40. Howell, *Trade Unions and the State*, 8. For classification of British labor policy as voluntarist, see also Alexander J. S. Colvin and Owen R. Darbishire, "The Emerging Anglo-American Model: Convergence in Industrial Relations Institutions?" DigitalCommons@ ILR, ILR School, Cornell University, August 2009, https://digitalcommons.ilr.cornell.edu/ cgi/viewcontent.cgi?article=1032&context=conference.

41. John Pencavel, "The Surprising Retreat of Union Britain," in *Seeking a Premier Economy: The Economic Effects of British Economic Reforms, 1980–2000*, ed. David Card, Richard Blundell, and Richard B. Freeman (Chicago: University of Chicago Press, 2004), 181–232, https://www.nber.org/chapters/c6748.pdf.

42. Industrial Relations Act 1971 (Commencement No. 4) Order 1972, http://www. legislation.gov.uk/uksi/1972/36/pdfs/uksi_19720036_en.pdf; Trade Union and Labour Relations Act 1974, Chapter 52, http://www.legislation.gov.uk/ukpga/1974/52/pdfs/ ukpga_19740052_en.pdf; Employment Protection Act 1975, Chapter 71, http://www. legislation.gov.uk/ukpga/1975/71/pdfs/ukpga_19750071_en.pdf. See also "Report of the Royal Commission on Trade Unions and Employers Association (Donovan)," *Relations Industrielles* 23, no. 4 (1968): 686–98; and Lord Wedderburn of Charlton, "Industrial Relations and the Courts," *Industrial Law Journal* 9, no. 1 (1980): 65–94.

43. Howell, *Trade Unions and the State*; Pencavel, "Surprising Retreat of Union Britain"; Ewing and Hendy, "New Perspectives on Collective Labour Law."

44. These factors were partly why union density grew by over 10 percentage points from the late 1960s to the late 1970s, and the reversal of these policies contributed to union decline. Chris Howell, "Unforgiven: British Trade Unionism in Crisis," chap. 2 in

The Brave New World of European Labor: European Trade Unions at the Millennium, ed. Andrew Martin and George Ross (New York: Berghahn Books, 1999).

45. Pencavel, "Surprising Retreat of Union Britain," 191.

46. Howell, *Trade Unions and the State*, 83, 89.

47. Ewing and Hendy, "New Perspectives on Collective Labour Law," esp. note 25.

48. Colvin and Darbishire, "Emerging Anglo-American Model"; Pencavel, "Surprising Retreat of Union Britain"; Ewing and Hendy, "New Perspectives on Collective Labour Law."

49. Ewing and Hendy, "New Perspectives on Collective Labour Law."

50. For a good summary of these and other changes, see Richard Freeman and Jeffrey Pelletier, "The Impact of Industrial Relations Legislation on British Union Density," *British Journal of Industrial Relations* 28, no. 2 (1990): 141–64; and Pencavel, "Surprising Retreat of Union Britain."

51. Howell, *Trade Unions and the State*; Freeman and Pelletier, "Impact of Industrial Relations Legislation on British Union Density"; Colvin and Darbishire, "Emerging Anglo-American Model."

52. Philip Bassett, "Unions Popular as Membership Falls," *Financial Times*, November 18, 1987; P. K. Edwards and George Sayer Bain, "Why Are Trade Unions Becoming More Popular? Unions and Public Opinion in Britain," *British Journal of Industrial Relations* 26, no. 3 (1988): 311–26.

53. Pencavel, "Surprising Retreat of Union Britain"; Freeman and Pelletier, "Impact of Industrial Relations Legislation on British Union Density."

54. Freeman and Pelletier, "Impact of Industrial Relations Legislation on British Union Density"; Pencavel, "Surprising Retreat of Union Britain."

55. Freeman and Pelletier, "Impact of Industrial Relations Legislation on British Union Density"; Colvin and Darbishire, "Emerging Anglo-American Model."

56. Freeman and Pelletier, "Impact of Industrial Relations Legislation on British Union Density."

57. Howell, *Trade Unions and the State*, esp. chap. 6; Paul Smith and Gary Morton, "Nine Years of New Labour: Neoliberalism and Workers' Rights," *British Journal of Industrial Relations* 44, no. 3 (2006): 401–20; Anna Pollert, "Britain and Individual Employment Rights: 'Paper Tigers, Fierce in Appearance but Missing in Tooth and Claw,'" *Economic and Industrial Democracy* 28, no. 1 (2007): 110–39; Linda Dickens, "Legal Regulation, Institutions and Industrial Relations" Warwick Papers in Industrial Relations 89, May 2008, https://warwick.ac.uk/fac/soc/wbs/research/irru/wpir/wpir_89.pdf.

58. Nancy Peters, "The United Kingdom Recalibrates the US National Labor Relations Act: Possible Lessons for the United States?," *Comparative Labor Law and Policy Journal* 25, no. 2 (2004): 227–56, https://papers.ssrn.com/sol3/papers.cfm?abstract_id=726947.

59. Alan Bogg, "The Death of Statutory Union Recognition in the United Kingdom," *Journal of Industrial Relations* 54, no. 3 (2012): 409–25.

60. Personal communication with the author, December 3, 2018.

61. Howell, *Trade Unions and the State*, 173; Howell, "Unforgiven"; Edmund Heery, John Kelly, and Jeremy Waddington, "Union Revitalization in the Britain," *European Journal of Industrial Relations* 9, no. 1 (2003): 79–97.

62. Pencavel, "Surprising Retreat of Union Britain"; Howell, *Trade Unions and the State*; Ewing and Hendy, "New Perspectives on Collective Labour Law."

63. *Prosperity and Justice: A Plan for the New Economy: The Final Report of the IPPR Commission on Economic Justice* (Cambridge, UK: Polity Press, 2018), https://www.ippr.org/files/2018-08/1535639099_prosperity-and-justice-ippr-2018.pdf.

64. Geoff Tily, "17-Year Wage Squeeze the Worst in Two Hundred Years," Trades Union Congress, May 11, 2018, https://www.tuc.org.uk/blogs/17-year-wage-squeeze-worst-two-hundred-years.

65. Andrew G. Haldane, "Labour's Share," speech, Trades Union Congress, London, November 12, 2015, 21, chart 15, https://www.bis.org/review/r151203a.pdf.

66. JRF Analysis Unit, *Poverty 2017* (York, UK: Joseph Rowntree Foundation, 2017), 32, https://www.jrf.org.uk/report/uk-poverty-2017.

67. Low Pay Commission: Non-compliance and Enforcement of the National Minimum Wage (London: Low Pay Commission, 2017), paragraphs 1.9 and 1.10, https://assets.publishing.service.gov.uk/government/uploads/system/uploads/attachment_data/file/645462/Non-compliance_and_enforcement_with_the_National_Minimum_Wage.pdf. See also Smith and Morton, "Nine Years of New Labour"; Pollert, "Britain and Individual Employment Rights"; John Goodman et al., "Procedures, Recruitment Methods and Management Style: Case Study Evidence from Three Industrial Sectors," *Employee Relations* 20, no. 6 (1998): 536–50, https://www.emeraldinsight.com/doi/abs/10.1108/01425459810247297; Robert Blackburn and Mark Hart, *Small Firms' Awareness and Knowledge of Individual Employment Rights*, Employment Relations Research Series 14 (Department of Trade and Industry, 2002), http://citeseerx.ist.psu.edu/viewdoc/download?doi=10.1.1.496.6367&rep=rep1&type=pdf.

68. "Top 1% National Income Share," World Inequality Database, accessed March 4, 2020, https://wid.world/world/#sptinc_p99p100_z/US;DE;CN;ZA;WO;GB/last/eu/k/p/yearly/s/false/5.487/30/curve/false/country. See also "Gini Coefficient, 2016," Compare Your Country, https://www1.compareyourcountry.org/inequality/en/0/313/datatable. For more information on inequality, see Adam Corlett and Stephen Clarke, *Living Standards 2017: The Past, Present, and Possible Future of UK Incomes* (Resolution Foundation, 2017), https://www.resolutionfoundation.org/app/uploads/2017/01/Audit-2017.pdf.

69. See David Bailey, Keith Cowling, and Philip Tomlinson, *New Perspectives on Industrial Policy for a Modern Britain* (Oxford, UK: Oxford University Press, 2015, 68, figure 4.1.

70. Stephen Machin, "The Decline of Labour Market Institutions and the Rise in Wage Inequality in Britain," *European Economic Review* 41, no. 3–5 (1997): 647–57; Amanda Gosling and Stephen Machin, "Trade Unions and the Dispersion of Earnings in British Establishments, 1980–90," *Oxford Bulletin of Economics and Statistics* 57, no. 2 (1995): 167–84; Card, Lemieux, and Riddell, "Unions and Wage Inequality"; Craig Holmes and Ken Mayhew, "Have U.K. Earning Distributions Polarised," INET Oxford Working Paper 2015-02, Employment, Equity and Growth Programme, Oxford Martin School, University of Oxford, https://www.inet.ox.ac.uk/files/WP2.pdf; *Working for the Economy: The Economic Case for Trade Unions* (New Economics Foundation, University of Greenwich, 2015), https://b.3cdn.net/nefoundation/5237986e74dd1368f5_51m6b4u2z.pdf; Özlem Onaran and Alexander Guschanski, "The Causes of Falling Wage Share: Sectoral and Firm Level Evidence from Developed and Developing Countries—What Have We Learned?," Greenwich Papers on Political Economy, University of Greenwich, Greenwich Political Economy Research Centre, 2018, https://ideas.repec.org/p/gpe/wpaper/19373.html; Richard Blundell, Claire Crawford, and Wenchao Jin, "What Can Wages and Employment Tell Us about the UK's Productivity Puzzle?," *Economic Journal* 124, no. 576 (2014): 377–407. See also Joe Dromey, *Power to the People: How Stronger Unions Can Deliver Economic Justice*, Discussion Paper (IIPPR Commission on Economic Justice, 2018), 9, figure 1.4, https://www.ippr.org/research/publications/power-to-the-people.

71. Trades Unions Congress, *Collective Bargaining Strategy for the 1990s* (London: TUC, 1991), 16, cited in Howell, *Trade Unions and the State*, 173.

72. Howell, *Trade Unions and the State*, 17.

73. Keith D. Ewing and John London Hendy, *Reconstruction after the Crisis: A Manifesto for Collective Bargaining* (Liverpool: Institute of Employment Rights, 2013). For supporters, see K. D. Ewing, John Hendy, and Carolyn Jones, *Rolling out the Manifesto for Labour Law* (Liverpool: Institute of Employment Rights, 2018). See also *Prosperity and Justice*.

74. Ewing and Hendy, *Reconstruction after the Crisis: A Manifesto for Collective Bargaining*; IPPR, "Prosperity and Justice."

75. "Manifesto for Labour Law," Institute of Employment Rights, http://www.ier.org.uk/manifesto#labourpartysupport.

76. Jim Stanford, "Fair Go No More: Neoliberalism and Australian Labour Market Policy," chap. 9 in *Wrong Way: How Privatisation and Economic Reform Backfired*, ed. Damien Cahill and Phillip Toner (Carlton, Australia: La Trobe University Press, 2018).

77. The discussion of the *Harvester* case relies largely on the decision itself, as well as some additional material such as "Harvester Judgement," Defining Moments in Australian History, National Museum Australia, http://www.nma.gov.au/online_features/defining_moments/featured/harvester_judgement; Peter Macarthy, "The Harvester Judgement: An Historical Assessment," PhD thesis, Australian National University, Canberra, 1967, https://openresearch-repository.anu.edu.au/handle/1885/10985; "Harvester Case," Waltzing Matilda and the Sunshine Harvester Factory, https://www.fwc.gov.au/waltzing-matilda-and-the-sunshine-harvester-factory/historical-material/harvester-case.

78. Commonwealth Conciliation and Arbitration Act 1904 (No 13 of 1904), Commonwealth of Australia Numbered Acts, http://www6.austlii.edu.au/cgi-bin/viewdb/au/legis/cth/num_act/ccaaa190413o1904441.

79. Excise Tariff 1906, Federal Register of Legislation (Australia), https://www.legislation.gov.au/Details/C1906A00020.

80. "The Strangling Tariff," *Age* (Melbourne), October 8, 1904, https://trove.nla.gov.au/newspaper/article/189435179; "New Wages Board," *Age*, August 9, 1906, https://trove.nla.gov.au/newspaper/article/189369554.

81. Ex Parte H. V. McKay, "Excise Tariff 1906 (No. 16 of 1906)" ("Application for declaration that wages are fair and reasonable—Test of fairness and reasonableness"), http://www.aph.gov.au/binaries/library/intguide/law/harvester.pdf.

82. All quotes and facts in this paragraph and the following about Harvester come from the decision itself. Ex Parte H. V. McKay, "Excise Tariff 1906 (No. 16 of 1906)." Note that this was a living wage for a white male. Women and Aboriginals did not receive the same standards.

83. "Harvester Case."

84. See, for example, Mark Bray and Johanna Macneil, "Reforming Collective Bargaining," chap. 6 in *Industrial Relations Reform: Looking to the Future: Essays in Honour of Joe Isaac AO*, eds. Keith Hancock and Russell Lansbury (Annandale, Australia: Federation Press, 2016).

85. Henry Bournes Higgins, *A New Province for Law and Order: Industrial Peace through Minimum Wage and Arbitration* (New York City: National Consumers' League, 1915), https://babel.hathitrust.org/cgi/pt?id=hvd.hnmdum;view=1up;seq=5.

86. See Rae Cooper and Bradon Ellem, "Cold Climate: Australian Unions, Policy, and the State," *Comparative Labor Law and Policy Journal* 38, no. 3 (2017): 415–36. See also Stanford, "Fair Go No More."

87. Joe Isaac, "Why Are Australian Wages Lagging and What Can Be Done about It?," *Australian Economic Review* 51, no. 2 (2018): 181.

88. Mark Bray and Jacques Rouillard, "Union Structure and Strategy in Australia and Canada," *Labour History* 71 (1996): 198–238.

89. The system was supported by significant factions of both labor and capital. See discussion in Bray and Macneil, "Reforming Collective Bargaining," 106. See also S. Macintyre and R. Mitchell, eds. *The Foundations of Arbitration* (Melbourne: Oxford University Press, 1987); and F. Castles, *Australian Public Policy and Economic Vulnerability* (Sydney: Allen & Unwin, 1988).

90. For union figures, see Isaac, "Why Are Australian Wages Lagging and What Can Be Done about It?," 175–90, figure 5; and Stanford, "Fair Go No More," figure 3. For coverage,

see Visser, "ICTWSS: Database on Institutional Characteristics of Trade Unions, Wage Setting, State Intervention and Social Pacts."

91. For example, the Australian system was highly legalistic and put the arbitral tribunal at the center, rather than workers and business. There were limits on strikes and lockouts, and the tribunal had almost limitless authority to decide whether a dispute needed to be resolved. The system placed great emphasis on collective rights but gave fewer rights to individuals. The extraordinary number of decisions—at the firm, industry, state, and national levels—added complexity and rigidity.

92. For inequality, see "Top 1% National Income Share, Australia, 1921–2015," World Inequality Database, accessed April 23, 2019, https://wid.world/country/australia.

93. Duncan MacDonald, Iaian Campbell, and John Burgess, "Ten Years of Enterprise Bargaining in Australia: An Introduction," *Labour and Industry: A Journal of the Social and Economic Relations of Work* 12, no. 1 (2001): 1–25.

94. Chris Briggs, "Australian Exceptionalism: The Role of Trade Unions in the Emergence of Enterprise Bargaining," *Journal of Industrial Relations* 43, no. 1 (2001): 27–43; Chris F. Wright, "The Prices and Incomes Accord: Its Significance, Impact and Legacy," *Journal of Industrial Relations* 56, no. 2 (2014): 264–72.

95. "Other policies . . . to undermine unions and collective bargaining": for example, by allowing enterprise flexibility arrangements—a type of collective agreement that could be made without a union being party to it.

96. Raymond Markey, "Tragedy or Farce: The Repetition of Australian Industrial Relations History, 1929 and 2007," *Labor History* 54, no. 4 (2013): 355–76. Note that this defeat of antilabor politicians echoed earlier Australian history. In 1929, the ruling party pushed legislation to significantly weaken unions and the arbitration system, but their legislative efforts were blocked, and soon after they were defeated from office.

97. Louise Thornthwaite and Peter Sheldon, "Fair Work Australia: Employer Association Policies, Industrial Law and the Changing Role of the Tribunal," *Journal of Industrial Relations* 53, no. 5 (2011): 616–31; Bray and Macneil, "Reforming Collective Bargaining"; and Kurt Walpole, "The Fair Work Act: Encouraging Collective Agreement Making but Leaving Collective Bargaining to Choice," *Labour and Industry: A Journal of the Social and Economic Relations of Work* 25, no. 3 (2015): 205–18.

98. See Cooper and Ellem, "Cold Climate." See also Tess Hardy, "The State Strikes Back: Supervision and Sanctioning of Unlawful Industrial Activity by Federal Government Agencies in Australia," chap. 9 in *Collective Bargaining Under the Fair Work Act*, ed. Shae McCrystal, Breen Creighton, and Anthony Forsyth (Leichhardt, Australia: Federation Press, 2018); and Stanford, "Fair Go No More."

99. "Australia's Industrial Relations Timeline," Fair Work Ombudsman (Australia), accessed April 15, 2019, https://www.fairwork.gov.au/about-us/legislation/the-fair-work-system/australias-industrial-relations-timeline.

100. See, among others, Isaac, "Why Are Australian Wages Lagging and What Can Be Done about It?"; Tess Hardy and Andrew Stewart, "What's Causing the Wages Slowdown?," chap. 4 in *The Wages Crisis in Australia*, ed. Andrew Stewart, Jim Stanford, and Tess Hardy (Adelaide: University of Adelaide Press, 2018).

101. Shae McCrystal, "Why Is It So Hard to Take Lawful Strike Action in Australia?" *Journal of Industrial Relations* 61, no. 1 (2019): 129–44.

102. Andreas Pekarek et al., "Old Game, New Rules? The Dynamics of Enterprise Bargaining under the Fair Work Act," *Journal of Industrial Relations* 59, no. 1 (2016): 44–64.

103. Bray and Macneil, "Reforming Collective Bargaining." See also Anthony Forsyth et al., "Establishing the Right to Bargain Collectively in Australia and the UK: Are Majority Support Determinations under Australia's Fair Work Act a More Effective Form of Union Recognition?," *Industrial Law Journal* 46, no. 3 (2007): 335–65.

104. Geoff Gilfillan and Chris McGann, "Trends in Union Membership in Australia," Parliamentary Library Statistical Snapshot, Research Paper Series, 2018–19, Parliament of Australia, October 16, 2018, https://www.aph.gov.au/About_Parliament/Parliamentary_Departments/Parliamentary_Library/pubs/rp/rp1819/UnionMembership.

105. Note that there is some variation in country minimum wage rankings depending on how prices are adjusted, and several countries have a higher ratio of minimum to median (and/or mean) wages. Still, by most any measure, Australia's minimum wage is high compared to most other countries.

106. See James Bishop, "The Effect of Minimum Wage Increases on Wages, Hours Worked and Job Loss," Research Discussion Paper 2018-06, Reserve Bank of Australia, 2018, 4 (figure 1), 2, https://www.rba.gov.au/publications/rdp/2018/pdf/rdp2018-06.pdf.

107. "Summary of Decision, Annual Wage Review 2017–2018," FairWork Commission (Australia), June 1, 2018, https://www.fwc.gov.au/documents/documents/summaries/2018fwcfb3500-summary.htm; "Decision: Annual Wage Review 2017–18," FairWork Commission (Australia), June 1, 2018, https://www.fwc.gov.au/documents/sites/wagereview2018/decisions/2018fwcfb3500.pdf.

108. Bishop, "Effect of Minimum Wage Increases on Wages, Hours Worked and Job Loss."

109. Margaret McKenzie, "The Erosion of Minimum Wage Policy in Australia and Labour's Shrinking Share of Total Income," *Journal of Australian Political Economy* 81 (2018): 52–77, https://d3n8a8pro7vhmx.cloudfront.net/theausinstitute/pages/2838/attachments/original/1532441298/Labour_Share_Symposium_McKenzie.pdf?1532441298.

110. McKenzie, "Erosion of Minimum Wage Policy in Australia." See also Brian Lawrence, "The Catholic Church as an Employer in Australia: An Antipodean Contribution to an American Audience," January 18, 2018 unpublished speech. Lawrence notes that the ratio of the minimum wage to the median wage was 62 percent in 1997.

111. For more on enterprise agreement coverage, see Alison Pennington, *On the Brink: The Erosion of Enterprise Agreement Coverage in Australia's Private Sector* (Canberra: Centre for Future Work at the Australia Institute, 2018), https://d3n8a8pro7vhmx.cloudfront.net/theausinstitute/pages/2905/attachments/original/1544650280/On_the_Brink_Formatted.pdf?1544650280; Hardy and Stewart, "What's Causing the Wages Slowdown?"; Jim Stanford, "Charting Wage Stagnation in Australia," chap. 2 in *The Wages Crisis in Australia*, ed. Andrew Stewart, Jim Stanford, and Tess Hardy (Adelaide: University of Adelaide Press, 2018).

112. "Trade Union [Density]," OECD.Stat, accessed April 15, 2019, https://stats.oecd.org/Index.aspx?DataSetCode=TUD; Stanford, "Charting Wage Stagnation in Australia"; Isaac, "Why Are Australian Wages Lagging and What Can Be Done About It?," 175–90, figure 5; Hardy and Stewart, "What's Causing the Wages Slowdown?"

113. See Jeff Borland, "Has Declining Union Density Contributed to Growing Earnings Inequality in Australia?," Labour Market Snapshot no. 43 (June 2018), 3, https://drive.google.com/file/d/1L-uryj0Af1MPAtJIWyEGgl_kAUZvkUp3/view.

114. Hardy and Stewart, "What's Causing the Wages Slowdown?," 58, table 4.1; Pennington, *On the Brink*; Hardy and Stewart, "What's Causing the Wages Slowdown?"; Stanford, "Charting Wage Stagnation in Australia"; Visser, "ICTWSS: Database on Institutional Characteristics of Trade Unions, Wage Setting, State Intervention and Social Pacts." See also "6306.0—Employee Earning and Hours, Australia, May 2018," Australian Bureau of Statistics, http://www.abs.gov.au/ausstats/abs@.nsf/mf/6306.0. Note that some figures, such as those by the OECD and Visser, indicate 60 percent coverage. But these coverage statistics significantly overstate the amount of collective bargaining because they include the government awards—which once were closer to collectively bargained agreements but now are essentially government-set minimum wages.

115. Wage increases from nonunion collective agreements are weak and significantly below that of even the relatively modest gains in union agreements. See Pennington, *On the Brink*. See also Rosalind Read, "The Role of Trade Unions and Individual Bargaining

Representatives," chap. 4 in *Collective Bargaining under the Fair Work Act*, ed. Shae McCrystal, Breen Creighton and Anthony Forsyth, eds. (Annandale, Australia: Federation Press, 2018); Fiona Macdonald, Sara Charlesworth and Cathy Brigden, "Access to Collective Bargaining for Low-Paid Workers," chap. 10 in *Collective Bargaining under the Fair Work Act*, ed. Shae McCrystal, Breen Creighton and Anthony Forsyth, eds. (Annandale, Australia: Federation Press, 2018).

116. Pennington, *On the Brink*.

117. *Industry Insights: Flexibility and Growth* (Canberra: Office of the Chief Economist, Department of Industry, Innovation, and Science, 2018), 9, figure 1.3, https://publications.industry.gov.au/publications/industryinsightsjune2018/documents/IndustryInsights_1_2018_ONLINE.pdf; Stanford, "Charting Wage Stagnation in Australia."

118. Jim Stanford, "Labour Share of Australian GDP Hits All-Time Record Low," Briefing Note, Australia Institute, Centre of Future Work, June 13, 2017, https://d3n8a8pro7vhmx.cloudfront.net/theausinstitute/pages/1500/attachments/original/1497298286/Labour_Share_Hits_Record_Low.pdf?1497298286.

119. *OECD Economic Surveys: Australia, March 2017, Overview* (Organisation for Economic Co-operation and Development, 2017), https://www.oecd.org/eco/surveys/Australia-2017-OECD-economic-survey-overview.pdf; and "Top 1% National Income Share, Australia, 1921–2015."

120. Roger Wilkins, "The Changing Socio-Demographic Composition of Poverty in Australia: 1982 to 2004," Melbourne Institute Working Paper Series, Working Paper 12/07, University of Melbourne, 2007, 11, figure 1, https://melbourneinstitute.unimelb.edu.au/downloads/working-paper-series/wp2007n12.pdf. Note that the share of the population in absolute poverty has decreased a few percentage points since the 1980s (see 11, figure 2).

121. Studies find, for example, that the linkages between formal qualifications and jobs and pay outcomes are less common and weaker in enterprise agreements than in the current awards. Damian Oliver and Kurt Walpole, "How Are Links between a National Qualifications Framework, Job Roles and Pay Mediated by Industrial Relations Institutions in Manufacturing?," *Journal of Vocational Education & Training*, 69, no. 4 (2017): 576–95; Damian Oliver and Kurt Walpole, "Subject to Qualification: Weakening Links between Job Roles and Qualifications in Australian Manufacturing Enterprise Agreements," *Journal of Industrial Relations* 60, no. 4 (2018): 517–37.

122. Damian Oliver, "Wage Determination in Australia: The Impact of Qualifications, Awards and Enterprise Agreements," *Journal of Industrial Relations* 58, no. 1 (2015): 69–92.

123. "Public Spending on Labour Markets: Total, % of GDP, 2000–2016," OECD Data, accessed April 15, 2019, https://data.oecd.org/socialexp/public-spending-on-labour-markets.htm.

124. See, for example, Isaac, "Why Are Australian Wages Lagging and What Can Be Done About It?, 185, as well as discussion in McKenzie, "Erosion of Minimum Wage Policy in Australia"; Hardy and Stewart, "What's Causing the Wages Slowdown?"; Laurie Berg and Bsasina Farbenblum, "Wage Theft in Australia: Findings of the National Temporary Migrant Work Survey," unpublished paper, 2017, https://papers.ssrn.com/sol3/papers.cfm?abstract_id=3140071.

125. "National Hospitality Industry Campaign Restaurants: Café's and Catering (Wave 2)," Fair Work Ombudsman, Australia, 2015; "Wage Repayment Program Closing to New Applicants," 7 Eleven, January 9, 2017, https://www.7eleven.com.au/media-centre/article/wage-repayment-program-closing-to-new-applicants; "Caltex Assistance Fund for Franchisee Employees," Caltex Australia, https://www.caltexassistancefund.com.au.

126. Louise Thornthwaite, "The Government Needs to Better Enforce the Laws It Creates, to Protect Franchise Workers," *Conversation*, March 2, 2017, http://theconversation.com/the-government-needs-to-better-enforce-the-laws-it-creates-to-protect-franchise-workers-73445.

127. Elsa Underhill et al., "Evaluating the Role of CFMEU OHS Representatives in Improving Occupational Health and Safety Outcomes in the Victorian Construction Industry: Interim Report," unpublished paper, Deakin University Australia, 2016.

128. Keith Hancock, "Enterprise Bargaining and Productivity," *Labor and Industry: A Journal of the Social and Economic Relations of Work* 22, no. 3 (2012): 289–301.

129. Justine Evesson et al., *"Lowering the Standards": From Awards to Work Choices in Retail and Hospitality Collective Agreements, Synthesis Report* (University of Sydney Workplace Research Center, 2007), https://www.pc.gov.au/inquiries/completed/retail-industry/submissions/subdr183-attachment.pdf.

130. Stanford, "Charting Wage Stagnation in Australia."

131. Hardy and Stewart, "What's Causing the Wages Slowdown?"; Stanford, "Fair Go No More."

132. Joe Isaac, an emeritus professor at Monash University in Melbourne and one of Australia's preeminent economists, explains, "Although a number of factors may be involved, an important explanation is to be found in the change in the balance of power [in favor of employers due to changes in industrial relations policies]." Isaac, "Why Are Australian Wages Lagging and What Can Be Done About It?" See also Hardy and Stewart, "What's Causing the Wages Slowdown?"

133. Cooper and Ellem, "Cold Climate."

134. Borland, "Has Declining Union Density Contributed to Growing Earnings Inequality in Australia?"

135. John Celliah and Serge Mukhi, "A Chronological Analysis of the Evolution of Industrial Relations in New Zealand," Proceedings of the 12th Annual Conference of the International Employment Relations Association: "Regionalism and Globalisation—The Challenge for Employment Relations," 2004, 77–84, https://opus.lib.uts.edu.au/bitstream/10453/7669/1/2004000719.pdf; Michael Barry, "Transforming Workplace Relations in New Zealand: A Retrospective," *Labour and Industry: A Journal of the Social and Economic Relations of Work* 28, no. 1 (2018): 82–92. See also Tracy Withers, "Workers in New Zealand Strike over Decade of Stagnant Wages," *Bloomberg*, July 31, 2018, https://www.bloomberg.com/news/articles/2018-07-31/workers-in-new-zealand-strike-over-decade-of-stagnating-wages; and Paul Dalziel, "New Zealand's Economic Reforms: An Assessment," *Review of Political Economy* 14, no. 1 (2002): 31–46.

136. Florence Jaumotte and Carolina Osorio Buitron, Inequality and Labor Market Institutions, IMF Staff Discussion Notes (International Monetary Fund, 2015), 26, figure 7, https://www.imf.org/external/pubs/ft/sdn/2015/sdn1514.pdf.

137. Alison Pennington, *Workplace Policy Reform in New Zealand: What Are the Lessons for Australia?* (Canberra: Centre for Future Work at the Australia Institute, 2019), https://apo.org.au/sites/default/files/resource-files/2019-03/apo-nid226936.pdf.

138. Philip Lowe, "Productivity, Wages, and Prosperity," address to Australian Industry Group, Melbourne, June 13, 2018, https://www.rba.gov.au/speeches/2018/sp-gov-2018-06-13.html#r1.

139. Peter Gahan, Andreas Pekarek, and Daniel Nicholson, "Unions and Collective Bargaining in Australia in 2017," *Journal of Industrial Relations* 60, no. 3 (2018): 337–57.

140. John Buchanan and Damian Oliver, "'Fair Work' and the Modernization of Australian Labour Standards: A Case of Institutional Plasticity Entrenching Deepening Wage Inequality," *International Journal of Employment Relations* 54, no. 4 (2016): 790–814. See also Stanford, "Fair Go No More."

141. See, for example, Isaac, "Why Are Australian Wages Lagging and What Can Be Done About It?"; Greg Jericho, "The Time Is Ripe for a More Activist Approach to Industrial Relations," *Guardian*, June 23, 2018; Jim Stanford, "A Turning Point for Labour Market Policy in Australia," *Economic and Labour Relations Review* (2019): 177–99.

142. Paul Karp, "Sally McManus Says Enterprise Bargaining Is 'Smothering' Wage Growth," *Guardian*, March 21, 2018; "Change the Government, Change the Rules," https://web.archive.org/web/20190410001010/https://changetherules.org.au/; Sally McManus, "Change the Rules: For More Secure Jobs and Fair Pay," Press Club speech, March 21, 2018, Australian Council of Trade Unions, https://www.actu.org.au/media/1033746/180320-national-press-club-speech-sally-mcmanus-march-21-2018.pdf; United Voice, "Our Industrial Relations System Has Failed Workers, Evatt Foundation Speech on Industry Bargaining," June 18, 2018, https://web.archive.org/web/20190228134421/https://www.unitedvoice.org.au/evatt_foundation_speech_on_industry_bargaining.

143. Paul Karp, "Labor Flags Industrial Relations Changes Including New Arbitration Power," *Guardian*, March 15, 2018. See also *Report of the Commission on Inclusive Prosperity* (Washington, DC: Center for American Progress, 2015), https://cdn.americanprogress.org/wp-content/uploads/2015/01/IPC-PDF-full.pdf, which the current national president of the Australian Labor Party, Wayne Swan, endorsed.

144. See, for example, *Future of Work and Workers Inquiry* (Australian Industry Group, 2018), http://cdn.aigroup.com.au/Submissions/Workplace_Relations/2018/AiGroup_Submission_Future_of_Work_Inquiry_feb2018.pdf.

CHAPTER 5. ANSWERING SKEPTICS

1. See Steven L. Willborn, "A New Look at NLRB Policy on Multiemployer Bargaining," *North Carolina Law Review* 60, no. 3 (1982), 456n7, http://scholarship.law.unc.edu/cgi/viewcontent.cgi?article=2863&context=nclr. See also the claim that "undoubtedly, the NLRB's early support of more inclusive units accelerated the ascendency of industrial unionism" in Jack Barbarsh, "Contemporary American Experience-A Commentary," in *Collective Bargaining: Contemporary American Experience*, ed. Gerald Somers (Madison, WI: Industrial Relations Research Association, 1980), 579.

2. "Industrial Welfare Commission," State of California Department of Industrial Relations, https://www.dir.ca.gov/iwc/wageorderindustriesprior.htm.

3. "Commissioner of Labor Opening Statement and Charge to the 2015 Fast Food Wage Board," New York State Department of Labor, May 20, 2015, https://www.labor.ny.gov/workerprotection/laborstandards/pdfs/5-20-charge.pdf.

4. For more details, see Kate Andrias, David Madland, and Malkie Wall, "A How-To Guide for State and Local Workers' Boards," Center for American Progress, December 11, 2019, https://www.americanprogress.org/issues/economy/reports/2019/12/11/478539/guide-state-local-workers-boards.

5. For example, in Sweden the manufacturing industry sets the industry norm that specifies a certain percentage of the upper wage increase for the whole economy. See Anders Kjellberg, "Sweden: Collective Bargaining under the Industry Norm," in *Collective Bargaining in Europe: Towards an Endgame*, vol. 3, ed. Torsten Müller, Kurt Vandaele, and Jeremy Waddington (Brussels: European Trade Union Institute, 2019), https://www.etui.org/publications/books/collective-bargaining-in-europe-towards-an-endgame-volume-i-ii-iii-and-iv. For the less formal German variant of using a key industry to pattern wages for other industries (and on its decline in recent years), see Torsten Müller and Thorsten Schulten, "Germany: Parallel Universes of Collective Bargaining," in Müller, Vandaele, and Waddington, eds., *Collective Bargaining in Europe: Towards an Endgame*, vol. 2, 254–55.

6. For a discussion of policy to promote employer associations to limit the effects of union power in the Canadian construction industry, see Joseph Rose, "Legislative Support for Multi-Employer Bargaining: The Canadian Experience," *ILR Review* 40, no. 1 (1986): 3–18.

7. Erin Blakemore, "The 1936 Strike That Brought America's Most Powerful Automaker to Its Knees," History Channel, September 17, 2019, https://www.history.com/news/flint-sit-down-strike-general-motors-uaw; "U.A.W. and the Auto Industry," *New York Times*, October 8, 2015; "This Day in History: June 20, 1941: Ford Signs First Contract with Autoworkers' Union," History Channel, https://www.history.com/this-day-in-history/ford-signs-first-contract-with-autoworkers-union.

8. Blakemore, "1936 Strike That Brought America's Most Powerful Automaker to its Knees"; "U.A.W. and the Auto Industry"; Steve Fraser, "The Good War and the Workers," *American Prospect*, September 20, 2009, https://prospect.org/special-report/good-war-workers; Quinn Mills and Janice McCormick, *Industrial Relations in Transition: Cases and Text* (John Wiley & Sons, 1985), 273, 348. For details on some of the history, see *The Termination Report of the National War Labor Board: Industrial Disputes and Wage Stabilization in Wartime: January 12, 1942–December 31, 1945*, vol. 1 (Washington, DC: US National War Labor Board, 1949).

9. Harry C. Katz, "Automobiles," in *Collective Bargaining in American Industry: Contemporary Perspectives and Future Directions*, ed. David Lipsky and Clifford Donn (Lexington, MA: D.C. Heath, 1987), 20. The International Union of Electronic, Electrical, Technical, Salaried and Machine Workers also represented a small percentage of workers in assembly and parts.

10. Katz, "Automobiles," 22–23.

11. _Ronald L. Seeber, "Agricultural Machinery," chap. 3 in Lipsky and Donn, eds., *Collective Bargaining in American Industry*; Mark D. Karper, "Tires," chap. 4 in Lipsky and Donn, eds., *Collective Bargaining in American Industry*.

12. Frank Levy and Peter Temlin, "Inequality and Institutions in 20th Century America," Massachusetts Institute of Technology Working Papers Series, 2007, https://inequality.stanford.edu/sites/default/files/media/_media/pdf/key_issues/politics_research.pdf.

13. *Industrial Relations in Transition*, 273.

14. Katz, "Automobiles," 30. See also Mills and McCormick, *Industrial Relations in Transition*, 273, 274.

15. Katz, "Automobiles," 14.

16. Katz, "Automobiles," 14, 32. The fact that bargaining largely covered the industry also helped.

17. Katz, "Automobiles," 14.

18. In 1983 and 1984, profits recovered, but there were still concerns about competition from Japan. Katz, "Automobiles," 14–15.

19. Mills and McCormick, *Industrial Relations in Transition*, 342.

20. Katz, "Automobiles," 33, 39, 45, 38, as well as chaps. 3 and 4.

21. Introduction to Lipsky and Donn, eds., *Collective Bargaining in American Industry*, 4.

22. See, for example, Kate Andrias, "GM Strike Exposes Anti-worker Flaws in US Labor Laws. Companies Have the Upper Hand," *USA Today*, September 21, 2019.

23. One hundred percent density was just among blue-collar workers in assembly and did not include white-collar workers. Katz, "Automobiles," 22.

24. Katz, "Automobiles," 21, 22.

25. Katz, "Automobiles," 19, 128, and table 2-1, 19.

26. Mills and McCormick, *Industrial Relations in Transition*, 345.

27. Auto assembly wages were over 50 percent higher than those of the average private-sector production worker in 1980 but only 30 percent higher in 1970 and less than 20 percent higher in 1950s and 1960s. Katz, "Automobiles," table 22, 27.

28. Mills and McCormick, *Industrial Relations in Transition*, 272, 274, 345, 348, 323–24.

29. See Mills and McCormick, *Industrial Relations in Transition*, 349, exhibit 5; Frederick E. Allen, "How Germany Builds Twice as Many Cars as the US While Paying Its Workers Twice as Much," *Forbes*, December 21, 2011, https://www.forbes.com/sites/frederick

allen/2011/12/21/germany-builds-twice-as-many-cars-as-the-u-s-while-paying-its-auto-workers-twice-as-much/#a1fd2946b789.

30. For a discussion of this research, see Stephen J. Silva, *Holding the Shop Together: German Industrial Relations in the Postwar Era* (Ithaca, NY: Cornell University Press, 2013).

31. Mills and McCormick, *Industrial Relations in Transition*, 349, exhibit 5.

32. Exhibit 5 in Mills and McCormick, *Industrial Relations in Transition*, exhibit 5.

33. See Katz, "Automobiles"; and Mills and McCormick, *Industrial Relations in Transition*.

34. Introduction to Lipsky and Donn, eds., *Collective Bargaining in American Industry*, 9.

35. For strike information, see Gerald Somers, ed., *Collective Bargaining: Contemporary American Experience* (Madison, WI: Industrial Relations Research Association, 1980), 181.

36. In steel, after initial resistance, employers generally supported multi-employer bargaining, in part as a way to limit union power. See Somers, *Collective Bargaining*, 166–67. For general information on collective bargaining in the steel industry, see Mills and McCormick, *Industrial Relations in Transition*, 317–40; and Jack Stieber, "Steel," chap. 4 in Somers, *Collective Bargaining*. For failure of industry to promote technological superiority, see Mills and McCormick, *Industrial Relations in Transition*, 272. For general success of collective bargaining in steel, see Somers, *Collective Bargaining*, 205.

37. See Somers, *Collective Bargaining*, 165–66.

38. Wallace Hendricks, "Telecommunications," in Lipsky and Donn, eds., *Collective Bargaining in American Industry*, 120.

39. Lipsky and Donn, eds., *Collective Bargaining in American Industry*, 119–21; and Chris Shelton, "The Future of American Labor," speech, Albert Shanker Institute, Washington, DC, February 8, 2019, https://georgetown.app.box.com/s/2jtwawgaows4gie5a1sn 0kmiqulg5r5u/file/402242107074.

40. Hendricks, "Telecommunications," 129.

41. Harry Rissetto and Thomas Reinert, "The Railway Labor Act from 15,000 Feet," unpublished paper, American Bar Association, 2009, https://www.americanbar.org/con tent/dam/aba/administrative/labor_law/meetings/2009/ac2009/096.pdf.

42. "Who Are the Parties?," National Railway Labor Conference, accessed December 12 2019, http://raillaborfacts.org/bargaining-essentials/the-parties.

43. William Miernyk, "Coal," chap. 1 in Somers, ed., *Collective Bargaining*.

44. Miernyk, "Coal," 25, 27.

45. Harold Levinson, "Trucking," chap. 3 in Somers, ed., *Collective Bargaining*.

46. Levinson, "Trucking," 104–6.

47. This paragraph is based on Mark Anner, Jennifer Bair, and Jeremy Blasi, "Towards Joint Liability in Global Supply Chains: Addressing the Root Causes of Labor Violations in International Subcontracting Networks," *Comparative Labor Law and Policy Journal* 35, no. 1 (2013): 1–43.

48. Anner, Bair and Blasi, "Towards Joint Liability in Global Supply Chains," 18, 19.

49. See chapter 4 for discussion of this estimate. See also Scott Legree, Tammy Schirle, Mikal Skuterud, "The Effect of Labour Relations Laws on Union Density Rates: Evidence from Canadian Provinces," CLSSRN Working Papers (2014), https://ideas.repec.org/p/ubc/clssrn/clsrn_admin-2014-42.html.

50. See chapter 3 for a discussion of the impact of the Ghent system. See also Bo Rothstein, "Labor-Market Institutions and Working-Class Strength," in *Structuring Politics: Historical Institutional in Comparative Analysis*, ed. Sven Steinmo, Kathleen Thelen, and Frank Longstreth (UK: Cambridge University Press, 1992); "Trade Union Density," OECD.stat, accessed May 22, 2019, https://stats.oecd.org/Index.aspx?DataSet Code=TUD.

51. See, for example, Karla Walter, "Public Sector Training Partnerships Build Power," Center for American Progress, 2019, https://www.americanprogress.org/issues/economy/reports/2019/10/03/475355/public-sector-training-partnerships-build-power.

52. "The Davis-Bacon Act: Institutional Evolution and Public Policy," Congressional Research Service, November 30, 2007, https://www.everycrsreport.com/reports/94-408.html. Note that federal standards are now based on 50 percent coverage.

53. For additional discussion of thresholds, see David Madland, "How to Promote Sectoral Bargaining in the United States," Center for American Progress Action Fund, July 10, 2019, https://www.americanprogressaction.org/issues/economy/reports/2019/07/10/174385/promote-sectoral-bargaining-united-states.

54. "Decoupling of Wages from Productivity: What Implications for Public Policies?," chap. 2 in *OECD Economic Outlook 2018*, issue 2 (Organization for Economic Cooperation and Development, 2018), http://www.oecd.org/economy/decoupling-of-wages-from-productivity.

55. Bruce Western and Jake Rosenfeld, "Unions, Norms, and the Rise in US Wage Inequality," *American Sociological Review* 76, no. 4 (2011): 513–37.

56. See "An Overview of Growing Income Inequalities in OECD Countries: Main Findings," in *Divided We Stand: Why Inequality Keeps Rising* (Organization for Economic Cooperation and Development, 2011), 25, figure 2, https://www.oecd.org/els/soc/49499779.pdf.

57. Benjamin Radcliff and Patricia Davis, "Labor Organization and Electoral Participation in Industrial Democracies," *American Journal of Political Science* 44, no. 1 (2000): 132–41; Roland Zullo, "Union Membership and Political Inclusion," *Industrial and Labor Relations Review* 62, no. 1 (2008): 22–38.

58. "National General Election VEP Turnout Rates, 1789–Present," United States Elections Project, accessed December 12, 2019, http://www.electproject.org/national-1789-present.

59. For example, researchers have found that right-to-work laws (which have a much smaller impact on union density than would the new labor system) reduce Democratic presidential vote shares by 3.5 percentage points and overall turnout by 2 to 3 percentage points. James Feigenbaum, Alexander Hertel-Fernandez, and Vanessa Williamson, "From the Bargaining Table to the Ballot Box: Political Effects of Right to Work Laws," unpublished paper, January 20, 2018, https://jamesfeigenbaum.github.io/research/pdf/fhw_rtw_jan2018.pdf.

60. See Frances Fox Piven and Richard A. Cloward, *Poor People's Movements: Why They Succeed, How They Fail* (New York City: Vintage Books, 1978) for the importance of disruption for less powerful groups.

61. Joseph McCartin, "Bargaining for the Future: Rethinking Labor's Recent Past and Planning Strategically for Its Future," Kalmotovitz Initiative for Labor and the Working Poor, Georgetown University, June 18, 2014, http://lwp.georgetown.edu/wp-content/uploads/Bargaining-for-the-Future.pdf.

62. Christian Lyhne Ibsen and Maite Tapia, "Trade Union Revitalisation: Where Are We Now? Where to Next?," *Journal of Industrial Relations*, 59, no. 2 (2017): 170–91. See also Bob Carter et al., "Made in the USA, Imported into Britain: The Organizing Model and the Limits of Transferability," *Research in the Sociology of Work* 11 (2003): 59–78.

63. Larry Mishel, "Private Sector Union Density Dynamics, 1951–2017," PowerPoint presentation, document in possession of author, February 21, 2019.

64. Henry S. Farber and Bruce Western, "Accounting for the Decline of Unions in the Private Sector, 1973–1998," *Journal of Labor Research* 22, no. 3 (2001): 459–85.

65. Kate Bronfenbrenner, "The Role of Union Strategies in NLRB Certification Elections," *Industrial and Labor Relations Review* 50 (1997): 195–212, https://digitalcommons.ilr.cornell.edu/cgi/viewcontent.cgi?article=1076&context=articles; Kate Bronfenbrenner et al., eds., *Organizing to Win: New Research on Union Strategies* (Ithaca, NY: Cornell University Press, 1998); Kim Voss and Rick Fantasia, "The Future of American Labor:

Reinventing Unions," *Contexts* 3, no. 2 (2004): 35–41; Rachel Sherman and Kim Voss, "'Organize or Die': Labor's New Tactics and Immigrant Workers," chap. 3 in *Organizing Immigrants: The Challenge for Unions in Contemporary California,* Ruth Milkman, ed. (Ithaca, NY: Cornell University Press, 2000).

66. Ibsen and Tapia, "Trade Union Revitalisation." See also McCartin, "Bargaining for the Future," which finds that union organizing "will require more than a greater commitment to new organizing."

67. For information on scale, see Maya Rhodan, "Here's Why West Virginia Teachers Are on Strike," *Time,* February 26, 2018; Christine Hauser, "West Virginia Teachers, Protesting Low Pay, Walk Out," *New York Times,* February 23, 2018.

68. Henry S. Farber et al., "Unions and Inequality over the Twentieth Century: New Evidence from Survey Data," NBER Working Paper 24587, National Bureau of Economic Research, May 2018, https://www.nber.org/papers/w24587.

69. Kate Cimini, "Teacher Strikes Are Illegal in West Virginia . . . So How Do They Strike?" *Medill News Service,* March 8, 2018, http://dc.medill.northwestern.edu/blog/2018/ 03/08/67017/#sthash.dRbblBh8.dpbs; Kelsey Hoak, "Kanawha County Board Approves Resolution to Support Teachers," WSAZ.com, February 14, 2018, https://www.wsaz.com/ content/news/Kanawha-County-Board-expected-to-vote-on-resolution-to-support-teach ers-474064363.html; Mark Walsh, "Are Teacher Strikes Illegal? Depends Where You Are and Who You Ask," *Education Week,* May 8, 2018, https://www.edweek.org/ew/articles/2018/05/09/ legalities-and-politics-collide-in-teacher-work.html; Matt Pearce, "In Oklahoma Schools, Bosses Are Helping Teachers Go on Strike," *Los Angeles Times,* March 29, 2018.

70. For more on the importance of the legal standards for apprenticeship, see the official comments of North America's Building Trades Unions (NABTU) on the US Department of Labor's Notice of Proposed Rulemaking: Apprenticeship Programs, Labor Standards for Registration, Amendment of Regulations, as well as the over three hundred thousand comment letters submitted. "Apprenticeship Programs, Labor Standards for Registration, Amendment of Regulations," Regulations.gov, accessed December 12, 2019, https://www. regulations.gov/docketBrowser?rpp=50&so=DESC&sb=postedDate&po=0&dct=PS&D= ETA-2019-0005.

71. See industry tables for 1983 and 2018 in Barry T. Hirsch and David A. Macpherson, "Union Membership and Coverage Database from the CPS," February 4, 2019, http:// unionstats.com/.

72. See metropolitan area and state tables for 1986 and 2018 in Hirsch and Macpherson, "Union Membership and Coverage Database from the Current Population Survey." Note that density declined in all industries except professional services, where it remained stable at around 6 percent. See Ryan Nunn, Jimmy O'Donnell, and Jay Schambaugh, *The Shift in Private Sector Union Participation: Explanation and Effects* (Hamilton Project, 2019), https://www.hamiltonproject.org/assets/files/UnionsEA_Web_8.19.pdf.

73. Hirsch and Macpherson, "Union Membership and Coverage Database." For cities, the author compared union density in the years 1986 and 2018 in the ten most populous metropolitan areas of 2017 based on the US Census Bureau, "New Census Bureau Population Estimates Show Dallas-Fort Worth-Arlington Has Largest Growth in the United States," March 22, 2018, https://www.census.gov/newsroom/press-releases/2018/popest-metro-county.html. Note that statistical area definitions changed over time. For 1986 the author used Metropolitan Statistical Areas (MSAs) and Primary Metropolitan Statistical Areas (PMSAs). For 2018 the author used Metropolitan Statistical Areas (MSAs).

74. Richard Freeman and Joel Rogers, *What Workers Want* (Ithaca, NY: Cornell University Press, 1999).

75. While it is theoretically possible that direct action could lead to American unions that are strong enough that they only need to threaten to strike to get employers to

negotiate, as in Sweden, this level of density has never been achieved in US history and seems extremely unlikely without favorable policy.

76. Matthew Dimick, "Productive Unionism," *UC Irvine Law Review* 4, no. 679 (2014): 679–724, https://www.law.uci.edu/lawreview/vol4/no2/Dimick.pdf.

77. See, for example, Joseph B. Rose and Gary Chaison, "Unionism in Canada and the United States in the 21st Century: The Prospects for Revival," *Relations Industrielles/Indus trial Relations* 56, no. 1 (2001): 34–65; John Godard, "Do Labor Laws Matter? The Density Decline and Convergence Thesis Revisited," *Industrial Relations* 42 (2003): 458–92; Scott Legree, Tammy Schirle, Mikal Skuterud, "The Effect of Labour Relations Laws on Union Density Rates: Evidence from Canadian Provinces," unpublished paper, September 2014, https://uwaterloo.ca/economics/sites/ca.economics/files/uploads/files/legree_schirle_skuterud_sept2014_2.pdf; Joseph B. Rose, "The Prospects for Union Renewal in Canada," in *Proceedings of the 60th Annual Meeting of the Labor and Employment Relations Association: LERA* (Labor and Employment Relations Association, 2008), 101–7, http://www.lerachapters.org/OJS/ojs-2.4.4-1/index.php/LERAMR/article/download/1341/1326; Eric Tucker, "Welcome to the Bottom: A North American Perspective on the Fair Work Act," chap. 12 in *Collective Bargaining under the Fair Work Act*, ed. Shae McCrystal, Breen Creighton and Anthony Forsyth, eds. (Annandale, Australia: Federation Press, 2018); Christopher Schenk, "Fifty Years after PC 1003: The Need for New Directions," in *Labour Gains, Labour Pains: 50 Years of PC 1003*, ed. Cy Gonick, Paul Phillips, and Jesse Vorst (Halifax, NS: Fernwood, 1995); Paul C. Weiler, *Governing the Workplace: The Future of Labor and Employment Law* (Cambridge, MA: Harvard University Press, 1990). See also Ethan Phillips, "The Unfinished Business of Labour Law Reform in Ontario: A Strategy for Implementing Sectoral Bargaining," *Canada Fact Check*, January 12, 2018, https://can adafactcheck.ca/bill148ontariolabourlawsectoralbargaining/.

78. Mishel, "Private Sector Union Density Dynamics."

79. Rebecca Rainey and Ian Kullgren, "1 Year after Janus, Unions Are Flush," *Politico*, May 17, 2019, https://www.politico.com/story/2019/05/17/janus-unions-employment-1447266.

80. While not all research shows positive productivity effects from works councils, most studies do. See Steffen Mueller, "Works Councils and Establishment Productivity," *Industrial and Labor Relations Review* 65, no. 4 (2012): 880–98; Steffen Mueller, "Works Councils and Labour Productivity: Looking beyond the Mean," *British Journal of Industrial Relations* 53, no. 2 (2015): 308–25; John T. Addison, Claus Schnabel, and Joachim Wagner, "Works Councils in Germany: Their Effects on Establishment Performance," *Oxford Economic Papers* 53, no. 4 (2001): 659–94; and Olaf Hübler and Uwe Jirjahn, "Works Councils and Collective Bargaining in Germany: The Impact on Productivity and Wages," *Scottish Journal of Political Economy* 50, no. 4 (2003): 471–91. See also "Co-determination: Works Council Pays Off," Hans-Böckler-Stiftun, June 2010, https://web.archive.org/web/20190719185852/http://www.boeckler.de/35927_35964.htm. For US-focused studies on general labor-management partnership, see Jody Hoffer Gittell, Andrew Von Nordenflycht, and Thomas A. Kochan, "Mutual Gains or Zero Sum? Labor Relations and Firm Performance in the Airline Industry," *Industrial and Labor Relations Review* 57, no. 2 (2004): 163–80; and Eileen Appelbaum, Jody Hoffer Gittell, and Carrie Leana, "High-Performance Work Practices and Sustainable Economic Growth," Center for Economic and Policy Research, March 20, 2011, http://cepr.net/publications/reports/high-performance-work-practices-and-sustainable-economic-growth.

81. Hübler and Jirjahn, "Works Councils and Collective Bargaining in Germany."

82. Richard B. Freeman and Edward P. Lazear, "An Economic Analysis of Works Councils," NBER Working Paper 4918, National Bureau of Economic Research, November 1994, https://www.nber.org/papers/w4918.pdf; Hübler and Jirjahn, "Works Councils and Collective Bargaining in Germany"; John Addison et al., "Worker Participation and

Firm Performance" *British Journal of Industrial Relations* 38, no. 1 (2000): 7–48; John T. Addison et al., "Collective Bargaining and Innovation in Germany: Cooperative Industrial Relations?" IZA Discussion Papers 7871, IZA (Institute for the Study of Labor), December 2013, http://ftp.iza.org/dp7871.pdf. Stefan Zagelmayer notes, "As far as bargaining centralization is concerned, multi-employer collective bargaining allows for the strategy of the institutional separation of co-operation at company level and conflict at higher levels, thus increasing the scope for co-operative strategies at lower levels." Stefan Zagelmayer, "The Employer's Perspective on Collective Bargaining Centralization: An Analytical Framework," *International Journal of Human Resource* Management 16, no. 9 (2005): 1623–39.

83. For a theoretical discussion of workers on corporate boards, see Isabelle Ferreras, *Firms as Political Entities: Saving Democracy through Economic Bicameralism* (Cambridge, UK: Cambridge University Press, 2017).

84. See, for example, Sigurt Vitols, "Board Level Employee Representation, Executive Remuneration and Firm Performance in Large European Companies," unpublished paper, March 2010, http://www.efesonline.org/Database%20of%20employee%20ownership/Users/2010_ceo_pay_paper.pdf; Felix Hörisch, "The Macro-economic Effect of Codetermination on Income Equality," Working Paper 147, University of Mannheim, 2012, https://www.mzes.uni-mannheim.de/publications/wp/wp-147.pdf; Robert Kleinknecht, "Employee Participation in Corporate Governance: Implications for Company Resilience," *European Journal of Industrial Relations* 21, no. 1 (2014): 57–72; E. Han Kim, Ernst G. Maug, and Christoph Schneider, "Labor Representation in Governance as an Insurance Mechanism," Working Paper 411, European Corporate Governance Institute Finance, 2014; and Franziska Boneberg, "The Economic Consequences of One-Third Co-determination in German Supervisory Boards: First Evidence for the Service Sector from a New Source of Enterprise Data," Working Paper Series in Economics 177, University of Lüneburg, June 2010, https://www.econstor.eu/bitstream/10419/57116/1/629529868.pdf. For firm performance, see Aline Conchon, *Board-Level Employee Representation Rights in Europe: Facts and Trends*, Report 121 (Brussels: European Trade Union Institute, 2011), https://www.etui.org/Publications2/Reports/Board-level-employee-representation-rights-in-Europe, which reviews the literature on board-level employee representatives in Germany. A majority found positive or no significant impacts on firm value, productivity, or corporate performance.

85. Kim, Maug, and Schneider, "Labor Representation in Governance as an Insurance Mechanism."

86. Simon Jäger, Benjamin Schoefer, Jörg Heining, "Labor in the Board Room," IZA—Institute of Labor Economics, November 2019, https://www.iza.org/publications/dp/12799/labor-in-the-boardroom.

87. Alice Kügler, Uta Schönberg, and Ragnhild Schreiner, "Productivity Growth, Wage Growth and Unions," European Central Bank Forum on Central Banking, 2018, https://www.ecb.europa.eu/pub/conferences/shared/pdf/20180618_ecb_forum_on_central_banking/Schoenberg_Uta_Paper.pdf.

88. See, for example, Caroline Pateman, *Participation and Democratic Theory* (Cambridge, UK: Cambridge University Press, 1976); and Robert Dahl, *A Preface to Economic Democracy* (Berkeley: University of California Press, 1986)

89. For a related argument about the downside of shifting some of the costs of supporting unions onto public-sector employers, see Martin H. Malin and Catherine Fisk, "After *Janus*," *California Law Review*, 2018, https://ssrn.com/abstract=3245522.

90. Neera Tanden et al., "Toward a Marshall Plan for America," Center for American Progress, May 16, 2017, https://www.americanprogress.org/issues/economy/reports/2017/05/16/432499/toward-marshall-plan-america.

91. Clive Belfield and Thomas Bailey, "The Labor Market Returns to Sub-Baccalaureate College: A Review," CAPSEE Working Paper, Center for Analysis of Postsecondary Education and Employment, March 2017, https://capseecenter.org/wp-content/uploads/2017/04/labor-market-returns-sub-baccalaureate-college-review.pdf; Anthony P. Carnevale, Stephen J. Rose, and Andrew R. Hanson, *Certificates: Gateway to Gainful Employment and College Degrees* (Washington, DC: Georgetown University Center on Education and the Workforce, 2012), https://cew.georgetown.edu/wp-content/uploads/2014/11/Certificates.FullReport.061812.pdf.

92. Jaison R. Abel, Richard Deitz, and Yaqin Su, "Are Recent College Graduates Finding Good Jobs?," *Federal Reserve Bank of New York Current Issues in Economics* 20, no. 1 (2014): 1–8, https://www.newyorkfed.org/medialibrary/media/research/current_issues/ci20-1.pdf.

93. Edward Wolf, *Does Education Really Help* (Oxford: Oxford University Press, 2006); Brad Hershbein, Melissa S. Kearney, and Lawrence H. Summers, "Increasing Education: What It Will and Will Not Do for Earnings and Earnings Inequality," Brookings Institution, March 31, 2015, https://www.brookings.edu/blog/up-front/2015/03/31/increasing-education-what-it-will-and-will-not-do-for-earnings-and-earnings-inequality.

94. For more details on how to make this work, see David Madland and Angela Hanks, "Better Training and Better Jobs," Center for American Progress, February 22, 2018, https://www.americanprogress.org/issues/economy/reports/2018/02/22/447115/better-training-better-jobs.

95. Jason Heyes and Mark Stuart, "Bargaining for Skills: Trade Unions and Training at the Workplace," *British Journal of Industrial Relations* 36, no. 3 (1998): 459–67; Sally Klingel and David B. Lipsky, "Joint Labor-Management Training Programs for Healthcare Worker Advancement and Retention," DigitalCommons@ILR, ILR School, Cornell University, 2010, http://digitalcommons.ilr.cornell.edu/cgi/viewcontent.cgi?article=1042&context=reports; Alison L. Booth, Marco Francesconi, and Gylfi Zoega, "Unions, Work-Related Training, and Wages: Evidence for British Men," Discussion Paper 737, IZA—Institute of Labor Economics, March 2003, http://ftp.iza.org/dp737.pdf; Christian Dustmann and Uta Schönberg, "Training and Union Wages," *Review of Economics and Statistics* 91, no. 2 (2009): 363–76; Daron Acemoglu and Jörn-Steffen Pischke, "Beyond Becker: Training in Imperfect Labour Markets," *Economic Journal*, 109, no. 453 (1999): F112–F142, https://economics.mit.edu/files/3810; Cihan Bilginsoy, "The Hazards of Training: Attrition and Retention in Construction Industry Apprenticeship Programs," *Industrial and Labor Relations Review* 57, no. 1 (2003): 54–67.

96. For research on the lack of training access for those with low skills, see Maureen Conway, Amy Kays Blair, and Catherine Gibbons, "Investigating Demand Side Outcomes: Literature Review and Implications," Aspen Institute, 2003, https://assets.aspeninstitute.org/content/uploads/files/content/docs/03-OP03.PDF.

97. Emmanuel Saez, "Income and Wealth Inequality: Evidence and Policy Implications," *Contemporary Economic Policy* 35, no. 1 (2017): 21, figure 17, https://eml.berkeley.edu/~saez/SaezCEP2017.pdf.

98. Dylan Matthews, "The Amazing True Socialist Miracle of the Alaska Permanent Fund," *Vox*, February 13, 2018, https://www.vox.com/policy-and-politics/2018/2/13/16997188/alaska-basic-income-permanent-fund-oil-revenue-study; Damon Jones and Ioana Elena Marinescu, "The Labor Market Impacts of Universal and Permanent Cash Transfers: Evidence from the Alaska Permanent Fund," December 2019, https://papers.ssrn.com/sol3/papers.cfm?abstract_id=3118343&utm_content=buffer0e9c8&utm_medium=social&utm_source=twitter.com&utm_campaign=buffer; Antti Jauhiainen and Joona-Hermanni Mäkinen, "Universal Basic Income Didn't Fail in Finland. Finland Failed It," *New York Times*, May 2, 2018; Leonid Bershidsky, "In Finland, Money Can Buy You

Happiness," *Bloomberg Opinion*, February 9, 2019, https://www.bloomberg.com/opinion/articles/2019-02-09/universal-basic-income-in-finland-money-can-buy-you-happiness.

99. See, for example, Hilary W. Hoynes and Jesse Rothstein, "Universal Basic Income in the US and Advanced Countries," NBER Working Paper 25538, National Bureau of Economic Research, February 2019, https://www.nber.org/papers/w25538.

100. Author's calculation using supplemental data from Congressional Budget Office, *The Distribution of Household Income and Federal Taxes, 2013* (Washington, DC: Congressional Budget Office, 2016), https://www.cbo.gov/publication/51361; "Table 1.9.3: Real Net Value Added by Sector, Quantity Indexes," FRED Economic Data, Federal Reserve Bank of St. Louis, 2017, https://fred.stlouisfed.org/release/tables?rid=53&eid=42088; "Index/Level and Office of Productivity and Technology and Work Hours: Nonfarm Business," U.S. Bureau of Labor Statistics, accessed January 2018, http://beta.bls.gov/dataViewer/view/timeseries/PRS85006033; "Trust Fund Data: Old-Age, Survivors, and Disability Insurance Trust Funds, 1957–2019," Social Security Administration, accessed April 26, 2019, https://www.ssa.gov/oact/STATS/table4a3.html.

101. Ljubica Nedelkoska and Glenda Quintini, "Automation, Skills Use and Training," Employment and Migration Working Paper 202, Organisation for Economic Co-operation and Development, 2018, https://www.oecd-ilibrary.org/fr/employment/automation-skills-use-and-training_2e2f4eea-en.

102. For a good review of some of this research, see Jason Furman and Robert Seamans, "AI and the Economy," NBER Working Paper 24689, National Bureau of Economic Research, June 2018, https://economics.harvard.edu/files/economics/files/furman-jason_2-25-19_ai-and-economy_nberwp24689.pdf.

103. John Harris, "Workers' Rights? Bosses Don't Care—Soon They'll Only Need Robots," *Guardian*, December 17, 2018; Matt Day and Benjamin Romano, "Amazon Has Patented a System That Would Put Workers in a Cage, on Top of a Robot," *Seattle Times*, September 7, 2018. See also Ceylan Yeginsu, "If Workers Slack Off, the Wristband Will Know (and Amazon Has a Patent for It)," *New York Times*, February 1, 2018.

104. Benjamin Fearnow, "Amazon Denies Forcing Employees to Urinate in Bottles as Bathroom Break Time-Saver," *Newsweek*, April 18, 2018, https://www.newsweek.com/amazon-fulfillment-centers-bathroom-breaks-pee-bottle-urination-workplace-887952.

105. Ellen Ruppel Shell, "The Employer-Surveillance State," *Atlantic*, October 15, 2018, https://www.theatlantic.com/business/archive/2018/10/employee-surveillance/568159; "Companies Start Implanting Microchips into Workers' Bodies," *Los Angeles Times*, April 3, 2017, https://www.latimes.com/business/technology/la-fi-tn-microchip-employees-20170403-story.html.

106. Jared Bernstein, "Is the US Labor Market Finally at Full Employment? Not According to the Inflation Numbers," *Washington Post*, May 5, 2017.

107. Author's analysis of "Median/Average Hourly Wages," *State of Working America Data Library*, Economic Policy Institute, last viewed: February 19, 2019, update, https://www.epi.org/data/#?subject=wage-avg.

108. David Autor, "Skills, Education, and the Rise of Earnings Inequality among the Other 99 Percent," *Science*, May 2014, https://science.sciencemag.org/content/344/6186/843.full.

109. For Britain, see *Prosperity and Justice: A Plan for the New Economy* (Cambridge, UK: Polity Press, 2018), https://www.ippr.org/files/2018-08/1535639099_prosperity-and-justice-ippr-2018.pdf; "Labour Market Economic Commentary: June 2018," Office for National Statistics (UK), https://www.ons.gov.uk/employmentandlabourmarket/peopleinwork/employmentandemployeetypes/articles/labourmarketeconomiccommentary/june2018. For Australia, see Industry Insights: Flexibility and Growth (Canberra: Office of the Chief Economist, Department of Industry, Innovation, and Science, 2018),

https://publications.industry.gov.au/publications/industryinsightsjune2018/documents/ IndustryInsights_1_2018_ONLINE.pdf; Jim Stanford, "Charting Wage Stagnation in Australia," chap. 2, in *The Wage Crisis in Australia*, ed. Andrew Stewart, Jim Stanford and Tess Hardy (Adelaide: University of Adelaide Press, 2018). For Canada, see Andy Blatchford, "Canada's Unemployment Rate Stays at 43-Year Low, but Wage Growth Fizzles," *HuffPost*, January 4, 2019, https://www.huffingtonpost.ca/2019/01/04/unemployment-canada-december-2018_a_23633502.

110. A jobs guarantee could be designed with prevailing wage standards, which are a sectoral strategy to maintain high wages where they prevail in the private sector. Tanden et al., "Toward a Marshall Plan for America."

111. "Employment by Major Industry Sector," US Bureau of Labor Statistics, https:// www.bls.gov/emp/tables/employment-by-major-industry-sector.htm; Antoine Gervais and J. Bradford Jensen, "The Tradability of Services: Geographic Concentration and Trade Costs," Center for Economic Studies, January 2014, https://www2.census.gov/ces/ wp/2014/CES-WP-14-03.pdf.

112. In 2018, the median hourly wage was $18.80, while the average was $25.60. See "Median/Average Hourly Wages"; and "Ratio of Minimum to Average Wages," International Labour Organization, accessed April 26, 2019, https://www.ilo.org/global/topics/ wages/minimum-wages/setting-adjusting/WCMS_439253/lang--en/index.htm. Research finds that bargaining is much more effective than minimum wage at reducing the share of low-wage workers in a country. Gerhard Bosch and Claudia Weinkopf, "Reducing Wage Inequality: The Role of the State in Improving Job Quality," *Work and Occupations* 44, no. 1 (2016): 68–88; Gerhard Bosch, "Shrinking Collective Bargaining Coverage, Increasing Income Inequality: A Comparison of Five EU Countries," *International Labour Review*, 154, no. 1 (2015): 57–66.

113. Arindrajit Dube, "Using Wage Boards to Raise Pay," Research Brief (Economists for Inclusive Prosperity), December 2018, https://econfip.org/wp-content/uploads/ 2019/02/4.Using-Wage-Boards-to-Raise-Pay.pdf.

114. David Kooper and Teresa Kroeger, "Employers Steal Billions from Workers' Pay-checks Each Year," Economic Policy Institute, May 10, 2017, https://www.epi.org/publi cation/employers-steal-billions-from-workers-paychecks-each-year. See also Annette Bernhardt et al., *Broken Laws, Unprotected Workers: Violations of Employment and Labor Laws in America's Cities* (Washington, DC: National Employment Law Project, 2009), https://www.nelp.org/wp-content/uploads/2015/03/BrokenLawsReport2009.pdf.

115. Philip Mattera, *Grand Theft Paycheck: The Large Corporation Shortchanging Their Workers' Wages* (Washington, DC: Good Jobs First and Jobs with Justice Education Fund, 2018), https://www.goodjobsfirst.org/sites/default/files/docs/pdfs/wagetheft_report.pdf.

116. For inadequacy of current enforcement, see Marianne Levine, "Behind the Minimum Wage Fight, a Sweeping Failure to Enforce the Law," *Politico*, February 18, 2018, https://www. politico.com/story/2018/02/18/minimum-wage-not-enforced-investigation-409644.

117. Janice Fine and Jennifer Gordon, "Strengthening Labor Standards Enforcement through Partnerships with Workers' Organizations," *Politics and Society* 38, no. 4 (2010): 552–85; David Madland and Alex Rowell, "How State and Local Governments Can Strengthen Worker Power and Raise Wages," Center for American Progress Action Fund, May 2, 2017, https://www.americanprogressaction.org/issues/economy/reports/2017/05/02/166640/ state-local-governments-can-strengthen-worker-power-raise-wages.

118. Karla Walter, David Madland, and Danielle Corley, "Capitalism for Everyone," Center for American Progress, July 21, 2015, https://www.americanprogress.org/issues/ economy/reports/2015/07/21/117742/capitalism-for-everyone/; David Madland and Karla Walter, "Growing the Wealth," Center for American Progress, April 2, 2013, https://www. americanprogress.org/issues/economy/reports/2013/04/02/57409/growing-the-wealth.

119. For a discussion of this research, see Walter, Madland, and Corley, "Capitalism for Everyone"; and Madland and Walter, "Growing the Wealth."

120. "Financial Accounts of the United States—L.117 Private and Public Pension Funds," Board of Governors of the Federal Reserve System, last modified September 20, 2018, https://www.federalreserve.gov/releases/z1/20180920/html/l117.htm; "Union Construction Job Creation," AFL-CIO Housing Investment Trust, last modified December 31, 2018, accessed August 18, 2019, http://www.aflcio-hit.com/wmspage.cfm?parm1=1794; Jay Miller, "Building Trades Put Financial Clout to Work," *Crain's Cleveland Business*, April 15, 2018, https://www.crainscleveland.com/article/20180413/news/158196/building-trades-put-financial-clout-work; "Union Labor Policies," AFL-CIO Housing Investment Trust, accessed April 26, 2019, http://www.aflcio-hit.com/wmspage.cfm?parm1 = 151; "Ullico Infrastructure Fund Responsible Contractor Policy," North America's Building Trades Unions, https://nabtu.org/wp-content/uploads/2017/03/UIF-Responsible-Contractor-Policy.pdf; "Corporate Accountability," AFL-CIO, https://aflcio.org/what-unions-do/social-economic-justice/corporate-accountability.

121. National Academies of Sciences, Engineering, and Medicine, *The Economic and Fiscal Consequences of Immigration* (Washington, DC: National Academies Press, 2017), https://www.nap.edu/catalog/23550/the-economic-and-fiscal-consequences-of-immigration; Michael Greenstone et al., "What Immigration Means for US Employment and Wages," Brookings Institution, May 4, 2012, https://www.brookings.edu/blog/jobs/2012/05/04/what-immigration-means-for-u-s-employment-and-wages.

122. Adriana Kugler and Patrick Oakford, "Comprehensive Immigration Reform Will Benefit American Workers," Center for American Progress, September 12, 2013, https://www.americanprogress.org/issues/immigration/reports/2013/09/12/74014/comprehensive-immigration-reform-will-benefit-american-workers.

123. In addition to more traditional remedies, some mergers that strongly promote efficiency could be allowed so long as workers benefit from those efficiencies through collective bargaining.

124. See a survey of recent research by Suresh Naidu, Eric A. Posner, and E. Glen Weyl, "Antitrust Remedies for Labor Market Power," *Harvard Law Review* 132 (2018): 537–600, https://chicagounbound.uchicago.edu/cgi/viewcontent.cgi?article=13776&context=journal_articles. See also José Azar, Ioana Marinescu, and Marshall Steinbaum, "Labor Market Concentration," NBER Working Paper 24147, National Bureau of Economic Research, December 2017, revised February 2019, https://www.nber.org/papers/w24147; Efraim Benmelech, Nittai Bergman, and Hyunseob Kim, "Strong Employers and Weak Employees: How Does Employer Concentration Affect Wages?," NBER Working Paper 24037, National Bureau of Economic Research, February 2018, https://www.nber.org/papers/w24307; Arindrajit Dube, Jeff Jacobs, Suresh Naidu, and Siddharth Suri, "Monopsony in Online Labor Markets," NBER Working Paper 24416 National Bureau of Economic Research, March 2018, http://www.nber.org/papers/w24416; "Labor Market Monopsony: Trends, Consequences, and Policy Responses," *Council of Economic Advisers Issue Brief*, October 2016, https://obamawhitehouse.archives.gov/sites/default/files/page/files/20161025_labor_mrkt_monopsony_cea.pdf; and Marshall Steinbaum, "How Widespread Is Labor Monopsony? Some New Results Suggest It's Pervasive," Roosevelt Institute, December 18, 2017, http://rooseveltinstitute.org/how-widespread-labor-monopsony-some-new-results-suggest-its-pervasive.

125. Josh Bivens, Lawrence Mishel, and John Schmitt, "It's Not Just Monopoly and Monopsony," Economic Policy Institute, April 25, 2018, https://www.epi.org/publication/its-not-just-monopoly-and-monopsony-how-market-power-has-affected-american-wages. For similar view, see Suresh Naidu and Eric A. Posner, "Labor Market Monopsony and the Limits of the Law," unpublished paper, October 14, 2018, https://irs.princeton.

edu/sites/irs/files/naidu%20posner%20limits%20of%20law%20conference%20draft. pdf as well as Anna Stansbury and Lawrence H. Summers, "Declining Worker Power and American Economic Performance," Brookings Institution, March 19, 2020, https://www. brookings.edu/wp-content/uploads/2020/03/Stansbury-Summers-Conference-Draft.pdf.

126. Benmelech, Bergman, and Kim, "Strong Employers and Weak Employees."

127. Brishen Rogers, "The Limits of Antitrust Enforcement," *Boston Review*, April 30, 2018, http://bostonreview.net/class-inequality/brishen-rogers-limits-antitrust-enforcement.

128. Steven Lukes, *Power: A Radical View* (London: Palgrave MacMillan, 1974).

129. John R. Hibbing and Elizabeth Theiss-Morse, *Stealth Democracy: Americans' Beliefs about How Government Should Work* (Cambridge, UK: Cambridge University Press, 2002).

130. Cheol-Sung Lee, "Labor Unions and Good Governance: A Cross-National, Comparative Analysis," *American Sociological Review*, 72, no. 4 (2007): 585–609.

131. For more extensive discussion of the stability of "political capitalism," see Branko Milonivic, *Capitalism Alone* (Cambridge, MA: Harvard University Press, 2019).

CHAPTER 6. CREATING THE NEW SYSTEM

1. Frank R. Baumgartner and Bryan D. Jones, *Agendas and Instability in American Politics* (Chicago: University of Chicago Press, 1993).

2. See, among others, William Domhoff, "The Rise and Fall of Labor Unions in the US," in *Who Rules America?* (Upper Saddle River, NJ: Prentice Hall, 1967), especially page 43. Even though business was opposed to the NLRA, the compromise to exclude many minority workers and thus not offend southern agricultural businesses was important to its passage.

3. Nick Hanauer and David Rolf, "Portable Benefits for an Insecure Workforce," *American Prospect*, February 23, 2017, http://prospect.org/article/portable-benefits-insecure-workforce.

4. For example, the Guffey-Snyder Act (1935) and the National Industrial Recovery Act (1933). More recently, see Lyft's concerns that New York City's high standards for drivers is helping Uber: Grace Dobush, "Lyft Claims that NYC's New Driver Minimum Wage Makes It Even Harder to Compete with Uber," *Fortune*, January 31, 2019, http://fortune.com/2019/01/31/lyft-uber-nyc-driver-minimum-wage-lawsuit. In the UK, Peter A. Swenson, *Capitalists against Markets* (Oxford, UK: Oxford University Press, 2002), 218, finds that the National Association of Manufactures was divided on the benefits of multi-employer bargaining throughout the 1950s.

5. Swenson, *Capitalists against Markets*; Kathleen Thelen, *Varieties of Labor Politics in the Developed Democracies* (Cambridge, UK: Cambridge University Press, 2014).

6. "Report of the Fast Food Wage Board to the NYS Commissioner of Labor," New York State Fast Food Wage Board, 2015, https://labor.ny.gov/workerprotection/laborstan dards/pdfs/Fast-Food-Wage-Board-Report.pdf

7. Sam Pizzigati, *The Case for a Maximum Wage* (Cambridge, UK: Polity, 2018).

8. Alan Brinkley, *Voices of Protest: Huey Long, Father Coughlin, and the Great Depression (New York: Penguin Random House, 1983).*

9. See, for example, David Leonhardt, "The Corporate Donors behind a Republican Power Grab," *New York Times*, December 9, 2018; Donovan Hicks, "Michigan Is the Latest Example of the Restaurant Lobby Subverting Democracy," *Talk Poverty*, December 7, 2018, https://talkpoverty.org/2018/12/07/michigan-restaurant-lobby-democracy.

10. See, for example, Alexander J. De Grand, *Italian Fascism: Its Origins and Development* (Lincoln: University of Nebraska Press, 2000); Gregory M. Luebbert, David Collier, and Seymour Martin Lipset, *Liberalism, Fascism or Social Democracy: Social Classes and the Political Origins of Regimes in Interwar Europe* (Oxford, UK: Oxford University Press, 1991).

11. See, for example, James F. Clarity, "Jacob Javits Dies in Florida at 81: 4-Term Senator from New York," *New York Times*, March 8, 1986. George Shultz, secretary of labor, OMB director, and secretary of the treasury during the Nixon administration and secretary of state during the Reagan administration, argued in support of trade unions that in "a healthy workplace, it is very important that there be some system of checks and balances." Leonard Silk, "Economic Scene; Worrying Over Weakened Unions," *New York Times*, December 13, 1991. Other examples of Republican support for unions include Nixon's appointment of union leader Peter J. Brennan as labor secretary in 1970 and Gerald Ford's appointment of union leader W. J. Usery Jr. in 1976 for the same position. See "Secretarial Portraits: Peter J. Brennan," US Department of Labor, https://www.dol.gov/general/aboutdol/history/brennan; "Hall of Secretaries: W. J. Usery Jr.," and US Department of Labor, https://www.dol.gov/general/aboutdol/history/usery.

12. See Michael Goldfield, "Radical Organization and New Deal Labor Legislation," *The American Political Science Review* 83, no. 4 (1989): 1257–82. See also Theda Skocpol, "Political Response to Capitalist Crisis: Neo-Marxist Theories of the State and the Case of the New Deal," *Politics and Society* 10, no. 2 (1980): 188, http://pluto.mscc.huji.ac.il/~mshalev/ppe/Skocpol_NewDeal_1980.pdf.

13. "Work Stoppages Summary," U.S. Bureau of Labor Statistics, press release, February 8, 2019, https://www.bls.gov/news.release/archives/wkstp_02082019.pdf.

14. The NLRA passed Senate, with votes from forty-nine Democrats, twelve Republicans, on Farmer-Labor Party member, and one Progressive Party member supporting. "Description of Key Votes, 1944–1919," In *CQ Almanac 1949*, 5th ed. (Washington, DC: Congressional Quarterly, 1950), https://library.cqpress.com/cqalmanac/document.php?id=cqal49-1402137.

15. Art Swift, "Labor Union Approval Best since 2003, at 61%," Gallup, August 30, 2017, https://news.gallup.com/poll/217331/labor-union-approval-best-2003.aspx. Union support has basically been high and steady for five decades, though the Great Recession temporarily decreased public support. David Madland and Karla Walter, "Why Is the Public Suddenly Down on Unions?" Center for American Progress Action Fund, 2010, https://www.americanprogressaction.org/issues/economy/reports/2010/07/20/8046/why-is-the-public-suddenly-down-on-unions.

16. Hannah Fingerhut, "More Americans View Long-Term Decline in Union Membership Negatively than Positively," Pew Research Center, June 5, 2018, http://www.pewresearch.org/fact-tank/2018/06/05/more-americans-view-long-term-decline-in-union-membership-negatively-than-positively.

17. Ruth Milkman, "A New Political Generation: Millennials and the Post-2008 Wave of Protest," *American Sociological Review* 82, no. 1 (2017): 1–31.

18. Alexander Hertel-Fernandez, Will Kimball, and Tom Kochan, "How US Workers Think about Workplace Democracy: The Structure of Individual Worker Preferences for Labor Representation," Working Paper Series, Washington Center for Equitable Growth, August 2019, https://equitablegrowth.org/working-papers/how-u-s-workers-think-about-workplace-democracy-the-structure-of-individual-worker-preferences-for-labor-representation. See also Alexander Hertel-Fernandez, Will Kimball, and Tom Kochan, "What Forms of Representation do American Workers Want? Understanding How Workers Think about Labor Organization," paper presented at American Economic Association, San Diego, January 3, 2020, 18 (fig. 1), 31 (fig. 6), https://www.aeaweb.org/conference/2020/preliminary/1885.

19. Alex Hertel-Fernandez, "What Americans Think about Worker Power and Organization: Lessons from a New Survey," Data for Progress, May 2020, http://filesforprogress.org/memos/worker-power.pdf; David Madland, "Broad Public Support for Wage Boards,"

Center for American Progress Action Fund, May 31, 2018, https://www.americanprogress action.org/issues/economy/news/2018/05/31/170396/broad-public-support-wage-boards.

20. "New PDK Poll Shows Far-Reaching Support for Teacher Strikes, Higher Pay," August 28, 2018, National Education Association, http://www.nea.org/home/73949.htm.

21. A ballot initiative to amend the state constitution of Virginia to enshrine right to work failed in 2016, likely in part because of voter reluctance to amend the constitution for any reason.

22. Sabrina Tavernise, "Ohio Turns Back a Law Limiting Unions' Rights," *New York Times*, November 8, 2011.

23. Kris Maher, "Missouri Overturns 'Right-to-Work' Law in Referendum," *Wall Street Journal*, August 8, 2018; David Madland, Twitter, August 9, 2018, https://twitter.com/DavidMadland/status/1027560704382066688.

24. Irving Bernstein, "The Wagner Act," chap. 7 in *The Turbulent Years: A History of the American Worker, 1933–1940* (Boston: Houghton Mifflin, 1969). See also Domhoff, "Rise and Fall of Labor Unions in the US," 47, 57.

25. David Rolf, former president of SEIU 775 has been a notable leader. See David Rolf, "A Roadmap to Rebuilding Worker Power," Century Foundation, August 9, 2018, https://tcf.org/content/report/roadmap-rebuilding-worker-power.

26. Dylan Matthews, "The Big New Plan to Save Unions Endorsed by Bernie Sanders and Pete Buttigieg, Explained," *Vox*, August 22, 2019, https://www.vox.com/policy-and-politics/2019/8/22/20826642/mary-kay-henry-seiu-sectoral-bargaining; Patricia Harty, "Mary Kay Henry: A New Deal for America's Working Poor," *Irish America*, June/July 2018, https://irishamerica.com/2018/05/mary-kay-henry-a-new-deal-for-americas-working-poor; Chris Opfer, "White House Hopefuls Find Labor Reform Pickle," Bloomberg Law, September 12, 2018, https://web.archive.org/web/20181011004345/https://www.bna.com/white-house-hopefuls-n73014482499; Chris Shelton, "The Future of American Labor," speech, Albert Shanker Institute, Washington, DC, February 8, 2019, https://georgetown.app.box.com/s/2jtwawgaows4gie5a1sn0kmiqulg5r5u/file/4022 42107074; and "CWA Shares Vision for Future of American Labor," Communications Workers of America, February 14, 2019, https://cwa-union.org/news/cwa-shares-vision-for-future-of-american-labor.

27. Richard L. Trumka, "Labor's Future: Bargaining for All," speech, National Press Club, Washington, DC, April 4, 2017, https://aflcio.org/speeches/labors-future-bargaining-all.

28. Bob King, "The Future of American Labor," speech, Albert Shanker Institute, Washington, D.C., February 8, 2019, https://georgetown.app.box.com/s/2jtwawgaows4 gie5a1sn0kmiqulg5r5u/file/402242107074; Larry Cohen, "The Time Has Come for Sectoral Bargaining," *CUNY New Labor Forum*, June 2018, https://newlaborforum.cuny.edu/2018/06/22/the-time-has-come-for-sectoral-bargaining.

29. Kamala Harris, Pramila Jayapal, and Ai-jen Poo, "Change Begins at Home—and on the Floor of Congress," CNN, November 29, 2018, https://www.cnn.com/2018/11/29/opinions/domestic-workers-bill-of-rights-harris-poo-jayapal/index.html.

30. See, for example, Domhoff, "Rise and Fall of Labor Unions in the US," 47. See also Goldfield, "Radical Organization and New Deal Labor Legislation."

31. See, for example, Irving Bernstein, *New Deal Collective Bargaining Policy* (Berkeley: University of California Press, 1950), 71–72; Domhoff, "Rise and Fall of Labor Unions in the US," 40; and Skocpol, "Political Response to Capitalist Crisis," 187.

32. See Skocpol, "Political Response to Capitalist Crisis," 188 (chart). Goldfield, "Radical Organization and New Deal Labor Legislation," argues that labor unrest was key but also that many supporters of the NLRA argued for one of the ideas behind the bill—that it was necessary to reduce and contain such unrest.

33. Janice Fine and Jennifer Gordon, "Strengthening Labor Standards Enforcement through Partnerships with Workers' Organizations," *Politics and Society* 38, no. 4 (2010):

552–85; Janice Fine, *Co-production: Bringing Together the Unique Capabilities of Government and Society for Stronger Labor Standards Enforcement* (Labor Innovations for the 21st Century Fund, n.d.), http://theliftfund.org/wp-content/uploads/2015/09/LIFTRe portCoproductionOct_ExecSumm-rf_4.pdf.

34. Rolf, "Roadmap to Building Worker Power"; David Rolf, *The Fight for Fifteen: The Right Wage for a Working America (New York: New Press, 2016); and David Rolf, "Labor: Building a New Future," Democracy 29 (Summer 2013): 42–46.*

35. "Jenny Durkan for Mayor," Labor Day 2017, https://web.archive.org/web/2017 1023235005/https://jennyforseattle.com/wp-content/uploads/2017/08/Jenny-Durkan-for-Seattle-%E2%80%94-Labor-Day-2017.pdf.

36. Kate Andrias, "The New Labor Law," *Yale Law Journal* 126, no. 1 (2016): 2–100, https://www.yalelawjournal.org/pdf/a.2.Andrias.100_sa4cc96k.pdf; and Kate Andrias, "Social Bargaining in States and Cities: Toward a More Egalitarian and Democratic Workplace Law," paper prepared for Harvard Law School Symposium, "Could Experiments at the State and Local Levels Expand Collective Bargaining and Workers' Collective Action?," 2017, https://repository.law.umich.edu/cgi/viewcontent.cgi?article=3000&context=articles; Matthew Dimick, "Labor Law, New Governance and the Ghent System," *North Carolina Law Review* 90, no. 2 (2012): 319–74; Matthew Dimick, "Productive Unionism," *UC Irvine Law Review* 4 (2014): 679–724; Brishen Rogers, "Libertarian Corporatism Is Not an Oxymoron," *Texas Law Review* 94, no. 7 (2016): 1623–46, http://texaslawreview.org/wp-con tent/uploads/2016/09/Rogers.pdf.

37. David Madland, "The Future of Worker Voice and Power," Center for American Progress, October 11, 2016, https://www.americanprogress.org/issues/economy/reports/2016/10/11/143072/the-future-of-worker-voice-and-power; Kate Andrias and Brishen Rogers, *Rebuilding Worker Voice in Today's Economy* (New York: Roosevelt Institute, 2018), http://rooseveltinstitute.org/wp-content/uploads/2018/07/Rebuilding-Worker-Voices-final-2.pdf; Mark Barenberg, *Widening the Scope of Worker Organizing* (New York: Roosevelt Institute, 2015), http://rooseveltinstitute.org/widening-scope-worker-organizing.pdf.

38. Brett Milano, "A 'Clean Slate' for the Future of Labor Law," *Harvard Law Today*, August 1, 2018, https://today.law.harvard.edu/clean-slate-future-labor-law. The author was an active participant in this process.

39. Sharon Block and Ben Sachs, Clean Slate for Worker Power: Building a Just Economy and Democracy (Boston: Labor and Worklife Program, Harvard Law School, n.d.), https://www.cleanslateworkerpower.org/clean-slate-agenda.

40. "The Future of American Labor: Initiatives for a New Era," Albert Shanker Institute conference, Washington, DC, February 8–9, 2019, http://www.shankerinstitute.org/event/future-american-labor.

41. Frank Newport, "Democrats More Positive about Socialism Than Capitalism," Gallup, August 13, 2018, https://news.gallup.com/poll/240725/democrats-positive-socialism-capitalism.aspx.

42. Donald Trump, "Remarks at the 2017 Conservative Political Action Conference," speech, Conservative Political Action Conference, Washington, DC, February 24, 2017, C-SPAN, https://www.c-span.org/video/?424395-1/president-trump-gop-party-american-worker; Tessa Berenson, "Read Donald Trump's Speech on Jobs and the Economy," *Time*, September 15, 2016, http://time.com/4495507/donald-trump-economy-speech-transcript.

43. Daily Kos and AFT, "Take Action: Tell Your Mayor to Pledge to Stand With Working Families," Action Network, accessed April 26, 2019, https://actionnetwork.org/letters/take-action-tell-your-mayor-to-stand-with-working-people-and-sign-the-pledge-2?source=MayorsJanus_SEIU&referrer=group-seiu-3; Governor's Office of New York, "In Response to Janus Decision, Governor Cuomo Signs Executive Order to Protect Union Members from Harassment and Intimidation," June 27, 2018, https://www.governor.

ny.gov/news/response-janus-decision-governor-cuomo-signs-executive-order-protect-union-members-harassment; Philip D. Murphy, "Governor's Statement upon Signing Assembly Bill No. 3686 (First Reprint)," May 18, 2018, https://nj.gov/governor/news/state ments/docs/A3686.pdf.

44. See, for example, S.B. 285: Public Employers: Union Organizing, sess. of 2017 (Cal. 2017), https://leginfo.legislature.ca.gov/faces/billTextClient.xhtml?bill_id=2017201 80SB285.

45. See, for example, US Congress, Senate, Workplace Democracy Act, S.2810, 115th Cong., 2nd sess., introduced in Senate May 9, 2018, https://www.congress.gov/115/bills/ s2810/BILLS-115s2810is.pdf; US Congress, House, Protecting the Right to Organize Act, H.R. 2474, 116th Congress, 1st sess., introduced in House May 2, 2019, https://edlabor. house.gov/imo/media/doc/PRO%20Act.pdf.

46. "Following the Supreme Court's Janus Decision, Hirono, Cartwright, Senate & House Democrats Introduce New Legislation to Strengthen Rights of Workers to Join Unions & Bargain Collectively," office of US Senator Mazie K. Hirono, press release, June 28, 2018, https://www.hirono.senate.gov/news/press-releases/following-the-supreme-courts-janus-decision-hirono-cartwright-senate-and-house-democrats-introduce-new-legisla tion-to-strengthen-rights-of-workers-to-join-unions_bargain-collectively.

47. US Congress, Senate, Domestic Workers Bill of Rights Act, S. 2112, 116th Cong., 1st sess., introduced July 15, 2019, https://www.congress.gov/bill/116th-congress/senate-bill/2112/text; Harris, Jayapal, and Poo, "Change Begins at Home—and on the Floor of Congress."

48. US Congress, House, Wage Theft Prevention and Wage Recovery Act, H.R. 3467, 115th Cong, 1st sess., introduced July 27, 2017, https://www.congress.gov/bill/115th-congress/house-bill/3467.

49. State of Washington, An Act Relating to Creating the Universal Worker Protections Act, S.B. 5690, 66th leg., reg. sess. (2019), http://lawfilesext.leg.wa.gov/biennium/2019-20/ Pdf/Bills/Senate%20Bills/5690.pdf.

50. City of Philadelphia, Bill No. 190607, introduced June 20, 2019, https://phila.legis tar.com/LegislationDetail.aspx?ID=3991789&GUID=C8CA6F0D-9748-4074-8E3E-CABD 3C840701&Options=ID|Text|&Search=190607.

51. Lawrence Mishel, "What Options Do Workers Have?," testimony, Democratic National Convention Platform Drafting Hearing, Washington, DC, June 9, 2016, https:// www.epi.org/multimedia/what-options-do-workers-have-testimony-before-the-dem ocratic-platform-committee; Mark DeSaulnier et al., "The Future of Work: Wages and Labor," 2018, https://desaulnier.house.gov/sites/desaulnier.house.gov/files/REPORT%20-%20Future%20of%20Work%2C%20Wages%2C%20and%20Labor%20-%2018.09.05.pdf.

52. Matthews, "The Emerging Plan to Save the American Labor Movement"; David Leonhardt, "A Time for Big Economic Ideas," *New York Times*, April 22, 2018; Noah Smith, "Stronger Labor Unions Could Do a Lot of Good," *Bloomberg Opinion*, December 6, 2017, https://www.bloomberg.com/opinion/articles/2017-12-06/stronger-labor-unions-could-do-a-lot-of-good.

53. Bernie Sanders, "The Workplace Democracy Plan," accessed December 12, 2019, https://berniesanders.com/en/issues/workplace-democracy; Elizabeth Warren, "Empow-ering American Workers and Raising Wages," accessed December 12, 2019, https:// elizabethwarren.com/plans/empowering-american-workers; Jay Inslee, "Organizing the American Dream," accessed December 12, 2019, https://www.jayinslee.com/issues/amer ican-dream; Beto O'Rourke, "A 21st Century Labor Contract," *Medium*, August 22, 2019, https://medium.com/@BetoORourke/a-21st-century-labor-contract-1a97b5f64a85; Pete Buttigieg, "A New Rising Tide," accessed December 12, 2019, https://peteforamerica.com/ policies/empower-workers; Cory Booker, "Opportunity and Justice for Workers," accessed

December 12, 2019, https://corybooker.com/issues/economic-security-and-opportunity/ opportunity-and-justice-for-workers; Julian Castro, "Workers First: A Fair Deal for a More Just Economy," *Medium*, October 2, 2019, https://medium.com/castro2020/wor kersfirst-391ff46bf9f9; Joe Biden, "The Biden Plan for Strengthening Worker Organizing, Collective Bargaining, and Unions," accessed December 12, 2019; https://joebiden.com/ empowerworkers; Mike Bloomberg, "Labor," accessed March 4, 2020, https://www.mike bloomberg.com/policies/labor.

54. Democratic Party, "Democratic Party Platform," 2020, https://www.demconvention. com/wp-content/uploads/2020/08/2020-07-31-Democratic-Party-Platform-For-Distribution.pdf.

55. Jonathan Berry et al., "Conservatives Should Ensure Workers A Seat At The Table," *American Compass*, September 6, 2020, https://americancompass.org/essays/ conservatives-should-ensure-workers-a-seat-at-the-table.

56. There is also a possibility that the Supreme Court is moving toward a neo-Lochner era, where it returns to early 1900s jurisprudence that regularly overturned economic regulation, and could strike down the entirety of the new labor system, along with many other progressive economic policies from the New Deal to the present, but that possibility is beyond the scope of this book. More optimistically, it is worth noting that courts sometimes make political decisions to back off from gutting popular legislation, and prevailing legal philosophies can change rapidly.

Index

AARP, 49
Acemoglu, Daron, 53
Act 10, 70
Affordable Care Act, 148
AFL-CIO, 54, 57, 59, 152–53
agriculture industry, 10, 23, 54, 59, 115, 117
Aidt, Toke, 83
air traffic controllers, 70
Alabama, 58, 127
Alaska, 127, 133
Albert Shanker Institute, 155
Alberta Federation of Labor, 91
Alliance of Motion Picture and Television
    Producers, 13
Amazon, 136
American Federation of Labor (AFL), 30–31,
    54, 57–58, 67, 151–52
American Federation of State, County and
    Municipal Employees (AFSCME), 58–59
American Federation of Teachers, 59
American Railway Union, 57
American Train Dispatchers Association, 120
Andrias, Kate, 154
apparel industry, 58, 121
Argentina, 50
Arizona, 151
AT&T, 119–20
Australia
    broad-based bargaining efforts, 7, 77–79,
        97–98, 101, 107–8
    Commonwealth Conciliation and
        Arbitration Act, 98–99
    economic inequality levels, 79, 87, 97–98,
        101, 104, 141
    enterprise bargaining disadvantages, 7, 79,
        86–87, 97–98, 101–7
    Fair Works Commission, 102
    Harvester case, 98–101
    Labor Party, 101–3, 107
    labor union density, 63, 71, 74, 78, 87, 98,
        101–7, 139
    Liberal Party, 106–7
    Liberal-National Coalition, 107
    minimum standard-setting policies, 95,
        98–105

multi-employer agreements, 78, 102
Reserve Bank, 106
strike rights, 74, 98, 102
training programs, 104–5
unemployment levels, 137
wage patterns, 97–107, 137, 139, 141
Austria
    broad-based bargaining efforts, 77–78, 80
    economic inequality levels, 80
    labor union density, 78
    multi-employer agreements, 77–78
automobile industry, 15, 58, 112, 114–19,
    125, 127

Baigent-Ready model, 19–21, 91–92
Bartenders Union Local 165, 28
Belgium
    broad-based bargaining efforts, 77–78
    economic inequality levels, 78
    Ghent system, 10, 24–25, 72, 78
    government funding, 24
    incentive structures, 4
    labor union density, 71–72, 78
    labor union policy support, 72–73
    multi-employer agreements, 77–78
    unemployment insurance (UI)
        management, 3, 10, 24–25, 72
    works councils, 72–73
Biden, Joe, 157
Bituminous Coal Conservation Act, 33
Black Car Fund, 25–26
Black Lives Matter, 57
Bloomberg, Mike, 157
Booker, Cory, 157
boycotts, 66, 94, 125, 128
Britain
    broad-based bargaining efforts, 77–78,
        92–97, 107–8
    Conservative Party, 94–95
    economic inequality levels, 38, 79, 96–97, 141
    enterprise bargaining disadvantages, 7, 79,
        83, 86–87, 92, 107
    labor union density, 63, 71, 78, 87, 92–97,
        107, 128, 139
    Labour Party, 93–97